The Success Principle

Ronald N. Yeaple

The Success Principle

Ronald N. Yeaple, Ph.D.

Macmillan/Spectrum
New York

Macmillan/Spectrum
A Simon & Schuster Macmillan Company
1633 Broadway
New York, NY 10019

MACMILLAN is a registered trademark of Macmillan, Inc.
Library of Congress Cataloging-in-Publication Data: 96-068556
ISBN: 0-02861-416-X

99 98 97   9 8 7 6 5 4 3 2 1

Interpretation of the printing code: the rightmost double-digit
number is the year of the book's first printing; the rightmost
single-digit number is the number of the book's printing. For
example, a printing code of 97-1 shows that this copy of the book
was printed during the first printing of the book in 1997.

Printed in the United States of America.

Book Design: Scott Meola
Cover Design: Kevin Hanek
Publisher: Theresa Murtha
Editor: Dick Staron

To David, Susan, Jodie, and Annie

Every individual necessarily labors to render the annual revenue of the society as great as he can. He generally indeed neither intends to promote the public interest, nor knows how much he is promoting it. . . . He intends only his own gain, and he is in this, as in many other cases, led by an invisible hand to promote an end which was no part of his intention. . . . By pursuing his own interest he frequently promotes that of society more effectually than when he really intends to promote it.

...Adam Smith

Do not accept any job offer that will not make you deliriously happy. Success will follow.

...An Anonymous Survey Respondent

CONTENTS

You must understand your own industry in great depth. Use this proven framework to determine who your key competitors are, how the companies in your industry compete, and how your company has positioned itself to satisfy its customers.

You will be outgunned in today's competitive workplace if you don't have a basic understanding of these analytical tools.

Personal computer use is now universal among professionals and managers at all levels. Learn what key software applications you should master to avoid being tagged as obsolescent — with the pink slip that often follows.

Accelerating the development of new products is one of the hottest areas in management today. Find out about the latest techniques for improving your company's time-to-market.

A manager's value is directly tied to how much he or she can accomplish in cooperation with others. With the decline of managerial hierarchy, you must learn these techniques to get things done by creating strategic alliances with your colleagues.

Your personal core competencies set you aside from others. Find out how to select core competencies that will be of great value to you and your company — and will also be personally satisfying.

To get the most value from your investment in your personal core competencies, people inside and outside of your company must be aware of them. Discover how some of our most successful survey respondents are marketing themselves.

Survey respondents reported that advice from senior managers who served as mentors was as valuable as the content of all the MBA courses they took. But successful mentoring relationships don't just happen—they have to be developed and managed as described in this chapter.

You can be very successful without earning an MBA degree, depending on what your goals are. But for many, the MBA is an efficient way to build your portfolio of Strategic Skills—and as this chapter shows, the financial payoff for investing in an MBA from a quality school can be very attractive.

Learn what our more than 450 successful survey respondents had to say about such important questions as how to get promoted, when to change companies, how to choose a mentor, whether or not to seek cross-functional experience, whether it pays to pursue a part-time MBA degree, and many other critical career issues.

One of the distinguishing characteristics of this book is that it is based on a scientific study of the careers of more than 450 successful men and women. In these pages you will find out how the research was done.

ABOUT THE AUTHOR

Ronald N. Yeaple is Executive Professor of Business Administration at the William E. Simon Graduate School of Business Administration at the University of Rochester. Before joining the Simon School faculty, Dr. Yeaple was Executive Vice President of the Ritter Company, a biomedical equipment company, where he was responsible for Marketing, R&D, Manufacturing and Quality Assurance. He began his career as Product Manager of Consumer Products for Stromberg-Carlson stereophonic equipment.

A high point of his early career was designing a custom stereo system for President John F. Kennedy, which he personally installed in the living quarters of the White House. Later, he moved to Xerox Corporation, where he held a number of positions in new product development, before joining the Ritter Company.

A four-time winner of the Superior Teaching Award, Dr. Yeaple's research and teaching interests center on professional career development, marketing research, new product development, and the strategic management of technology. He is the author of a 1994 book, *The MBA Advantage: Why It Pays to Get an MBA,* that compares the leading business schools in terms of the financial returns to students earning the MBA. His recent research study, "Why Are Small R&D Organizations More Productive?" was published in the *IEEE Transactions on Engineering Management.* He has also published a number of articles on biomedical instrumentation, and he is the inventor of a patented electronic biomedical instrument for diagnosing periodontal disease that has been accepted by leading universities throughout the world as a standard instrument for clinical research. In recent years he has consulted with more than 40 companies, and he serves on the board of directors of Ameritherm, Inc.

Dr. Yeaple is also director of the Simon School's Business Innovation Team, which is sponsored by a grant from the New York State Science and Technology Foundation, in which teams of students and faculty analyze markets and develop business strategies for high-tech companies. He holds bachelor's and master's degrees in electrical engineering from Cornell University, and an MBA degree and a Ph.D. in electrical engineering from the University of Rochester.

Acknowledgments

My thanks to the many people who encouraged me to write this book about Strategic Skills, who contributed ideas, provided important information, read early drafts, and made hundreds of suggestions and helpful comments.

First, my thanks to the faculty and staff at the William E. Simon Graduate School of Business Administration at the University of Rochester, particularly Karen Amico, Rajiv Dewan, Faith Diehl, Julian Keilson, Amy Lill, John Long, Larry Matteson, George McIsaac, Ron Schmidt, Steve Schwartz, Kathryn Seely, Avi Seidmann, Len Schutzman, Melinda Smith, George Tomczyk, Peter Waasdorp, and Jerry Zimmerman. Thanks also to Dean Charles Plosser, Associate Deans Ron Hansen, Charlie Miersch, and Dick West, and Assistant Deans Priscilla Gumina and Lee Junkans for their ideas and support of this project. I would also like to thank faculty and deans at other business schools who shared their thoughts with me, particularly Professor Larry Robinson at the S. C. Johnson Graduate School of Management at Cornell University, and Dean Ed Moses at the Roy E. Crummer Graduate School of Business at Rollins College. My appreciation also to Brad Salai for reviewing the section on intellectual property, to Nancy Hessler, to the several anonymous reviewers who read the entire manuscript and made a number of exceptionally valuable suggestions, and to Cathleen Zdyb, for suggesting the title *The Success Principle*.

Second, I would like to express my deep appreciation to the 481 men and women who took time from their busy lives to fill out the surveys that form the basis for this book. Their stories of hard work, planning, and perseverance will provide much encouragement and inspiration for the readers of this book who recognize that others have faced similar challenges and have succeeded, often beyond their expectations.

Third, I thank my agent, Mike Snell, for recognizing the potential for this book and for his excellent advice as the book began to take shape; my editor, Dick Staron at Macmillan, for his guidance, patience, and skill in transforming the manuscript into a finished book; and my copy editor, Carol Sheehan, for her many excellent suggestions and recommendations.

And finally, I thank my family. To my wife, Bev, for her love and advice from the very beginning of this project; to my four adult children, David, Susan, Jodie, and Annie, and their spouses, Debi, Juan, and Eric, who continue to ask all the right questions; and to my mother, who at age 93 still has plenty of advice for her son.

INTRODUCTION

As a business school professor, I admire good teaching. The best teachers I ever had were not in business school but were in the freshman physics and chemistry courses I took as an engineering student at Cornell.

In the physics course, Doctor Grantham had a wonderful demonstration of the principle of the conservation of energy. One morning we came to class to find a solid brass spherical pendulum six inches in diameter hanging a few feet above the floor in the center of the demonstration area of the large lecture hall, suspended from a thin steel cable that disappeared high in the dim rafters of the ceiling. Grantham began by explaining how a pendulum has maximum potential energy at the top of its swing and maximum kinetic energy as it passes through the lowest part of its arc, and that it neither gains nor loses its total energy during a swing, except for a tiny loss to windage. The distinguished white-haired professor then walked over to the wall at the front of the room and turned to face the audience. His assistant pulled the heavy brass sphere over to where Grantham stood facing the audience, with the back of his head firmly against the front wall. Grantham brought the sphere up to the tip of his nose, and with a flourish, released it.

As the massive weight swung majestically out over the audience in a huge arc, every eye followed the polished brass sphere. When the sphere reached the highest point of its arc somewhere out over the middle of the audience, it seemed to hang motionless for a moment before it slowly began to swing back toward where Grantham stood, the back of his head still firmly against the wall. Picking up speed as it approached the low point of its arc, the massive pendulum rushed toward Grantham's face. He never flinched. Then, as if an invisible brake were being gently applied, the heavy sphere gradually slowed until it was barely moving as it approached the end of its arc, coming to a complete stop within a fraction of an inch of Grantham's nose, before it slowly began its swing back again toward the audience. A gasp came from the audience, followed by enthusiastic applause. And decades later, everyone who was in that lecture hall remembers the principle of the conservation of energy, how it is transformed from potential energy at each end of the arc to kinetic energy in the middle of the arc, and how energy is neither gained nor lost in the transformation.

But for high drama, the lectures in freshman chemistry were hard to beat. One day Doctor Sienko was describing how hydrogen explosions can occur only when the proper mix of hydrogen and oxygen is present. To illustrate, he picked up a pipe connected to some hoses from his bench at the front of the room and blew a small plastic bubble filled with a mixture of hydrogen and oxygen, perhaps four inches in diameter, at the end of the pipe. Using a gas flame on the end of a long wand, he ignited the mixture, which detonated with a sharp concussion that rattled the windows of the large lecture hall, startling the audience. Then, without comment, he slowly began to blow another bubble, at first just a few inches in diameter, then a foot, then eighteen inches across . . . .

As the clear plastic bubble gradually swelled to three feet in diameter, a wave of panic swept the audience. People began shouting. Students in the front rows dropped their notebooks and ran for the exits. Concerned that Sienko had lost his mind and was about to commit suicide, taking the north wing of Baker Hall with him, those of us further back sought protection by sliding down between the rows of folding seats. As we peered over the wooden seat backs, we watched Sienko slowly bring the gas flame toward the huge bubble, which wobbled menacingly in the air currents at the end of its pipe. But to our astonishment, at the instant of contact the bubble merely flared with a soft poof, disappearing in a cloud of mist. Unlike the first bubble, this one was filled with pure hydrogen. Without oxygen in the bubble, it would only flare and burn but would not explode. Again, a lesson we would never forget.

TEACHING BASED ON EVIDENCE FROM THE REAL WORLD

One of the reasons that Grantham and Sienko were so effective is that they were able to present an abstract theory like the conservation of energy, and then nail the concept with a vivid classroom demonstration of a real-world application of the theory. Their teaching was supported by graphic evidence from the real world.

As a business school professor, I teach about market opportunities and business strategies. Like my colleagues in the physical sciences, what I teach is based on evidence from the real world. I support the concepts I teach, not with demonstrations of swinging pendulums and exploding hydrogen bubbles, but with real-world evidence from companies like Microsoft and Honda Motors and, in the case of this book, with extensive survey data from hundreds of successful professional people.

There are many books about developing career strategies and how to cope with the uncertainties of today's job market. Some of these books are based only on the subjective opinions and personal experiences of the author. This book is different. It is based on hard evidence about what works and what doesn't; the evidence comes from the real world, from the actual experiences of nearly 500 professional men and women at various stages in their careers.

Suppose you had the opportunity to spend an evening sitting at a conference table with a small group of advisors, men and women your age or perhaps a few years older, who were eager to share their job experiences with you, and to offer you information and advice about how you could achieve the same degree of success that many of them have achieved. What would this experience be worth to you?

Now suppose you could meet with an entirely new group each evening for the next couple of months—a total of nearly 500 advisors. Think of the fresh insights and great ideas for career opportunities that you would gain.

SURVEYING THE ALUMNI

In the spring and summer of 1995, I conducted comprehensive mail surveys of alumni of the Simon Graduate School of Business Administration and of the Department of Electrical Engineering, both at the University of Rochester.[1] A total of 550 questionnaires were mailed out to a random sample of Simon School alumni, all of whom have MBA degrees, and another 500 to a random sample of electrical engineering alumni, over half of whom have graduate degrees. Between the two alumni groups, there were 481 usable responses for an overall response rate of 46%, which is considered excellent for a mail survey. To ensure the privacy of the respondents, all replies were anonymous.

DISCOVERING THE SUCCESS PRINCIPLE

By analyzing the replies to these surveys, I discovered that the most successful respondents were doing well—in some cases, spectacularly well—because they had developed a set of skills for making the changes that are taking place in today's turbulent job market actually work *for* them. These successful men and women have taken responsibility for their own careers and have made investments of time and money in a a set of strategic skills for leveraging change to make it work on their behalf. I call this the Success Principle.

Books have been written about the MBA programs and alumni of such top business schools as Harvard and Stanford.[2] While such books are interesting and informative, these business schools are among the most elite, and the findings are of limited practical value to the typical hard-working young professional who is trying to decide whether or not it pays to invest in an advanced degree from a high-quality regional school, either full-time or through a part-time program. In this sense, the experiences of MBA and engineering alumni from the University of Rochester, a high-quality regional university, are much more relevant and therefore more useful for personal career planning.[3]

CONCEPT OF THE BOOK

This book was written for the hundreds of thousands of men and women whose dreams for an interesting and productive career are being increasingly frustrated by corporate reengineering and downsizing. The overall premise of this book is based on published studies showing that there are jobs everywhere for those who qualify.[4] But to cope with today's turbulent job market, you must learn to think of yourself as the CEO of a "company of one"—yourself—and you can thrive and prosper in this market by developing a set of Strategic Skills for success, just as our most successful survey respondents have done. As it turns out, many of these Strategic Skills are adaptations of the strategic planning techniques that top corporations have used for years—concepts that will apply equally well to managing the success of your personal "company of one."

From time to time in this book, I talk about "turbocharging your career." For those of you who are not automobile buffs, a turbocharger is a device that can be added to the engine of a high-performance automobile to dramatically improve its acceleration. When I use the phrase "turbocharging your career," I am referring to an action or a strategy that my research shows can dramatically improve the acceleration of your career, to get you out in front of the pack.

I have drawn on a number of sources for this book:

First and foremost, this book is based on the career experiences of nearly 500 alumni of a high-quality regional university, many of whom faced choices and opportunities very much like those you face today.

In more than 20 years of teaching, I have taught many outstanding young men and women who were not included in the survey sample, and on occasion I have drawn on the stories and experiences of a number of them to illustrate career strategies that have turned out to be particularly effective.

Throughout, I have filled the book with quotations and brief passages from selected books and articles on career management and corporate strategy to illustrate the applicability of the concepts presented, and to add depth and interest. Many of these have been chosen from materials used in my MBA courses that my students have found to be exceptionally useful.

Prior to teaching, I held a number of managerial positions in industry, and in recent years I have also done consulting, served on some boards of directors, and run a small company as a part-time enterprise to complement my teaching. To round out the book, I have included a few personal war stories and experiences from these activities to show how some of these key concepts have helped me in my own career.

To summarize, I hope you will look upon this book as being like a course about strategies for investing in yourself, strongly supported by evidence from the real world, and potentially of great practical benefit to your long term professional success. This program requires planning, commitment, and hard work. But you can do it, and, believe me, it is worth it.

....

1   See Appendix B for a discussion of the research methods used.

2   Two of the most recent are John Kotter's *The New Rules* (The Free Press, 1995), about alumni of the Harvard Business School, and Peter Robinson's *Snapshots from Hell: the Making of an MBA* (Warner Books, 1994), about the MBA program at Stanford.

3   To the extent that such rankings are meaningful, the University of Rochester was ranked 29th in the country by *U.S. News & World Report* in 1995, and the Simon School was ranked 23rd among graduate schools of business by *U.S. News* in 1996. For a discussion of the limitations of the various schemes for ranking business schools, see my previous book, *The MBA Advantage: Why It Pays to Get an MBA* (Bob Adams Inc., 1994), particularly Appendix B.

4   See, for example, Markels, A., "Restructuring Alters Middle-Manager Role but Leaves It Robust," *The Wall Street Journal,* September 25, 1995, p. A1; and Arnst, C., "Out One Door and In Another," *Business Week,* January 22, 1996, p. 41.

THERE ARE PLENTY OF GREAT JOBS— IF YOU QUALIFY

'K athy,' age 26, is an Operations Manager at a major telecommunications company, where she has 15 employees in Network Operations reporting to her.[1] She makes $54,000 a year.

It's a great job, with plenty of responsibility, unlimited potential, and an excellent salary for someone who is only 26. How did she qualify for it?

Graduating from college with a liberal arts degree, Kathy went to work for a well-known package delivery company, where she was assigned to an entry-level managerial position. When it became apparent that her growth in salary and responsibilities would be very limited, she began to investigate other options, and soon realized that she needed to upgrade her professional qualifications in order to get the kind of job she really wanted.

Her first move was to take a couple of night courses in accounting and economics at a local business school, which she paid for herself because her employer did not offer a tuition reimbursement plan. She did well in the courses and was accepted into the part-time MBA degree program. When scheduling changes at the package delivery company made it impossible to continue with her night courses, she quit her $18,000 a year job and transferred to the full-time MBA program, taking out student loans to pay her tuition.

Kathy decided to major in Marketing. In one of her elective courses, she and two of her classmates carried out an extensive marketing research project for the local phone company to develop a marketing plan for pre-paid long distance calling cards.

When she graduated with her MBA degree at age 25— which is two years younger than the age at which most full-time MBA students *start* their MBA studies—she initially had difficulty getting job offers because she was so much younger than the other students. But she persisted, and by leveraging the knowledge and experience she gained from her marketing research project for the phone company, she eventually received an offer from her new employer, a major regional telecommunications company.

TURBOCHARGING HER CAREER

Kathy qualified for such a great job because she took stock of her situation, realized that things were not going to improve at the package delivery company, and made a major investment of time and money to upgrade her professional qualifications.

The payoff from her investment has been enormous. Her salary rocketed up by a factor of *three* times, from $18,000 to $54,000, in just over two years. Moreover, she now has a challenging job with professional supervisory responsibilities, and a bright future with a top company. Kathy turbocharged her career.

Kathy has some advice for other young professionals who are pursuing a career in management: "First, it's never too early to start your job search. Second, cross-train in different functional areas. I majored in Marketing, but I'm actually working in Operations. Third, seek and evaluate a lot of advice from people with more experience."

MIDDLE MANAGER ROLE SURVIVES DOWNSIZING

Contrary to what the press has been reporting, middle management in America is surviving and, in many places, prospering. Government statistics cited in *The Wall Street Journal* show that there are plenty of high-quality middle management jobs like Kathy's:[2]

- "Reports of middle management's demise are much exaggerated," says *The Wall Street Journal*. Government data shows that the number of managerial jobs in Fortune 500 and other companies reporting to the Equal Employment Opportunities Commission *has remained almost unchanged* since peaking at nearly five million in 1990.

- In the decade from 1983 to 1993, the government reports that the total number of executives, managers, and administrators in the whole workforce *grew* by 28.8%.

- While the very largest corporations—those with payrolls of more than 50,000—have fewer management jobs than in 1989, small- and medium-size companies have *added* about 180,000 management jobs since 1989. Small, high-tech firms have fueled spectacular growth in management

Pursuing a Dream: From Staff Accountant to Screenwriter

'Craig,' 29, graduated in 1987 with a bachelor's degree in economics and finance. After working for a year as a staff accountant for a department store at a salary of $23,000, he resigned to attend graduate school, earning an MBA in 1990.

His first job after graduation was as an associate director for a bank in New York City, at a starting salary of $46,000—twice his pre-MBA pay.

But Craig soon discovered that banking and big companies in general were not for him. His dream was to become an independent screenwriter for the Hollywood film industry. After a year as a banker, he left New York to pursue his dream, working by himself to develop his craft. Within three years he established himself in his new profession, earning $100,000—more than four times his pre-MBA pay.

Like Kathy, Craig has turbocharged his career. He believes that while his MBA degree has allowed him to bring an analytical framework to a creative field, his success as a screenwriter is mainly the result of "discipline, will, learning about and listening to myself, and heart."

His advice to other young professionals: "Think very hard about what you want professionally and personally in this life, and meet as many people as possible in your field of interest."

jobs. Says one manager in a small telecommunications firm, "The industry is exploding. *There is so much opportunity in the marketplace, it's incredible.*"

Kathy is well on her way to success as a middle manager in a large telecommunications corporation. But perhaps middle management is not your goal.

Kathy and Craig are not geniuses or superstars. In many ways, they may be very much like you. The reason they are doing so well is that they took charge of their careers and made strategic investments of time and money to upgrade their professional qualifications—something you can do as well.

A GRADUATE DEGREE: DESIRABLE BUT NOT ESSENTIAL

No Time for Grad School

'Rick,' age 36, earned his undergraduate degree in electrical engineering in 1980 and began graduate studies that were to lead to a Ph.D. degree in biomedical engineering. But he was in a hurry, and he soon learned that the slow, scholarly pace of a Ph.D. program was not for him. Instead, he dropped out of the program to become an entrepreneur.

Today, Rick earns $120,000 a year as president of his own company that manufactures electronic medical devices. Although he hires subordinates with advanced degrees, he has no regrets about dropping out of the Ph.D. program. He took charge of his career, decided that he really wanted to run his own company, and made it happen.

Although many of our success stories are about men and women who invested in graduate degrees to improve their Strategic Skills, there are some important exceptions. These include people who were highly-focused and who gained their Strategic Skills from self-study and, in some cases, by hiring subordinates with graduate degrees to fill in the gaps in their own formal education.

A NEW MIX OF SKILLS FOR TODAY'S WORKPLACE

There are exceptional opportunities for managers who qualify. But to succeed in today's demanding workplace, managers need a new mix of Strategic Skills:

- <u>Multifunctional skills</u>: The narrow specialist is obsolete. Managers are being assigned to get things done in multifunctional teams, which requires them to master a wide breadth of knowledge to be effective.

- <u>Decision-making skills</u>: The leaner, flatter organizations of today are wiping out purely 'advisory' staff jobs. Today, managers at all levels need the analytical skills to make solid management decisions on their own, without comprehensive staff support.

- <u>Enhanced people skills</u>: The reduction in corporate hierarchy requires people to work together without command authority. Today's manager has to become an expert at building constructive personal strategic alliances with others.

- <u>Personal marketing skills</u>: Corporations are unable to promise lifetime employment. The only real security comes from managers' core competencies and their professional reputations—which means knowing how to market themselves.

Let's look at each one of these new skills in more detail.

MULTIFUNCTIONAL SKILLS

Years ago, large companies were made up of departments of functional specialists—accountants, salespeople, engineers. These people spent most of their time working in their own little groups, seldom talking with people in other parts of the company, or with customers.[3] Coordination between groups was orchestrated by layers of middle managers. Decisions were made slowly and cautiously, with multiple signoffs by each layer of management.

In today's competitive environment, decisions have to be made much more quickly and accurately than in the past. In their best selling book, *The Wisdom of Teams*, McKinsey & Company consultants Jon Katzenbach and Douglas Smith make the case for organizing the company into multifunctional teams. They find that teams consistently outperform collections of individuals organized by traditional job functions. Citing examples from Motorola, Ford, 3M, and General Electric, Katzenbach and Smith show that the multifunctional team has become a critical element in the new product strategies of these top firms.[4]

What is the difference between a team and a committee? Both are made up of individuals from various parts of the organization. But the individual contributions of members of a *committee* are based solely on their personal expertise. In the case of a *team*, their contributions are combined into a joint product that embodies the collective wisdom of all the members.

For example, a multifunctional new product development "team" typically will consist of individuals from Marketing, Engineering, Manufacturing, and Accounting. If the person from Marketing is concerned only with what Marketing wants from the new product program, and shows no empathy for the tradeoffs that Engineering and Manufacturing face in developing and starting up the new product within the overall constraints of project time and cost, then the group operates as a *committee*. But if Marketing shows an understanding of the problems of the other members and a willingness to work together to make the entire project a success, then the group operates as a *team*. In the second case, Marketing is concerned not with scoring points for Marketing, but in making the whole project a success—even if Marketing has to make some compromises.

To be effective, the individuals on the team must have multifunctional skills—a working knowledge of the functional areas outside their personal area of expertise. If, for example, the Marketing person on the team is uninformed and naive about the development and startup processes in Engineering and Manufacturing, he or she could get taken for a ride and end up making unnecessary compromises, or could insist on product features that are technically unreasonable. I will illustrate with the following story from my own experience.

Years ago, I worked for a marketing manager who had come up through the sales organization and had no awareness or sympathy for the kinds of tradeoffs that engineers face in developing new products. 'Frank' was a great salesman and a compulsive winner—he had to win every argument, even when he was wrong.

One time we were negotiating with Engineering about whether or not a recently-developed solid state component should be used in one of our new products. Frank argued that incorporating this new component in the design would give the product a big sales advantage with potential customers. Engineering resisted, pointing out that the new component was untried and untested, and might fail in the field.

Frank pounded the table with such fury that the engineers finally gave up and agreed under duress to incorporate the untried component which, as they predicted, turned out to be unreliable. Some 25,000 of the new products were manufactured and delivered to customers—and all 25,000 failed in the field and had to be returned, creating a major embarrassment and a large financial loss for the company.

Specialize, but also Understand How the Whole Business Operates

'Doug' graduated from college in 1978 with an undergraduate degree in English. His first job was as a Medical Records Clerk in a hospital, at $7,500 per year. In 1980, he earned an MBA degree with a concentration in information systems management, and went to work for a major systems consulting firm, at an annual salary of $22,000.

Fifteen years later, Doug is still with the same systems consulting company, but today he is a senior executive with 150 people reporting to him. His total compensation is $400,000 per year. His advice to aspiring young managers: "Take additional courses in information systems and finance, but also be sure to gain an overall understanding of how a business operates."

The objective when serving on a new product development team is not to win for your personal functional organization, but to win for the company as a whole. Sometimes this means having enough knowledge about the other functions of the company to know when to back off.

Many of the highest-paying jobs in the new economy require a wide breadth of knowledge, as well as specialized skills. Consider the case from the management survey responses above.

To survive and prosper in today's team-oriented environment, managers must have multifunctional skills as well as expertise in their own specialized area. Chapter 3, "Obtaining General Business Knowledge," will explore ways to acquire a working knowledge of how the various parts of the business work beyond your own functional area.

DECISION-MAKING SKILLS

In the hierarchical organizations of the 1980s and early 1990s, you didn't make many decisions without checking with your boss—and often your boss would have to check with his or her boss. In today's leaner organizations, the authority to make decisions is being delegated to those in lower levels of the organization. A Xerox Corp. executive says, "The reality of re-engineering is that many more people are in a decision-making mode."[5] You are much more likely to be given the responsibility for making your own decisions, and for being completely accountable for the outcomes. As one young manager reported recently, " . . . I used to have to go through my manager to implement anything I needed to do. Now I have a lot more latitude."[6]

To compound the problem, in the old organization of the 1980s, typically there were legions of staff experts available for consultation on everything from marketing research to office layout. But many of these purely advisory staff jobs have been eliminated in today's flatter, leaner organizations. If you have to make an important decision, it is likely that you will have to do it without the help of internal staff support.[7] You will be on your own, perhaps with support from a computerized decision-support system.

With less staff support available, managers who are personally skilled at structuring and analyzing complex decisions have a critical competitive advantage in today's organizations. Chapter 5, "Sharpening Your Analytical Abilities," will help you develop fundamental approaches to become more skilled in structuring and analyzing business problems.

PEOPLE SKILLS

People skills—the ability to get things done through other people—are what distinguish managers from individual contributors. People skills include leadership, and the ability to work with a team and to persuade others through written and oral communications. The star loner is of little value in today's organizations.

In the hierarchical organizations of the past, information about critical operating variables, such as sales and shipments, was gathered at the bottom of the organization and then summarized, refined, and selectively edited by layers of middle managers as it was passed up the line to top management. Then, after reflection, orders based on this information would come down from the top, again layer-by-layer, staff meeting-by-staff meeting, until they reached the troops in the field or on the production line.

For example, if sales were lagging behind budget, this information would work its way to the top over a period of days or weeks. A decision would be made at the vice presidential level to cut prices by 5%, which would then be transmitted back down the organization over a period of days or weeks to the people in sales, who would see to its implementation. The whole process might take a month or more, during which the situation in the field might have changed, and the 5% price cut would be either too late or, perhaps, completely unnecessary.

In today's marketplace, information technology has revolutionized the flow of information in organizations. Virtually all managers have computers in their offices.[8] By consulting their computers, senior management—and everyone else in the organization—know within a matter of hours how sales are going. The need for layers of middle managers to collect and summarize information has disappeared.

To speed up decision-making, senior management has delegated the authority to make decisions to first line managers, who have the most expertise to deal with the problem and who have the most to gain or lose by the results. The middle management hierarchy for command and control is gone.

With the decline of hierarchy, the basis for managerial decision-making is changing, from "Do it because I'm the boss" to "Do it because we agree it's the right thing to do." The emphasis is on persuasion of colleagues, not on command of subordinates.[9] This means that today's manager will greatly benefit from becoming skilled in the art of persuasion. Chapter 8 will discuss the development of specific approaches for

Change Careers to Find a Job You Love—"Success Will Follow"

'Thomas,' 29, is in the midst of a major career change. In 1987, with a freshly-minted BS degree in optics, he went to work for a laser manufacturer, where his annual pay rose to $41,000. But he soon found that he did not want to spend the rest of his career working as an optical engineer. In 1991, he took the Graduate Management Admissions Test (GMAT), scoring a very respectable 650, and in 1992 he left the laser company to begin work on an MBA in Finance and International Management.

Following receipt of his MBA in 1994, Thomas joined a very small money-management firm as an equity analyst, where he puts in about 50 hours a week at the office and another 2-3 hours a week working at home. Although his current pay, at $47,000, is not much higher than his pre-MBA pay, he's very satisfied with the long-run potential of his new career path in Finance, giving his new job a satisfaction rating of "5" on a scale of 1-to-5. His five-year goal is to grow professionally and to take on managerial responsibilities.

Thomas says that the most important skills he gained from his MBA program were in the fields of Accounting and Finance. As to leveraging the MBA as a means for a career change, he says the following: "Do not compromise when choosing your new job. A fresh MBA graduate has immense power to change the course of his or her life."

enhancing your skills of persuasion and communication.

MARKETING YOUR STRATEGIC SKILLS

You can't count on spending your entire career with one employer, or even in one industry.

In today's environment, companies are unable to promise lifetime employment. As Walter Kiechell, *Fortune's* Executive Editor, has pointed out, "Honest companies will avoid organizational co-dependency."[10]

Not only must you develop and refine your managerial skills for the changing environment, but you must also think about how you are going to market them. To get the most value from your investment in these skills, people have to be made aware of them.

One way to market yourself is to polish your writing skills and to document your ideas in writing. Your written work has the potential to reach a much larger audience within the company than your day-to-day oral communications, as I learned early in my career.

In the course of my work as a young systems engineer at Xerox Corporation, I wrote a report for my manager about a new telecommunications system that the company was developing, called high speed facsimile. This system required special dedicated wideband long-distance telephone lines that were very costly. In my report, I

His advice to other aspiring managers: "Do not accept any job offer that will not make you deliriously happy. Success will follow."

Like Craig, the accountant-turned-screenwriter, Thomas is following his dream.

pointed out that most of the profit from the proposed system would be made by the long distance telephone carriers, not by Xerox. At the time, I shared a cubicle with 'Bob,' another young engineer, and I gave him a copy of my rather critical report.

A few months later, Bob was given a temporary assignment in the Corporate Office, and in the course of his work, he passed along a copy of my report to Joe Wilson, the legendary Chairman of the Board of Xerox. Mr. Wilson found the report of great interest, particularly the part about how most of the profits would go to the phone companies, and proceeded to ask some hard questions of Xerox's senior R&D management. My boss, who had a stake in the continuance of the project, was not pleased, and I was embarrassed. Not long after, the project was phased out by top management.

The moral of this story is to keep in mind that once a written report of yours is out of your hands, it can end up anywhere in the organization. Before you send out that controversial memo, set it aside overnight and read it again in the cold light of morning. Be sure about what you write — it may end up being read by the Chairman of the Board.

To enhance your reputation outside the company, join a professional organization in your field and attend meetings. Become an officer. Develop an area of expertise in your field that will provide the subject for presentations at conferences, and for written articles for professional journals. Chapter 10, "Learning to Market Your Strategic Skills," will expand on ways to market yourself within your company and within your profession outside your company.

BEGIN TO THINK OF YOURSELF AS A "COMPANY OF ONE"

In this chapter, we have presented a brief overview of what it takes to qualify for the great jobs that are out there. The chapters that follow will develop a conceptual framework for developing these skills. The first step in creating this conceptual framework, which is the subject of Chapter 2, is to envision yourself as the CEO of a "company of one"—yourself. Over the next several chapters, we will develop a corporate strategy for your "company of one," and an organization chart in which each box contains a Strategic Skill needed for success in today's fast-changing world.

Welcome to your new job, as CEO of your "company of one."

....

[1] In keeping with my promise not to identify individual respondents, 'Kathy's' name and a few of the details of her case history have been disguised, but the important facts as she related them in her survey response have not been changed. This is also true of the other case histories described in this book.

[2] Markels, A., "Restructuring Alters Middle-Manager Role but Leaves It Robust," *The Wall Street Journal*, September 25, 1995, p. A1, emphasis added.

[3] A few years ago, I published an article showing how infrequently engineers in large companies in the mid-1980s talked with people outside of their own organizations. Most of their meetings were with other engineers, and typically only 3% of all the time they devoted to meetings was spent talking with customers. Yet they freely acknowledged that customers were their best source for successful new product ideas. See Yeaple, R.,

"Why are Small R&D Organizations More Productive?," *IEEE Transactions on Engineering Management*, Vol. 39, No. 4, November, 1992, pp. 332-346.

4 Katzenbach, J. and Smith, D., "The Wisdom of Teams," Harvard Business School Press, 1993, p. 15.

5 Markels, A., p. A1.

6 Ibid.

7 Many of these experts are now working for small consulting companies that service large corporations. You still may be able to get their advice—but now you will have to pay for it by the hour.

8 One of the interesting findings from our survey of managers was that virtually all—95%—have a computer in their office that they use on a daily basis.

9 For a number of years, I have devoted part of one lecture in my marketing courses to a discussion of the job of Product Manager. A Product Manager has responsibility for the success of a product line but no formal authority over those in the organization, such as Sales, who can determine its success. Without command authority, Product Managers have to learn to excel at persuasion. As I tell my students, this is wonderful training for young managers, because when they become senior managers, they will still emphasize persuasion over command.

10 Kiechell, W., "A Manager's Career in the New Economy," *Fortune*, April 4, 1994, p. 70.

2

TAKING CHARGE AS CEO OF YOUR "COMPANY OF ONE"

'Peter,' age 36, earned a bachelor's degree in printing technology in 1982, and went to work as a sales representative for a printing company. Over the next four years he took a number of evening courses at a local business school and eventually decided that he wanted to make a career move, into the area of Finance. In 1986, he quit his $50,000 a year sales job to finish up his MBA full time. He graduated a year later with concentrations in Finance and Accounting. Following graduation, he accepted a job as a credit analyst for a bank at a salary of $35,000, substantially less than the $50,000 he earned as a salesman.

Peter quickly recouped his initial setback in salary and moved ahead to achieve his goal of building a career in the financial industry. Today he earns $200,000 a year as a partner in an investment brokerage firm. He puts in long hours, typically 55 hours a week, but he loves what he is doing. On a job satisfaction scale of 1-to-5, he rates his job a "5."

After deciding that he didn't want to spend the rest of his life as a printing company salesman, Peter took charge of his career. He credits his MBA with increasing his self-confidence, but he believes that the biggest factor in achieving his goal was his inner motivation, his "fire in the belly," as he puts it. His advice to others: "Be aggressive. Decide what you want. Go for it. Don't take 'no' for an answer. If you are smart and competent, the sky's the limit."

EARNINGS INCREASED BY 3½ TIMES IN FIVE YEARS

Another case history from the survey beautifully illustrates the process of taking charge of your career.

In 1986, 'Barbara' earned a liberal arts degree in English literature at Columbia University, where she met her future husband, an aspiring actor. The week after graduation, at age 21, she was married. She and her husband moved to Hollywood, where she tried to sell screenplays and her husband searched for work as an actor. A year and a half later, Barbara became pregnant with their first child.

To generate enough income to pay the bills, the young couple managed residential real estate and Barbara also ran a word-processing service from their one-bedroom apartment. At the same time, she began thinking about graduate school. A month after the birth of their son, Barbara took the Graduate Management Admissions Test (GMAT) and scored 590. A few months later, she took it again and scored 650. Then she applied to a number of MBA programs and was offered a substantial scholarship at the University of Rochester's Simon School, which she decided to accept.

In the summer of 1990, she quit her $20,000 a year job as a property manager for a real estate company, and she and her family moved to Rochester, NY, to pursue her MBA in Marketing. She also accepted a part-time job working for a physician at the University of Rochester Medical Center.

As the result of her part-time work at the Medical Center, Barbara identified pharmaceutical marketing as the area in which she wanted to build her career. Working with the business school's Career Services office, she targeted a number of pharmaceutical companies, and during the summer between the first and second year of her MBA program, she secured a summer internship with an internationally renowned pharmaceutical company. Subsequently, this same company offered her a full-time Marketing job after she graduated in 1992, at $62,000 a year.

Today, Barbara, at age 30, makes $70,000—3½ times what she was earning five years ago—as a Brand Manager for a West Coast pharmaceutical company. As a rising young star in her company, she puts in long hours, averaging 52 hours a week at the office and another six hours a week at home. Since graduation, she has been the sole financial support for her family while her husband returned to school. In the spring of 1995, she had her second child and took a 2½ month maternity leave.

Despite the long hours, she rates her job satisfaction as a "5." If she had to do it over again, she would again pursue an MBA at the Simon School. She says that the most important skill she learned at business school was how to structure and solve complex problems. Regarding the value of her MBA, she says: "The MBA degree has enabled me to secure my family's financial future. It has also enabled me to use my creative talents to the benefit of my company as well as myself. As a female in business, I feel the MBA has given me training and a credential which garners respect and makes it a little easier to prove myself—which I have done."

Her advice to others: "Manage your own career. No one else will."

YOU CAN'T EXPECT YOUR COMPANY TO TAKE CARE OF YOU

Peter and Barbara are representative of the hundreds of survey respondents who have taken charge of their careers. To succeed in today's job market, you cannot rely on your employer to manage your career. In our survey of MBA graduates, many of whom are outstandingly successful, a mere 22% of the respondents agreed with the statement, "If you do excellent work, you can trust your company to promote you." As Barbara said, "Manage your own career. No one else will." You are on your own.

THE SUCCESS PRINCIPLE: INVESTING IN THE 10 STRATEGIC SKILLS FOR PERSONAL SUCCESS

Okay, at this point you might say, "how do I manage my career?"

Analysis of the survey results shows that there are 10 Strategic Skills that are essential for success in today's environment. Some jobs require more knowledge of one Strategic Skill than another (for example, proficiency with data analysis software is very important for marketing researchers, somewhat important for brand managers, and relatively unimportant for sales managers). But because of the new emphasis on multifunctional teams, effective professionals of all kinds need some degree of knowledge of every one of these 10 Strategic Skills:

1. <u>Taking charge of your career as CEO of your "company of one</u>." As we noted, only 22% of the survey respondents agreed with the statement, "If you do excellent work, you can trust your company to promote you." In today's workplace, you are on your own. The first Strategic Skill is learning to manage yourself as a "company of one."

2. <u>Obtaining general business knowledge</u>. The narrow functional specialist is obsolete, according to the survey respondents. To be effective as a member of a multifunctional team, you must have a basic knowledge of how the various parts of the business work, beyond your own functional area.

3. <u>Acquiring specific industry knowledge</u>. You must understand your own industry in great depth—who your key competitors are, how the companies in your industry compete, and how your company has positioned itself to satisfy its customers.

4. <u>Sharpening your analytical abilities</u>. You won't be able to compete in today's workplace if you think that business decisions can be based solely on intuition and experience. The most successful of the survey respondents ranked analytical problem-solving as the number one Strategic Skill for managerial success.

5. <u>Building computer competence</u>. According to the survey, personal computer use is universal among managers of all levels and ages, with 95% reporting that they use a computer in their office on a regular basis. Because today's youth have grown up with computers, young managers have a huge natural advantage to be at the leading edge in their companies in the application of computers to business opportunities.

6. <u>Learning to manage innovation</u>. Thriving companies are incorporating the latest technology into new products and services. Accelerating the development of profitable new products and services is one of the hottest areas in management today, and to be successful, you must understand how the R&D process works. *The Wall Street Journal*, reporting on a recent American Management Association survey on job creation, stated, "[There] is a strong indication that newly created jobs require . . . a new range of skill sets with heavy emphasis on technological know-how."[1]

7. <u>Developing skills for working with people</u>. The star loner is of little value in today's organizations. A manager's value is directly tied to how much he or she can accomplish in cooperation with others. With the decline of corporate hierarchy, you must also learn to manage strategic alliances with your peers outside of your immediate organization.

8. <u>Polishing your personal core competencies</u>. Core competencies are what you offer the company that clearly set you apart from other employees. It may be your Strategic Skill in designing new software, writing advertising copy, or laying out a new production line. This is the area where you must work hard to be the very best that you can be—perhaps even world class. But you must guard against being too free in sharing your hard-earned knowhow with others, lest your Strategic Skills be "hollowed out." And you must be concerned about the portability of your core competencies if you leave the company—be sure to pick an area that has value to more than just your current employer. Finally, you should be quick to upgrade any of your core competencies that would be made obsolete by emerging technologies.

9. <u>Learning to market your Strategic Skills</u>. To get the most value from your investment in your personal core competencies, people have to be made aware of them. You must learn to market your Strategic Skills within your organization and on the outside, among those in your professional field. This can be accomplished by writing articles

for journals and by holding office and giving talks at professional meetings. One of the most effective ways to promote your skills is by obtaining third party certification, in the form of a certificate of completion for a professional short course. An even better way to promote your skills is by earning an MBA degree from a recognized business school.

10. <u>Selecting and cultivating mentors</u>. Survey respondents reported that advice from senior managers who served as mentors was as valuable as the content of all of the MBA courses they took. But successful mentoring relationships don't just happen—they have to be developed and managed.

TAKING CHARGE AS CEO OF YOUR "COMPANY OF ONE"

As a conceptual framework for building these 10 Strategic Skills, visualize yourself as competing in the job market as the CEO of a "company of one"—yourself. This underscores the point that "the buck stops here:" you really are on your own in managing your career. You—not your company—are the boss.

To help you, as CEO, to see the big picture, over the next several chapters we will develop an organization chart of your "company of one." Each Strategic Skill will occupy a box in your new organization chart. For a preview of what your completed organization chart will look like when we have finished, see Figure 2.1.

CORPORATE STRATEGY FOR YOUR "COMPANY OF ONE"

Welcome to the Executive Suite. As they say, it's lonely at the top (see Figure 2.2).

Before beginning the process of filling in the empty boxes in the organization chart of your "company of one," it is important to give some serious thought to developing an overall

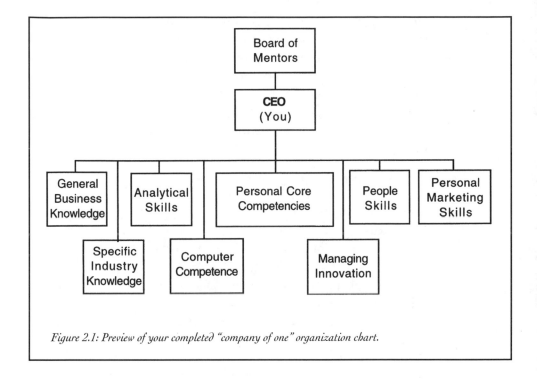

Figure 2.1: Preview of your completed "company of one" organization chart.

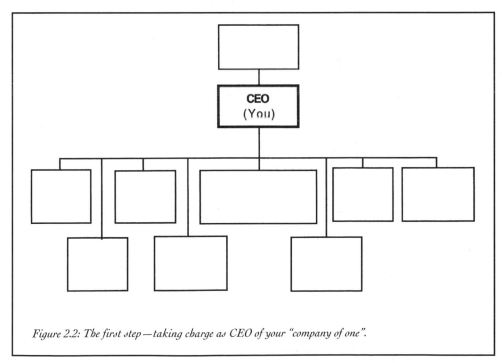

Figure 2.2: The first step—taking charge as CEO of your "company of one".

strategy for your "company of one." In the course of developing this strategy, we will introduce a number of state-of-the-art corporate strategic planning concepts that are used by today's major corporations—objectives and mission statements, strategic intent, multifunctional teams, the strategic management of innovation, core competencies, loose bricks, hollowing out, market positioning, protecting the value of intellectual property, and strategic alliances.

THE CONCEPT OF STRATEGY

Strategy is not the same as forecasting. Forecasting is an attempt to predict the future, something that, in most cases, is difficult if not impossible to do accurately. Forecasting deals with uncertainty. Attempts to forecast the stock market or the growth rate of the economy or the size of next year's market for automobiles are wrong as often as they are right. As someone once said, we need to have a strategy because of our inability to forecast.

Developing a strategy, whether for companies or for individuals, is useful for a number of reasons:

- We need some kind of rules for sorting out all the opportunities that come our way. Otherwise, the choices become unmanageable.

- From time to time, we need a prod to force us to think about what is really important to us, versus spending all of our time fighting fires. Developing and periodically updating our strategy provides this prod.

- Sometimes, when faced with an unexpected opportunity, we need help to avoid making a purely emotional decision. At such times, we can ask, "Does this really fit my strategy?"

- A well-developed strategy includes a time line, a series of target dates that define when key milestone events should occur, such as getting promoted, or completing a certain course. The strategy then provides a mechanism for checking progress toward these milestones.

- A personal strategy gives focus to your life, so that all the choices you make tend to move you in the general direction of your goals.

- A strategy gives consistency of purpose over time. We all know people who work very hard but who are constantly changing their mind about what they want to do, and end up accomplishing little or nothing. A strategy reminds us to "stay the course" long enough to achieve our objectives.

- Developing a strategy is a dynamic process that is never completed. As such, the strategy process recognizes that change is inevitable, and that we can often prosper by taking advantage of such changes if we recognize them as opportunities.

- Finally, the development of a strategy provides a sense of commitment, and from this commitment we can often accomplish much more than we originally thought possible (see the discussion of *strategic intent* later in this chapter).

What, then, is a strategy? Think of a strategy as a set of objectives—those things you want to accomplish—and a set of flexible rules or action steps for achieving those objectives. Corporate strategies also are characterized by a long planning horizon, usually measured in years, and by an emphasis on understanding and responding to problems and situations originating from outside the firm. Bear this in mind as we review the meaning of various strategic concepts that we will apply to your "company of one."

Objectives and Mission Statements

The first step in the development of a strategy for your "company of one" is to determine what will constitute success. Think of your *objectives* as measures of success for yourself and your family, and think of your *mission statement* as defining the kind of person you want to be. These two concepts are related, but they are not the same.

Your *mission statement* defines your vision and your values. Decades ago, some of our most successful companies developed mission statements, defining the basis on how they were going to do business. Examples are Hewlett-Packard's "HP Way" and Johnson & Johnson's "Credo." In his recent book, *The HP Way*, founder David Packard describes the role of the HP Way at Hewlett-Packard:

> *Any organization, any group of people who have worked together for some time, develops a philosophy, a set of values, a series of traditions and customs. These, in total, are unique to the organization. So it is with Hewlett-Packard. We have a set of values—deeply held beliefs that guide us in meeting our objectives, in working with one another, and in dealing with customers, shareholders, and others. Our corporate objectives are built upon these values.*[2]

For some, a personal mission statement might be as simple as "to make a contribution to the lives of others." For others, it may be more complex, with individual statements relating to family, friends, professional colleagues, and society. As Stephen Covey suggests in his best-selling book, *The Seven Habits of Highly Effective People*, think of your mission statement as addressing the question of how you want to be remembered after your death. Covey goes on to devote a large part of his book to the development of personal mission statements. *"The Seven Habits"* is a highly recommended source for help in working through the process of creating a personal mission statement.[3]

Covey notes that for many, a personal mission statement serves the same purpose as the Constitution does for the country, specifying the groundrules for what behavior and activities are and are not acceptable. Your mission statement defines your personal ethical standards, those things you will and will not do in pursuing your objectives.

Your *objectives* define what you want to achieve. Your personal objectives might involve starting a small software company, writing a successful book, inventing a new medical instrument, becoming the general manager of your division, or making enough money to be able to retire from corporate life at age 45 and become a college teacher. Your objectives define how you measure success.

For companies and for individuals, there is often the tendency to shoot too low in setting objectives. James Collins and Jerry Porras, in research for their book, *Built to Last*, found that companies with "audacious goals" consistently outperformed more timid companies in the same industries.[4] The same is true for individuals. You need to set goals that will stretch yourself. As Theodore Roosevelt said almost a century ago:

> *"Far better it is to dare mighty things, to win glorious triumphs, even though checkered by failure, than to take rank with those poor spirits who neither enjoy much nor suffer much, because they live in the gray twilight that knows not victory nor defeat."*[5]

At right is an example of a young professional from our survey who has set a high objective, a top management position in five years, and is well on her way to achieving it.

The bottom line: Make sure the professional objectives for your "company of one" are appropriate for you and your

Setting a Personal Stretch Goal

'Cindy', at 31, is leveraging the combination of her technical undergraduate degree and her recently-acquired MBA in Finance and Marketing to shoot for her five-year objective as a top manager of a major East Coast telecommunications firm. She graduated with a bachelor's degree in electrical engineering in 1986 and was hired as an assistant engineer at a telecommunications company, at an annual salary of $32,000. That fall, she began her part-time MBA program at a local business school, where 100% of her tuition was paid by her employer.

After completing her MBA in 1991, Cindy was promoted to Engineering Manager at a salary of $55,000. Within three years she was promoted again, this time to Director of Network Strategy. She works an average of 50 hours a week at the office, spends another five hours a week on company travel, and brings home an hour's worth of work every night. She also manages to squeeze in another 10 hours a week for tennis and golf. She earns $75,000 a year (an 18% increase over the prior year), supervises 33 employees, and rates her job satisfaction as a "5".

Asked about the most valuable skills she acquired in business school, she lists general business acumen, as well as financial and marketing skills. In retrospect, she wishes that she had taken more case-oriented courses to give her more practice in applying her new skills. While she values the skills she learned in her MBA courses, she also gives much

(continued)

credit for her rapid rise in the company to senior managers who took an interest in her career and served as her mentors.

Overall, Cindy is very satisfied with the value of her part-time MBA degree and would definitely do it again if she had to do it over. She says, "It has given me a broader business perspective which has assisted me in career advancement."

Incidentally, her advice to up-and-coming managers, appropriately is: "Network, network, network!"

family, and resist the temptation to set them too low. If in doubt, be like Cindy, and aim high. You may surprise yourself with what you are able to accomplish.

Strategic Intent

Strategic intent captures the essence of leadership and winning. It involves striving to make your "company of one" the "best in class" in your chosen field. Think of strategic intent as enhancing and focusing the objectives of your "company of one."

In their landmark article introducing the concept of strategic intent, Gary Hamel and C.K. Prahalad showed that by capturing the essence of winning as the cornerstone of their strategies, some companies have achieved success out of proportion to their initial resources.[6] For example, in 1970, Honda was a small automotive producer and had not yet begun to export cars to the U.S. By 1987, Honda's worldwide sales of cars nearly matched those of Chrysler. Similarly, Canon was initially tiny compared to Xerox, yet in the 1980s, Canon matched Xerox's global unit market share of the office copier market. (For the details of Canon's successful strategy, see Chapter 9.)

A classic example of strategic intent is John F. Kennedy's call to action, which came, in a speech to Congress in 1961, at a time of great national uncertainty during the height of the Cold War:

> *"I believe this nation should commit itself to achieving the goal, before this decade is out, of landing a man on the moon and returning him safely to earth."*[7]

Given the limited technology of the early '60s and the lead that the Soviet Union already had achieved in putting men into orbit, the goal seemed outrageous at the time. Yet the national commitment was made, and in 1969, before the decade was out, men did land on the moon and return safely. The United States won the race with the Soviet Union and achieved global recognition as "best in class" in space exploration.

For your "company of one," strategic intent means choosing an area where you have the opportunity to be truly outstanding in your company or your community, and then concentrating your resources and your efforts to become the "best in class." Chapter 9 will show how the development of your personal core competencies will provide the means for achieving your strategic intent.

Multifunctional Teams

Chapter 1 spoke of the widespread introduction of multifunctional teams as a way to improve both the speed and the quality of decisions in large organizations, particularly in such cross-functional areas as new product development. The use of such teams has become an important operational strategy for many of today's fastest growing companies, such as Hewlett-Packard and Motorola.

To be an effective member of such a multifunctional team, you need a working knowledge of how the various parts of the business operate, beyond your own functional specialty. Chapter 3 will discuss how you can acquire such knowledge.

Managing Innovation

Economists have learned that, in recent years, the most important factor in the economic growth of many companies has been the development of new technologies.[8] Explosive growth may result from the creation of totally new products and entire new industries, such as personal computers, cellular telephones, and direct satellite broadcasting. Or it may involve the manufacturing of traditional products — steel, for example — by new, lower cost, higher quality production technologies such as continuous casting. Service industries, such as banking and healthcare, are another area where alert companies are profitably employing new technological innovations.

While we usually think of Bill Gates and Michael Dell when we think of successful technical entrepreneurs, there are thousands

Technological Innovation, Not Management, is His Goal

'George,' age 27, makes $123,000 a year as a software engineer. A young, highly-paid technical entrepreneur, he writes programs for electronic games.

George graduated in 1989 with a bachelor's degree in electrical engineering and is currently pursuing a master's degree in computer science part-time at a local university. He enjoys his present job so much that he would not consider taking time off to study full-time for a graduate degree. He is not interested in management as a career path and his professional goal for the next five years is to advance as a highly-respected specialist in his technical field. The total focus of his career is technological innovation.

of others, often quite young, who are turbocharging their careers by participating in the process of technological innovation.

You don't have to be an engineer or scientist to participate in the rapid growth that is being fueled by new technology, but you should have a working knowledge of the innovation process for the development of new products and processes. Every manager should be familiar with strategies for accelerating the R&D process, such as multifunctional new product teams and fast-cycle development programs. This is where many of today's best companies, such as Intel and Hewlett-Packard, are making most of their money. Chapter 7 will discuss the elements of the innovation process that you need to know about.

Core Competencies

Core competencies are the cornerstone of corporate and personal strategy. In the corporate world, according to C.K. Prahalad and Gary Hamel, core competencies are defined as the collective learning of an organization.[9] Core competencies are those few things that a company does better than anyone else. A well-known example is 3M's core competency for coating all kinds of materials on various kinds of substrates—sandpaper, Post-It™ Notes, Scotch™ tape, and reflective highway signs.

For your "company of one," your core competencies are those things that you do better than anyone else in the company. They may involve writing software for electronic games, developing new pricing plans for financial services, or laying out a new production line for the factory. Your core competencies set you apart from everyone else in your firm. And because your core competencies are the focus of your career, they must involve doing something you truly enjoy.

Your core competencies enhance your value to the company because they make your company's products and services more valuable to your company's customers. Chapter 9 will provide a roadmap for developing and polishing your personal core competencies.

Loose Bricks

The strategic concept of the *loose brick* means that although an established competitor at first may appear to be impregnable, somewhere in his wall of defenses there may be a loose brick. Once that loose brick is discovered, it may be possible to pry it out — and then pry out others adjacent to it — until you have created a big enough hole to gain access to his customers.

Discovery of a loose brick is often the way a small competitor successfully enters a mature market. An example is Southwest Airlines' discovery of their competitors' loose brick, their high cost structures. By emphasizing simplicity — standardizing on only one kind of aircraft (the Boeing 737), no food service, and fast turnaround at the gate to maximize aircraft productivity — Southwest was able to offer good service at a much lower price than its competition, and make money in a market characterized by price wars and huge losses by other airlines. The company has grown rapidly and is highly profitable.

In choosing among alternatives for developing your personal core competencies, it pays for you to look for the loose bricks within your company and in your industry.

Hollowing Out

Personal core competencies involve your professional knowledge, skills, and knowhow. Because they are intellectual property rather than physical assets, they can be copied.

Hollowing out is a strategic term that refers to a company that learns everything it can from a partner in some venture, and, when there is nothing more to learn, it dumps the partner and uses what it has learned to its own advantage, without compensation. In the worst case, hollowing out is the theft of intellectual property.

To protect the value of the core competencies of your "company of one," you must be careful about being hollowed out, either by your peers or by persons outside your firm. While most of your colleagues are trustworthy, it is better to be cautious than sorry.

Market Positioning

Market positioning describes how companies want prospective customers to think about a certain product, in terms of its attributes. For example, a Corvette is clearly positioned in the market as a sports car, whereas a Cadillac is clearly positioned as a luxury car. Sometimes a product can be positioned to have more than one attribute. A BMW, for instance, is positioned as a luxury car with sporty performance.

How you position your "company of one" can have major implications for your career. Do you want people to think of you primarily as an engineer, as a salesperson, or as a number cruncher?

Peter Senge has written that our mental models, sometimes highly stereotyped, tend to dominate how we see people.[10] For example, "he's an engineer and therefore must be a nerd"; or "she's in sales and therefore probably very aggressive." Once formed, such stereotypes are hard to change, even in the face of new information about the person.

It is important, therefore, as you develop a marketing strategy for your "company of one," to think carefully about how you want to position—or reposition—yourself in the minds of those who can influence your success. We'll have more to say about this in Chapter 10.

Strategic Alliances

With the decline of organizational hierarchy, interpersonal relationships are based less on vertical authority of command ("do it because I'm the boss"), and more on horizontal cooperation among peers, both inside and outside your firm.

Such cooperative associations are much like strategic alliances between companies. Without a formal organizational structure and a central authority figure to settle differences, strategic alliances can be difficult to manage. Yet in today's team-oriented organizations, your skills in building and maintaining strategic alliances with your peers are essential to the success of your "company of one."

THE BOTTOM LINE

In this chapter we have developed the concept of thinking of yourself as a "company of one" in today's competitive environment. You are the CEO, and your job is to lay out a workable competitive strategy for your "company of one." We have identified the 10 Strategic Skills needed for managerial success — the boxes in your organization chart — and have introduced a number of powerful strategic concepts from the corporate world that we will apply to your "company of one" as we begin creating its plan for success.

THOUGHT QUESTIONS AS YOU TAKE CHARGE AS CEO

1. <u>Your objectives and mission statement</u>: Develop a mission statement that defines success for you and your family. Have you set your goals high enough? What values are important to you? What personal ethical standards are specified by your mission statement?

   What are your personal objectives, short term (within five years) and long term (beyond five years)? Prioritize your objectives (first things first). What tradeoffs are implied by your set of objectives (for example, income versus quality of life)?

   What do you want to be doing professionally five years from now? How much does this activity pay? (You may have to do some research on this, by checking newspaper ads, libraries, or computerized databases to see how much similar jobs pay now.) What are the qualitative aspects that you like about this job (e.g., challenge, location, type of work, hours)? What are the qualitative aspects that you *don't* like about this job (e.g., having to move, long hours, stress)? How much risk is implied by your plan—what is the worst that can happen if you try and fail?

What is your backup plan in case your first choice is not achievable? What will happen if you do nothing and stay in your present situation—is this an acceptable option? If your present job is acceptable now, will it still be acceptable to you five years from now? Will your present job even exist five years from now?

2. <u>Your core competencies for achieving your objectives</u>: What are your personal core competencies now? What new core competencies would you like to possess five years from now? What strategy will you follow to gain these core competencies?

3. <u>Mentors</u>: Who are your mentors? (Think of these people as prospective members of the board of directors of your "company of one.") List the names of these senior people and the most valuable input you have received from each of them in the past five years.

4. <u>Alliances</u>: List persons with whom you have strategic alliances. This does not include your boss or your subordinates, but individuals at your level in other parts of the company or in other firms or organizations, who are in a position to help you achieve your objectives, and vice versa.

---

[1] Lublin, J., "Corporate Survey Finds Fewer Layoffs, Increase in New Jobs to Balance Cuts," *The Wall Street Journal*, October 23, 1995, p. A2.

[2] Packard, D., *The HP Way*, HarperBusiness, 1995, p. 82.

[3] Covey, S., *The Seven Habits of Highly Effective People*, Fireside, 1989.

4   Collins, J. and Porras, J., *Built to Last*, HarperBusiness, 1994, pp. 81 - 114.

5   Speech before the Hamilton Club, Chicago, April 10, 1899.

6   Hamel, G. and Prahalad, C.K., "Strategic Intent," *Harvard Business Review*, May-June 1989, pp. 63 - 76.

7   Address to a joint session of Congress, May 25, 1961, as quoted in *Bartlett's Familiar Quotations*, Justin Kaplan, general editor, 16th edition, Little, Brown and Company, 1992, p. 741.

8   For a very readable account of how a leading young economist, Paul Romer, characterizes the importance of technology in today's economy, see Peter Robinson's "Paul Romer in the Shrine of the Gods," *Forbes ASAP*, June 5, 1995, pp. 67 - 72.

9   Prahalad, C. and Hamel, G., "The Core Competence of the Corporation," *Harvard Business Review*, May-June 1990, p. 82.

10   Senge, P., *The Fifth Discipline*, Doubleday Currency, 1990, pp. 174 - 204.

OBTAINING GENERAL BUSINESS KNOWLEDGE

The narrow functional specialist is obsolete. To improve the speed and quality of decisions, firms increasingly are forming multidisciplinary teams and task forces to carry out assignments ranging from new product development to improved customer service.

'James,' a Marketing Product Manager for a line of stereo equipment, was assigned to a multidisciplinary product development team, along with representatives from Engineering, Manufacturing, and Accounting, to develop a new stereo line. As the development project proceeded, James was informed that the direct labor cost of his new stereo assembly line would carry a factory overhead burden of 250%, which would make the new products only marginally profitable. (For every $1.00 of assembly labor cost, Accounting would allocate another $2.50 of factory overhead burden cost to his product line.) To make matters worse, an automobile radio line located in the same factory only 30 feet away from his stereo assembly line currently carried an overhead burden of only 100%.

When James protested, he was buried in accounting gobbledegook (he did not know that such cost allocations can be rather arbitrary). Without a clue as to how Accounting people allocate fixed costs to establish overhead burden rates, James lost the argument and was forced to set the prices on his new stereo line higher than he felt was appropriate. The result of the higher prices? Lower sales of the new line, less profit for the company, and a smaller year-end bonus for James—all because he did not have enough general business knowledge to win his point with Accounting.

To be effective as a member of a multidisciplinary team, you must have a basic knowledge of how the various parts of the business work, beyond your own functional area. The output of a successful multidisciplinary team is an integrated joint work product, not just a collection of unrelated inputs from various specialists.[1] Like James, you may work in Marketing, but you need a basic knowledge of Cost Accounting. If you are in Finance, you should understand the tradeoffs between selling your product directly through your own sales force versus the use of dealers. And in today's environment, everyone in the organization must understand the principles of Quality Management.

WHAT DO BUSINESS MANAGERS NEED TO KNOW?[2]

A good place to address this question is to examine what the leading business schools are teaching. While there has been criticism about the material that business schools teach, most business school graduates come to realize, after a few years on the job, that much of what they learned in business school turns out to be very useful. When our survey respondents were asked if they would still go for an MBA if they had to do it over, 92% said yes.

For many years, businesses operated on the apprentice system. Young men and women joined a firm and were taught what they needed to know by their supervisors, just as novice silversmiths were apprenticed to master craftsmen at the time of Paul Revere. Business was seen as a trade rather than as a science. There was no agreed upon general body of knowledge for the conduct of a business.

Nowhere was this more apparent than in the universities. In the 1960s and '70s, while university research was ascending in importance in the physical sciences, such as physics and engineering, the business schools of the time were under attack for being dull and unscientific. Looked upon with disdain by the "real scientists" on campus, business schools were often regarded as little more than trade schools, teaching case histories based on one-of-a-kind "war stories" that were of questionable generalizability to other business situations. Business was a course of study for students who couldn't make it in engineering or pre-med.

But during this period, a few business schools took a hard look at what was being taught and came up with sweeping new changes. At MIT and the University of Chicago, research on the behavior of stock prices led to an entirely new way of teaching about the stock market. At Wharton, an innovative marketing research technique was developed that allowed new product concepts to be scientifically broken down into attributes that could be analyzed individually, much as a chemist breaks down a new compound into its elements. A sophisticated formula for valuing financial options was developed at Stanford. At the University of Rochester, new theories were proposed to explain why corporate managers often make decisions that harm their stockholders. At MIT, research was initiated to better understand the process of innovation in high technology companies, and a systematic study of corporate competitive strategy was undertaken at Harvard.

Much of this research was done by business school professors who had undergraduate degrees in engineering, as well as PhDs in business or economics. They set standards for the same rigorous analysis demanded in the physical sciences.

Some of these professors subsequently went on to make a fortune by applying their mathematical "financial engineering" theories in the stock market. Others became wealthy and famous as consultants to industry. By applying their theories to real management problems, over time business school faculty learned which theories were most useful for the solution of the practical problems that managers face in the running of a business. From this real-world experience came a common body of knowledge in various fields, such as Finance and Marketing, that eventually found its way into the textbooks and into the classrooms. The practice of management was on its way to becoming less of a trade and more of a science.

Not all of this business school research was useful to business managers. Much was excessively arcane and detached from the practice of management. But this is true of basic research in any field—physics, electrical engineering, medicine. Only a very small percentage has significant impact, and it is difficult to predict which research studies will make an impact. That small percentage—perhaps only 1%—can have such a great impact that it more than justifies the other 99%.

There is evidence that having a faculty that is interested in doing research really does provide benefits to their MBA students. In my book, *The MBA Advantage: Why It Pays to Get an MBA*, I showed that for a sample of leading business schools, the economic value of the MBA degree is higher for the more research-intensive schools.[3]

THE FOUR COMPONENTS OF GENERAL BUSINESS KNOWLEDGE

In time, as the results of this business school research found its way into the classroom, the content of business education changed dramatically. As William H. Meckling, the former dean of the University of Rochester's Simon School, noted more than 20 years ago, the most effective management education has four components:[4]

1. *Principles or theories*: These are statements about cause and effect. When a manager advertises, he or she has a theory about how the advertising will affect sales. Much of what managers do is based on theories about such cause-and-effect relationships. Sometimes these theories are wrong.

    Business research has tried to make these theories explicit, and to test them with actual data from the business community. In this way, faculty have some assurance that when they teach such things as the effect of advertising on sales, the students will get meaningful results when they apply these concepts on the job.

2. *Techniques and methodology*: *Techniques* are the tools of analysis. A widely-used statistical technique is known as regression analysis. In its simplest form, it is just a computerized technique to fit a line to a set of data points.

Suppose, for example, I am due to have a performance review with my boss next week, and I would like to know ahead of time how fast the average salaries in my professional field have increased as a function of years of work experience. If I have the raw data, regression analysis will fit a line and provide the answer.[5]

Techniques like regression analysis are very useful to managers. With the widespread availability of spreadsheets and user-friendly statistical packages for personal computers, these techniques are inexpensive, powerful, and—believe it or not—can be fun to use. Managers need a toolbox of these techniques of analysis along with a good understanding of their limitations.

Methodology is the application of the scientific method—hypothesis, test, modified hypothesis, test some more—to business problems. Much of this has to do with the structuring of problems—determining the actual problem, stating the problem in a way that it can be scientifically evaluated, and determining what kind of data or evidence will be needed to get an answer. Our survey respondents reported that the ability to structure complex business problems is the single most valuable critical skill that a manager can possess.

If sales are dropping, what's the cause? (There may be many possible causes: a price-cut by competitors, quality problems with the product, a lull in the economy, and ineffective advertising, to name a few.) What kind of information do we need to check this out? When we're done, what assurance do we have that we got the right answer? And what are we going to do to get sales back on track? What evidence do we have that this proposed solution will work? This way of thinking about problems—using a scientific approach with a stubborn insistence on evidence—should be second nature to today's professional manager.

3. *Institutional knowledge*: Like every profession, management has its own jargon. Financial analysts talk about *P/E ratios* and *yield curves*. Advertising managers talk about *reach* and

frequency and *CPMs*. In the past, much of business education consisted of the teaching of such institutional knowledge. It is still very important. If you don't know what the words mean, your knowledge of regression analysis will be of no help.

In their enthusiasm to make a complete break with the past, some research-oriented business schools de-emphasized the teaching of institutional material to the point where graduating MBAs were illiterate in their chosen field.[6] Many students graduated without the slightest idea of how to write a marketing plan or what the inside of a factory looked like.

Fortunately, the pendulum has swung back. Today, teams of MBA students carry out projects with companies where they run focus groups in shopping malls and analyze production lines on the factory floor. They learn the jargon and the institutional concepts before they graduate, as they should.

4. *Communications skills*: The ability of managers to communicate orally and in writing remains a critical skill. Young managers, with a toolkit full of advanced analytical techniques, often know more about a particular problem-solving approach than their boss. Much of what a new hire presents will not be fully understood by the boss. Consequently, the quality of what is presented will be judged in large part by the quality of its packaging.

Every piece of work must not only be professional, it must *look* professional. This means that managers must be articulate and persuasive in oral presentations, and lucid in written reports. They should also be fully competent in running the latest computerized graphics presentation programs.

In addition to these four components of general business knowledge, which most business schools teach effectively, there is another component of managerial competence that business schools do not teach very well—people skills. Leadership, teamwork, emotional intelligence, and persuasiveness—the ability to get things done through other people — are the skills that distinguish managers from individual contributors. More will be said about these important people skills in Chapter 8.

THE SIX BASIC AREAS OF GENERAL BUSINESS KNOWLEDGE

In addition to the 10 Strategic Skills that were introduced in Chapter 2, there are a number of basic areas of general business knowledge that you have to be familiar with if you are going to function successfully in today's corporations.

Many of our survey respondents emphasized the importance of acquiring this across-the-board general business knowledge, as well as the more specialized skills. (See box at upper right.)

Another survey respondent similarly underscored the importance of acquiring general business knowledge (at right).

In business school, these general business concepts are covered in the 'core courses' taken by all students during the first year of an MBA program. In the second year, students choose from a variety of elective courses in Banking, Marketing Research, Production Management and the like, to prepare

Learn General Business Concepts

'Philip,' age 45, is Vice President of Finance for a medium-sized plastics manufacturer. With more than 100 people reporting to him, he earns $170,000 a year.

He received his undergraduate degree in Philosophy in 1971 and worked for three years as an Assistant Store Manager for a paint retailer at $8,500 a year before returning to school to pursue a full-time MBA program. Upon graduation with his MBA, he accepted a position with a CPA firm at $14,000 a year.

Philip's highest-priority advice to young managers is to "learn general business concepts." He credits his MBA education with introducing him "to economic concepts, which is the way business works."

Covering All the Basics

'Jane,' 42, earned a bachelor's degree in Mathematics in 1973 and, without pausing to gain work experience, continued directly on to pursue an MBA, majoring in Finance and Accounting.

Today, Jane is Manager of Audit at a very large document processing company, with a salary of $82,000 a year. She found that the most valuable part of her MBA experience was that it provided her with a "broad business background, covering all the basics."

for the specific job they intend to pursue after graduation. But first they have to learn the basics.

According to our survey respondents, these are the six basic areas where general business knowledge is most useful to practicing managers:

- Cost Accounting
- Financial Accounting
- Economics
- Finance
- Marketing
- Operations Management

Cost Accounting

Accounting is the language of business. *Net sales, cash flow, allocated fixed costs, and depreciation* are terms that you will use throughout your professional career. In a very real sense, these are the words by which your success as a manager is measured. You need to know what they mean, how they are calculated, and what assumptions are behind them.

As a manager, you are concerned with two kinds of accounting: 1) External (or Financial) Accounting, that periodically informs the stockholders and the banks how the business is doing; and 2) Internal (or Cost) Accounting, that is designed to track and control the day-to-day operations of the business. Of the two, Cost Accounting is more important. In fact, a number of our survey respondents said that Cost Accounting was the most important course they took in business school. Yet, a lack of understanding of the assumptions and limitations of Cost Accounting can create a minefield for the uninformed manager, where inappropriate accounting measures can lead to bad decisions, and hidden and unexpected accounting surprises can injure or kill a manager's otherwise good reputation.

In Eliyahu M. Goldratt's best selling book, *The Goal*, the story is told of a manufacturing plant that sinks deeper and deeper into chaos as its managers strive day and night to improve its performance, as measured by Cost Accounting numbers.[7] After struggling for months, the managers finally realize that trying to maximize the Cost Accounting performance numbers is what is destroying the operation, and the plant is saved from closure. There is probably no area of management that is more misleading or more misunderstood than Cost Accounting.

For example, if you are running a manufacturing company and sales are poor, common sense tells you it is risky to continue to build inventory. You would be tying up your cash, and you may end up with a warehouse full of obsolete product in a year from now. Yet, traditional Cost Accounting often rewards managers for building inventory, even if sales are lagging, because the manufacturing process of building goods "absorbs overhead costs" and thus enhances accounting profits.[8] But it does not put more cash in the cash register, which is what running a business is all about.

Or suppose you are introducing a very successful new product. In fact, it is so successful that you can't make it fast enough. You have to choose between filling an order for one customer who always pays you promptly, or filling a somewhat larger order from another customer who seldom pays in less than three months and is considered a real credit risk, so much so that you may have trouble collecting your payment. Common sense tells you that if you have to choose, ship to the first customer, who always pays promptly, because you are assured of getting your cash quickly. But traditional Cost Accounting will show a higher profit if you favor the larger order from the slow-paying, high-risk second customer, even though there is a significant chance that you will have real trouble collecting what he will owe you. This is because by conventional accounting standards, profit is recorded when you ship the goods, not when the customer pays, which could be much later or even never. It doesn't make sense, but that is how the accountants do it.[9]

Finally, consider this example of two division general managers, both of whom are rewarded with large bonuses based on maximizing return on assets, which is defined as profit divided by the book value of assets. 'Mary' is working very hard to build her division by expanding new product R&D, which reduces short-term profits, and by investing in modern production equipment, which increases assets. 'Mike,' on the other hand, is milking his division for accounting profits. He cuts R&D to the bone, thereby raising short-term profits, and refuses to replace his antiquated production equipment, causing the book value of his assets to automatically decrease year-by-year as their value is written off through depreciation. Guess who gets the bigger bonus? Mike, who lies awake at night hoping he will be promoted before his division collapses. This management incentive system, which is based on traditional accounting numbers, is destroying the corporation.

These are but three examples of the distortions that traditional Cost Accounting creates. The intelligent manager must be aware of these limitations of Cost Accounting and be prepared to fight back when they lead to obviously bad business decisions.

In recent years, alternative Cost Accounting methods have been proposed to reduce these problems. The best known of these, Activity Based Costing (ABC), has triggered a lot of interest. But tradition is a powerful force among the green eyeshade crowd, where year-to-year consistency is highly valued, and ABC has not been widely adopted.

As a manager, your bonuses and your promotions almost certainly will be influenced by traditional Cost Accounting numbers. If you intend to play to win, you must understand where these numbers come from, and the assumptions by which they are calculated. Of all the things you need to understand in the field of general business knowledge, Cost Accounting should be at the very top of your list. You don't have to become an accountant, but you must be able to defend yourself.

The best way to learn the material is to take an evening course in Cost Accounting at your local college. If you prefer studying on your own to learn how Cost Accounting works, its limitations, and how it can affect the organization's effectiveness, I recommend you obtain a copy of *Accounting for Decision Making and Control*, by Jerold L. Zimmerman (Richard D. Irwin, Inc., 1995).

Financial Accounting

Financial Accounting is the means by which companies disclose their financial condition to banks and stockholders, through quarterly and annual reports.

Although knowledge of Financial Accounting is less important to most operating managers than Cost Accounting, it is nonetheless useful to be able to read and understand the financial statements of your company and your competitors. For senior management, who communicate with the investment community as an essential part of their jobs, a comprehensive knowledge of Financial Accounting is absolutely indispensable.

A good source to learn about the basics of financial statement analysis is *Financial Accounting*, by Robert Libby, Patricia Libby, and Daniel G. Short (Richard D. Irwin, Inc., 1996).

Microeconomics

Economics is the basic science of business. It is to the field of management as physics is to engineering.

There are two kinds of economics courses taught in business schools: 1) Microeconomics, which deals with economic concepts at the level of the individual firm; and 2) Macroeconomics, which describes how the national and world economic systems work. Microeconomics is a required core course in virtually every MBA program, and Macroeconomics may be either a required course or an elective, depending on the school. Of the two, knowledge of Microeconomics is much more important for managers.

A course in Microeconomics describes how individual companies do business in a collection of markets. These include markets in which they sell their products and services and markets from which they buy raw materials, production and professional labor; capital assets such as buildings and machinery; and financial assets. The concept of marginal analysis is particularly valuable. "Micro" provides a conceptual framework for understanding one of management's most important tasks, the design and administration of organizational compensation and incentive systems. Microeconomics also shows how firms within an industry compete in various kinds of market structures, ranging from pure competition to oligopolies and monopolies.

A good working knowledge of Microeconomics is valuable because it provides many insights into all aspects of how a company runs. For an interesting and very readable introduction to the basics of Microeconomics and its relationship to managerial decision-making and organizational design, see *Organizational Architecture: A Managerial Economics Approach*, by James A. Brickley, Clifford W. Smith, Jr., and Jerold L. Zimmerman (Richard D. Irwin, Inc., 1996).

Finance

The most popular area of concentration in business school is Finance, a field that covers a wide range of professional opportunities—from a fast-paced, high-paying investment banking job on Wall Street to that of Chief Financial Officer of a large manufacturing company.

Finance develops methods for evaluating alternative investments, whether that investment is a new computerized machine tool for your factory, or the stock of a new biotechnology company for the investment portfolio of your venture capital firm. The concept of Net Present Value (NPV) is fundamental for choosing among such investment alternatives. Evaluating such investments under conditions of uncertainty are among the most important decisions that managers make, and you will use the underlying principles from this course repeatedly throughout your professional career.

To get a sense of the subject of Finance, subscribe to *The Wall Street Journal*, and take a few minutes every day to read it. The stories are well-researched, and all but the simplest financial concepts in their articles are explained in non-technical terms. To learn more about the stock market, tune in to CNBC and PBS's *Wall Street Week*. *Forbes* magazine is another good source. The best introductory textbook for learning the basics of Finance is Brealey and Myers' *Principles of Corporate Finance* (McGraw-Hill, 1991).

Marketing

Companies exist to serve customers and, ultimately, these customers determine whether or not the company stays in business.

Marketing analyzes how firms serve their customers. Regardless of the kind of organization—consumer goods, industrial goods, financial services, medical services—success depends on satisfying these customers better than competitors. Marketing managers have a variety of means for reaching and serving customers, including advertising and promotion, new product development, pricing strategies, and distribution channels. But every manager in the company has a stake in understanding how the firm relates to its customers.

A good way to become familiar with the concepts of Marketing is to attend meetings of your local chapter of the American Marketing Association. (Check with the Marketing Department of your local college for the time and place.) The second section of *The Wall Street Journal* is devoted mostly to marketing stories, and *Fortune* magazine features in-depth stories on the marketing strategies of national and international firms. (*Fortune* also runs outstanding articles on personal career strategy.) The *Harvard Business Review* is another good source of non-technical articles on marketing issues. (Before you lay out a lot of money for subscriptions, spend an afternoon going through back issues at your local library.) The most widely-used introductory Marketing textbook is Philip Kotler's *Marketing Management: Analysis, Planning, Implementation, and Control*, (Prentice-Hall, 1995).

Operations Management

Whatever a company produces—whether it's products such as automobiles and computers, or services such as portfolio management and medical care—Operations Management is concerned with the process by which the firm manages physical, financial, and human resources to create and deliver these goods and services to customers.

Over the past decade, worldwide competition has focused intense interest on how firms manage their operations. Not only must the existing product be of outstanding quality at a competitive price, but the process for developing new products must be faster and more effective as product life cycles become shorter and shorter. Excellence in Operations Management has become an increasingly important factor in the corporate strategies of world-class companies.

For an unusual and fascinating view of what life is like in Operations Management, read Eliyahu M. Goldratt's *The Goal* (North River Press, Inc., 1992). One of the best textbooks on the subject is Krajewski and Titzman's *Operations Management: Strategy and Analysis*, Addison Wesley, 1993.

THE BOTTOM LINE

As shown in Figure 3.1, General Business Knowledge is the first of the 10 Strategic Skills for Managerial Success to be added to the organization chart of your "company of one."

The best way to learn about general business practices is to take courses—either short courses for managers, or evening courses at your local college. And if you are really serious about taking courses, consider signing up for an MBA program so that you will get the credentials, as well as the knowledge (for more on the value of MBA degrees, see Chapter 12).

In the meantime, read, read, read. This includes *The Wall Street Journal*, *Forbes*, *Fortune*, and *Business Week*. Look for books

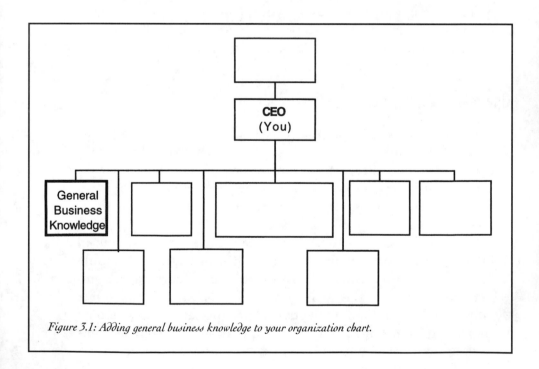

Figure 3.1: *Adding general business knowledge to your organization chart.*

by or about successful business leaders such as David Packard, Sam Walton, and Bill Gates—and when you are tired of reading, watch CNBC. You'll be surprised how much you will learn about the practice of business.

SELF ASSESSMENT OF GENERAL BUSINESS KNOWLEDGE

To test your general business knowledge, discuss each of the following terms (these are concepts you need to know to survive and prosper in today's organizations):

Cost Accounting

- ☐ Fixed versus variable costs
- ☐ Sunk costs
- ☐ Cost allocation
- ☐ FIFO (First In, First Out)
- ☐ Profit center
- ☐ Absorption cost system
- ☐ Straight-line depreciation
- ☐ Activity based costing
- ☐ Variance
- ☐ Transfer price

Financial Accounting

- ☐ Net revenue
- ☐ Common stock
- ☐ Cost of goods sold
- ☐ Bond
- ☐ Stockholders' equity
- ☐ Profit

Microeconomics

- ☐ Price elasticity
- ☐ Incentive system
- ☐ Marginal analysis
- ☐ Oligopoly

☐ Cross elasticity

☐ Opportunity cost

☐ Agency theory

☐ Diminishing returns

☐ Comparative advantage

☐ Decision rights

Finance

☐ Cash flow

☐ Net present value

☐ Capital budgeting

☐ Options

☐ Efficient market hypothesis

☐ Discount rate

Marketing

☐ Channel of distribution

☐ Product attributes

☐ Limitations of marketing research

☐ Marketing strategies for challenger firms

☐ Product life cycle

☐ How to measure the response to advertising

Operations management

☐ Learning curve

☐ Economies of scale

☐ Total quality management (TQM)

☐ Queuing and bottlenecks

☐ Just-In-Time

☐ Statistical process control

----

1   See "The Wisdom of Teams," by Katzenbach and Smith, *Harvard Business School Press*, 1993.

2   This section and the following two sections are adapted from my book, *The MBA Advantage: Why It Pays to Get an MBA*, Bob Adams Inc., 1994.

3   Ibid. pp. 232 - 241.

4   Adapted from Meckling, W. H., "Education for Business and Business Policy," unpublished paper, Graduate School of Management, University of Rochester, August 7, 1973.

5   For some reason, a few business school professors like to teach these techniques using lots of Greek letters and subscripts, perhaps so that it will look more like physics. The fact is that the underlying mathematics are really very simple, and if you got through high school algebra, you can handle it. Fortunately, most professors now teach these techniques not as a set of mathematical abstractions but rather as a practical way to attack real business problems, the solutions of which become the focus of their lectures.

6   The argument for not teaching institutional material in business school is that the companies can teach this more efficiently after the graduates are hired. This is similar to the argument that General Motors used to make about cars—they would ship cars to the dealers that were half-finished, expecting the dealers to correct all the problems, because the dealers—guided by customer complaints—were "more efficient" at finishing the cars. This kind of thinking cost General Motors almost half of its market share. Customers today—whether they are buying cars or MBAs—expect a fully functional product from day one. New MBA hires are expected to "hit the ground running."

7   Goldratt, E., *The Goal*, second revised edition, North River Press, Inc., 1992.

8   This assumes that average unit costs are continuing to decline with increasing volume.

9   If your accountants are concerned that there is a significant likelihood that your slow-paying customer will
never pay, they will hedge by setting up an account called
"Allowance for Bad Debts" to reduce some or all of the
recorded sales and profits.

ACQUIRING SPECIFIC INDUSTRY KNOWLEDGE

A number of years ago, 'Ed,' a research engineer at Eastman Kodak Company, had an idea for improving home movie cameras that would eliminate the need for the powerful floodlights that were required at the time for shooting indoor home movies. If you wanted to take home movies of little Johnnie's birthday party, you not only had to load the camera but you also had to set up a bank of floodlights. It was awkward and distracting, and the hot reflector bulbs were a hazard to be around.

Ed's idea was to redesign the camera and the movie film to be sensitive enough to take home movies with just the normal room lighting—he called the proposed system "available light home movies." Unfortunately, his superiors in the company were doubtful that Ed's idea would work, and the project was never authorized.

One day, the chairman of the board, Dr. Chapman, visited the Research Department, and as is usually the case with such visits from top management, was treated to a dog-and-pony slide presentation by the research group to showcase what they were developing. After the presentations were finished, Dr. Chapman went around the room shaking hands with everyone and thanking them for the presentation. Eventually, he got around to Ed, who had been running the projector, and inquired conversationally, "How are things going?"

"I'm glad you asked, sir," said Ed. "I have an idea for a new home movie system." Intrigued, Dr. Chapman wanted to know more. So Ed proceeded to outline his idea for the new technology for "available light home movies," along with facts and figures about the market and a set of arguments about how this innovation would fit in with the company's long-range strategy. Impressed, Dr. Chapman jotted down a few notes.

A few weeks later, the project was mysteriously funded. Doors were quietly opened around the corporation so that the "available light home movie" project received priority in product development, and in due course, Ed's innovation was introduced to the market with great success. For a number of years, until it was replaced by the new technology of video camcorders, available light home movies thrived as an important and profitable line of business for the company. Ed was widely recognized for his innovation, and his reputation in the company flourished.[1]

Ed was successful, not only because he had a good idea, but because he had thought out how his idea fit in with the overall goals of the company. He had done his homework and when the chance came, he was able to describe to the Chairman an informal business plan for his idea that made sense.

Ed's experience is more common than you might think. It is easy for senior managers to become isolated from what is really going on in the company, and so, like the Chairman, they make time to get out and talk with the troops. At Hewlett-Packard, they even have a name for it: Management By Walking Around (MBWA).[2]

WHY YOU NEED TO UNDERSTAND YOUR COMPANY'S COMPETITIVE POSITION

There is a message to this story. Someday, perhaps soon, you may find yourself in a discussion with a senior executive from your company, in which he or she asks your opinion on a matter that involves overall company strategy. This may be in a meeting, or over lunch, or perhaps in an informal setting and without prior notice. The executive wants to learn two things: 1) What is going on in your part of the company, and 2) How qualified a person are you, as a possible candidate for promotion? Are you able to think beyond the boundaries of your immediate job? Do you have a sense of where the company is headed, and what top management is trying to accomplish? Do you understand the competitive situation the company is facing? Do you have some constructive ideas on how the company might do better? As Dr. L. J. Thomas, former senior vice president of Eastman Kodak and director of the Kodak Research Laboratories said, "Never underestimate the power of a quiet lunch with the right people."[3]

To come across effectively, you must be prepared. Be ready for this opportunity. As a professional person, you should know where your organization fits within the company, and you should be aware of where the company fits within its industry. And most important, you have to think about these matters ahead of time.

Bill Gates, founder and CEO of Microsoft Corporation, is both admired and feared as a technical genius and a business strategist. Employees called upon to make presentations to him know that they will be grilled mercilessly, not only on the technical aspects of their project but also on its market potential and profitability. Around Microsoft, the word is, "Do your homework before meeting with Gates—otherwise he will destroy you."[4]

There is another important reason to understand your company and how it competes within its industry. In today's flatter, leaner organizations, important decisions are being made by lower level employees in the company, who have specific expertise. For example, in years past, the features in a new product design might have had to be approved by multiple layers of senior managers, a process that could take months. Today, those decisions may be delegated to members of a multidisciplinary product development team.

But to make the best decisions, the specific product expertise of the team members must be expanded to include knowledge about the company's overall competitive strategy. If, for example, the company's competitive strategy is to be the low-cost, no-frills producer in its industry, the individual product designs should reflect this strategy. The more you understand about your company's competitive strategy, the better the decisions you will make.

Finally, remember that your personal success is your responsibility, not the company's. As a professional employee, you are investing your time and talent in your firm. As CEO of your "company of one," you should spend some time keeping track of how well this investment is doing. As an insider, you will see any threatening storm clouds on the horizon long before they become apparent to those on the outside of the company. If you find that your company is losing ground within its industry, you should do whatever you can to help restore the company's competitive strength. But as CEO of your "company of one," you should also begin to develop some options in case it becomes necessary to move elsewhere.

UNDERSTANDING YOUR INDUSTRY

Professional people may move from company to company, but they tend to stay in a given industry (e.g., the computer business or the pharmaceutical industry). They build expertise and contacts in a given industry and it is usually difficult and costly to start over.

In a landmark article, Harvard Business School Professor Michael E. Porter showed how the competitive forces in an industry shape the strategy of individual companies within that industry.[5] We will use Porter's article as a framework for this discussion on how to better understand your industry and your company. To illustrate the usefulness of Porter's concepts, as we go through the discussion we will apply these concepts to a well-known personal computer company, Compaq Computer Corporation. At the end of the chapter, we will provide a checklist for developing these same concepts for your own company.

The Porter model of industry competition is diagrammed in Figure 4.1. The strength of each of these forces determines the state of competition in an industry.

In a few industries, such as agriculture, there are so many producers and the goods they produce are so similar that it is not possible for a company to develop a meaningful competitive strategy. In such an industry, producers can sell as much as they want at the prevailing market price. Entry of new producers is relatively easy. Economists refer to this kind of industry

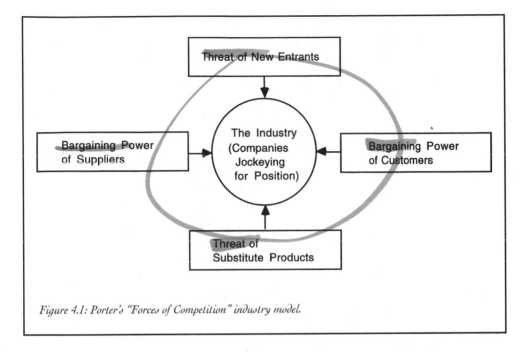

Figure 4.1: Porter's "Forces of Competition" industry model.

as "perfect competition." Under such conditions, where the products are commodities, unless you as a producer have a significant cost advantage, it is difficult to make much of a profit.

For the great majority of industries, however, products and services are at least somewhat differentiated in the minds of customers, and the number of producers is limited. Under such conditions, the strategies of companies interact. For example, if Ford cuts the price on its Explorers, it will sell more Explorers but Chevrolet will sell fewer Blazers. Under such conditions, competitive strategy becomes very important.

In today's management literature, there is much emphasis on understanding your customers. Certainly it is important to understand your customers—but to be successful, it is also important to understand your suppliers and your competitors, current and potential.

BARGAINING POWER OF SUPPLIERS

Powerful suppliers can squeeze the profit out of an industry, particularly if the companies in the industry are unable, for competitive reasons, to recover their cost increases in their own prices. Consider, for example, the situation faced by personal computer manufacturers like Compaq, who are dependent on two giant suppliers: Intel Corporation for their microprocessors, and Microsoft Corporation for their operating systems.

<u>Single source</u>: Although Compaq has made arrangements to procure some of its microprocessors from AMD and others who clone the Intel chips, these alternative suppliers have difficulty keeping up with Intel's high rate of innovation in bringing out new versions. And to the extent that Compaq finds that customers demand the latest version of the Pentium microprocessor in its PCs, it has no choice but to buy them from Intel.

<u>Locked in by industry standards</u>: Another very large company, Motorola, also makes microprocessors, but at this time, the Motorola PowerPC chip, which is used in the Apple Macintosh, is incompatible with the industry standard operating system, Microsoft's Windows 95. There has been so much software written for Windows that Compaq has no choice but to incorporate the Windows operating system in its PCs. So Compaq, at least for the time being, is locked in by industry standards to Intel as its primary supplier of microprocessors, and to Microsoft as its supplier of operating systems.

<u>Threat of forward integration</u>: One of Compaq's greatest concerns is that Intel will decide to integrate forward, bringing out its own Intel brand of PCs to compete with Compaq and others. The first step toward this strategy, according to Compaq, was Intel's successful "Intel Inside" advertising campaign, which established the Intel brand name with consumers. Compaq also complained that the "Intel Inside" campaign reduced the value of the Compaq name as a quality manufacturer by implying that all the leading brands were identical under the hood because they all sported the "Intel Inside" label.[6]

Moreover, in recent years, Intel has become a major supplier to the entire PC industry of motherboards, the large printed circuit boards that hold most of the critical circuitry, including the Pentium chips, that determine a PC's performance. Because the motherboard designers at Intel have advanced knowledge of new versions of the Pentium, which gives them an early opportunity to optimize the layout of the motherboard to squeeze the maximum performance out of the microprocessor and its supporting chips, companies such as Compaq have had trouble competing using their own in-house motherboards. It is much easier to buy them from Intel. Furthermore, Intel has announced plans to incorporate many of the functions of the support chips currently made by other companies into its own core microprocessor chip.[7] As Intel takes over production of more of the hardware inside a PC, Compaq's concern that Intel might integrate forward has some basis.

Given this structure of the PC industry, it is not surprising that Intel and Microsoft are making most of the industry's profits. Microsoft is reported to have a gross profit margin exceeding 80% on its Windows operating system, and Intel enjoys gross margins in the 50% range on its microprocessors. The leading PC manufacturers are said to have gross profit margins in the range of 8% to 14% and are struggling to make any net profit after selling expenses. IBM is reported to have lost $1 billion on PCs in 1994.[8]

Thus we see that the bargaining power of suppliers can squeeze industry profitability and can dominate the strategies of the various industry participants.

Question: As you think about your own industry, to what extent do powerful suppliers, like Intel and Microsoft, dominate the competitive structure?

THREAT OF NEW ENTRANTS

New entrants to an industry compete for market share, expanding capacity and often depressing the profits of the companies already in the industry. Furthermore, in a dynamic industry such as the PC business, the traditional barriers to entry may not be sufficient to keep out new entrants.

Financial resources as a barrier to entry: In many industries, such as automobile manufacturing, it is impossible to enter without enormous financial backing. But, in some industries a requirement for strong financial resources may not be enough to discourage entry. If having vast financial resources were sufficient as a barrier to entry in the personal computer business, IBM would control the PC business today. Instead, the business is split among such newcomers as Packard-Bell, Dell, Gateway and Compaq—companies that did not exist when IBM rolled out its first PC in 1981. And as we saw, most of the profit in the industry is being made by two other young companies, Intel and Microsoft.

Brand equity as a barrier to entry: In the days when the word 'computer' referred to a mainframe computer, data processing managers used to say that if they purchased an IBM computer system and there were problems, they would be forgiven because "they had bought the best," but if they specified some other brand of mainframe and there were problems, people would say, "Why didn't you stick with IBM?" The IBM name had value—what marketing people refer to as "brand equity."

In many businesses today, brand equity is still very important. But it is not an absolute barrier to entry. The rapid rise of Compaq, Dell, and Gateway in the PC business demonstrates the ease with which new entrants can penetrate an industry.

The latest 'new entrant' to the PC industry is Hewlett-Packard. Although HP has offered a line of PCs since the early 1980s, it is only recently that the company, spurred on by the huge success of its laser and inkjet printers, has taken a very aggressive approach to the PC business, announcing to the industry that it intends to become the number 3 supplier. With HP's technical resources and its highly-respected brand name, it has a good chance of reaching its goal.

Entry through innovation: New entrants often use innovation and product differentiation to challenge the existing companies. This, in fact, is how Compaq Computer got started. In 1981, IBM introduced its first desktop PC, using an early Intel microprocessor chip and Microsoft's MS-DOS operating system. In 1983, Compaq Computer, a startup company, developed the first portable version of the PC that was compatible with software developed for the IBM PC. The Compaq portable was a big hit, and Compaq's sales soared. In 1986, Compaq developed a desktop machine with an advanced Intel 386 microprocessor and had it on the market six months before IBM. Through the rest of the 1980s, Compaq stayed ahead of IBM by continual product innovation.

By the early 1990s, product differentiation among the major brands was fading. PCs were beginning to all look alike. But innovation for market entry does not always have to involve the product itself. Michael Dell, who started selling

PCs out of his college dorm room, made innovations in *distribution* by offering his PCs by mail order, cutting out the retailers so that he could trim prices. In the meantime, Compaq's strategy of selling high-performance, high-priced machines only through dealers began to falter, and the company went deeply into the red. It was only after a complete management shakeup and the hasty development of a very cost-competitive line of PCs that sales recovered and the company survived.

Question: How strong are the barriers to entry in your industry? Have new entrants made significant inroads in the past few years?

BARGAINING POWER OF CUSTOMERS

Customers exert bargaining power by forcing down prices, demanding higher quality or more service, and playing competitive suppliers against each other.

<u>Large buying power</u>: As giant retail organizations, such as Sears, Roebuck & Co., increase their PC sales to consumers, they become a larger and larger fraction of the total sales of PC producers such as Compaq. With their enormous buying power, they are able to demand the most favorable prices and terms from the PC manufacturers.

<u>Undifferentiated products</u>: To the extent that all brands of PCs are seen by consumers to be very similar—they all contain Pentium chips and Intel motherboards, and they all come with the Windows 95 operating system installed—it becomes easier for retailers to play one PC supplier against another. The retailers need PCs at various price points, but they may not care very much whether they carry the Packard-Bell brand, the Compaq brand, or the IBM brand, and they are likely to opt for whichever manufacturer gives them the best deal.

Question: Who has the real power in your industry—the producers or their customers?

JOCKEYING FOR POSITION AMONG COMPETITORS

Existing competitors in an industry jockey for position through price competition, new product introductions, and barrages of advertising. Rivalry among producers is related to a number of factors.

Having the best product as a competitive advantage: Having a great product certainly helps to maintain a company's competitive position in an industry, but sometimes even this is not enough to ensure success. Consider the case of Apple Computer, which is generally recognized as offering the best operating system (in terms of user-friendliness) and the easiest setup of any personal computer brand. These are competitive advantages that Apple has had for more than ten years. It is generally acknowledged that Windows 95, the Microsoft operating system introduced in 1995 by almost all other PC manufacturers, has barely caught up to the performance of the operating system Apple introduced in 1988. Yet Apple currently has only 9% of the total PC market, and the Windows-based PCs have almost all of the rest. Where industry standards—in this case, the dominance of the Windows operating system—have effectively locked out alternative product configurations, having the best product will not be enough to ensure success.

Slowing industry growth: In 1995, PC sales to home buyers grew about 26%, but the growth rate may drop sharply in future years.[9] When sales are growing rapidly, all the producers are busy just keeping up with orders, but when sales decline, competition between producers can become fierce—a problem that is made worse if customers believe that there is little difference in product features and quality between the various brands.

No one dominant market leader to set industry prices and practices: Market leadership, in terms of having the largest market share, has rotated among the various PC manufacturers. In the late 1970s, Apple was the dominant brand. But it was soon challenged by IBM for market leadership when the first IBM PCs were introduced in the early 1980s. More recently, Compaq became the number one brand because of strong sales to business customers. However, Packard-Bell is slashing prices and selling through mass-merchandise outlets to gain market share, a strategy that other manufacturers complain is depressing prices and profitability for the entire industry.

Question: Among the existing competitors in your industry, is your company the dominant market leader? Or is it a small player that has little power to set its own policies?

THREAT OF SUBSTITUTE PRODUCTS

Over the long run, the most powerful threat to any industry is that the products or services of all of the producers may be made obsolete by lower cost alternatives or by new technologies.

Lower cost alternatives: In 1995, about 6 million home PCs were sold, versus about 36 million TV sets. The average amount spent on a home PC is about $1,700, and some industry observers believe that the PC will not become a true mass-market product until its price drops to around $500. Larry Ellison, chairman of software maker Oracle Corp., believes that the time is right for a stripped down $500 PC for surfing the Internet—a view that is hotly rejected by traditional PC manufacturers, who fear that it could topple the economic structure of the entire industry.[10]

Technological replacement: Another alternative being talked about is to greatly simplify or even do away with the PC, replacing it with a basic keyboard and display that would be hooked to a plug on the wall connected to a networked information utility. IBM CEO Louis V. Gerstner has a vision of "network-centric computing"—reengineering the information systems business to get rid of the need for low-profit PCs, at least in the commercial market. Commercial customers would plug in a very simple "dumb" terminal and buy only the computing they need, the way they currently buy electricity and telephone service. Applications software, such as word processors and spreadsheets, would no longer reside within the user's PC. Instead, they would be rented from servers on the network on a per-usage basis.[11]

Although the concept of the centralized information utility is not new—time-shared mainframes were in use more than 30 years ago—the rapid growth of the Internet suggests that IBM's vision of network-centric computing represents a real long-term threat to the PC industry as it is configured today. And IBM's investment of $3.5 billion to acquire Lotus Development Corporation and its Notes® "groupware" is strong evidence of its commitment to the future of networked systems. (Lotus® Notes® is software that allows employees to send memos or documents over the computer network to be reviewed by co-workers without having to get together at meetings.)

The implication of network-centric computing for a PC company like Compaq is that the company will have to move rapidly to establish itself in the network server and communications business or be left behind.

Question: Looking down the road, what are the potential substitutes for the products and services your company produces? Is your company preparing to lead in this transition, or will it lag behind the rest of the industry and face possible obsolescence?

THE BOTTOM LINE

Your industry may not be as dynamic as the PC business and your company may not face the competitive and technological challenges that Compaq Computer faces, but as we add the Strategic Skill of "Specific Industry Knowledge" to your

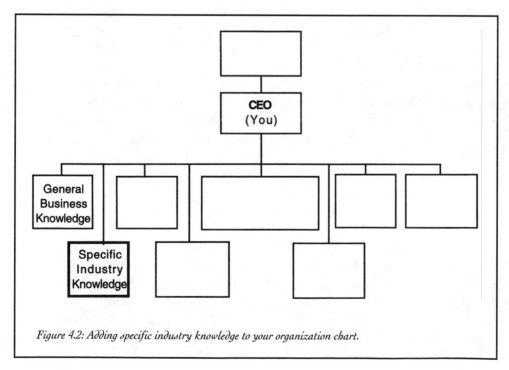

Figure 4.2: Adding specific industry knowledge to your organization chart.

organization chart in Figure 4.2, it is important that you understand the basics of your industry, and how your company competes within that industry. After all, you never know when you might be stopped in the hall or invited to lunch by a senior executive of your company who wants to know what you think about these issues—a conversation that could have a momentous impact on your career.

A CHECKLIST OF YOUR SPECIFIC INDUSTRY KNOWLEDGE

1. Bargaining power of suppliers

   ☐ Is your company dependent on any powerful single-source supplier of key components, as Compaq is dependent on Intel for microprocessor chips? Who are these powerful single-source suppliers?

   ☐ Are your competitors also dependent on these same single-source suppliers for critical components or raw materials?

   ☐ Are your product features and characteristics required to conform to industry standards, or is your company free to innovate its own standards?

   ☐ Is there any reason to believe that your suppliers may integrate forward so that they might someday become your competitors?

   ☐ In general, which group has the most power to dominate the competitive structure of your industry—your suppliers, your competitors, or your customers? Or is your company the dominant firm in your industry?

2. Threat of new entrants

☐ Is entry to your industry restricted to only those firms with large financial resources? Or have small companies been able to carve out niches for themselves?

☐ How important is brand equity in your industry as a barrier to entry? Which brand names are the most powerful in your industry? Are recognized brand names important or unimportant to customers?

☐ How important is product innovation in your industry as a means of entry? Have outsiders been able to enter in recent years by introducing innovative products or services? Which companies in your industry are the most innovative?

3. Bargaining power of customers

☐ Are your customers concentrated into a few major groups or firms with sufficient power to dictate industry prices and terms? Who are your most powerful customers? Or do you serve many small customers, none of whom by itself has much bargaining power?

☐ Are the products and services highly differentiated in your industry, in the minds of your customers?

4. Jockeying for position among competitors

☐ Which company has the largest market share in your industry? Is this company powerful enough to influence pricing strategy for the whole industry? What is your company's market share — is your company the market leader, or is it a small player that has little power to set its own policies?

☐ Are there only a few major firms in your industry, or are there many small firms that all compete with each other?

- ☐ Which company offers the highest quality products and services?

- ☐ Which company has the lowest manufacturing costs in your industry?

- ☐ Is your industry growing rapidly, so that all the suppliers are busy just keeping up with demand? Or is company growth possible only by taking sales away from a competitor?

- ☐ How would you characterize competition among the firms in your industry? Live and let live? Intense price wars? Follow the leader?

5. Threat of substitute products

- ☐ Are there low-cost substitutes under development that could undermine the demand for your products and services?

- ☐ Are there major technological developments on the horizon that could make your product or service obsolete?

....

1   Thomas, L. J., "Available Light Movies—An Individual Inventor Made It Happen," *Research Management*, November, 1980, pp. 14 - 18.

2   Packard, D., *The HP Way*, HarperBusiness, 1995, p. 155.

3   Thomas, p. 17.

4   Moody, F., *I Sing the Body Electronic*, Viking, 1995, p. 25.

5   Porter, M., "How Competitive Forces Shape Strategy," *Harvard Business Review*, March/April 1979, pp. 137 - 145.

6   Kirkpatrick, D., "Why Compaq is Mad at Intel," *Fortune*, October 31, 1994, pp. 171 - 178.

7   Young, J., "Digital Octopus," *Forbes*, June 17, 1996, pp. 102 - 106.

8   Ziegler, B., "PC Makers' Big Push Into the Home Market Comes at Risky Time," *The Wall Street Journal*, November 1, 1995, p. A1.

9   Ibid. p. A1.

10   Ibid. p. A9.

11   Sager, I., "The View from IBM," *Business Week*, October 30, 1995, p. 144.

SHARPENING YOUR ANALYTICAL ABILITIES

S ome people think that business decisions can be based solely on intuition and experience, but this is no longer true.

To illustrate how intuition can be very misleading in business decision-making, consider the following question: How thick is a piece of typing paper that is folded on itself 32 times? Is it an inch, two feet, or more?

The correct answer is 271 miles![1] You won't get that answer by intuition or experience.

But what does folding paper have to do with management, you might ask? Suppose you are a manager in a venture capital firm and you are evaluating a small, high-tech startup company as a possible investment. Company sales are currently $1 million. The CEO tells you that he expects to double his sales every year for the next ten years. Does this make sense? Better not trust your intuition on this one either.

The setup of the problem is identical to that of the paper folding problem. In year one, sales would be $2 million; in year two, $4 million, and so on. Sales in the tenth year will be $1 million times 2 to the 10th power. Using a hand calculator, you find that sales in the tenth year would be $1 million times 1024, which is $1.024 billion.

Plausible? Probably not, although this kind of soaring growth actually has been achieved by a very few startup companies, such as Compaq Computer and Sun Microsystems. If you really believe the CEO of the startup company, this could be the investment opportunity of a lifetime, and you had better grab it.

As we will see later in this chapter, intuition and experience are very important in business decision-making. But to depend only on intuition and experience is to put yourself at a serious disadvantage in today's managerial job market. You will be outgunned by people who know how to do the kind of analysis shown above.

ANALYTICAL SKILLS—"THE MOST VALUABLE OF THE 10 STRATEGIC SKILLS"

The highest-paid 10% of our research survey respondents—all making $200,000 or more—ranked analytical problem-solving skills as the most valuable Strategic Skill for managers, based on their own personal career growth. Analytical skills are vitally important because managers are regularly called upon to make decisions under conditions of uncertainty—forecasts of next year's sales, estimated profitability of a proposed new product, or future returns on investment opportunities in the securities markets. In today's flatter, leaner organizations, managers at all levels must be proficient in analytical skills to make decisions on their own, without staff support.

The Strategic Skill of Analysis always requires rigorous, logical thinking and may or may not involve mathematics (which, incidentally, can be mastered by anyone who got through high school algebra). The results are usually in the form of numbers, but with the availability of powerful spreadsheet programs for personal computers, the solutions to these problems are achievable with a minimum of mathematical drudgery.

As Lord Kelvin said,

"When you can measure what you are speaking about, and express it in numbers, you know something about it; but when you cannot measure it, when you cannot express it in numbers, your knowledge is of a meager and unsatisfactory kind."

Putting it more succinctly, business has become too complex for you to succeed by "winging it."

HOW TO ANALYZE AN IMPORTANT PERSONAL INVESTMENT DECISION

To provide a framework for our discussion of desirable analytical skills for managers, let's consider a decision that could be very important to you personally: whether or not you should pursue an MBA degree.

The decision about whether to go for an MBA is a major personal investment decision. If you give up your job to go full-time, you will invest two years and, typically, more than $100,000 in tuition and foregone earnings.[2] Is it worth it? Even if you go part-time and your employer pays for your tuition, you will still make a major commitment of time and effort.

How do you want to go about making this decision? By experience? Not likely, since most people earn only one MBA degree during their careers—although you could talk with others about *their* experiences in pursuing an MBA degree. By intuition? Perhaps, but wouldn't it be a good idea to also look at some numbers before you commit to investing $100,000? (Don't be put off by the math—we will be working at the Ninth Grade level.)

To assess this decision, we will introduce three of the most frequently used analytical techniques that managers employ in making major business investment decisions:

- Net present value

- Regression analysis

- Decision analysis

SETTING UP THE PROBLEM

From a financial standpoint, is it worth it to go to business school? The best way to answer that question is to estimate how much you will make over the next several years if you quit your present job to go full-time to business school, less the cost of tuition. Then make an estimate of how much you will make over the same period if you stay at your present job and don't go to business school. The difference is the additional value acquired by getting the MBA.

To do this, estimate your yearly income (which we will call your personal "cash flow") for each of the two choices: going to business school and not going to business school.

Figure 5.1 is a diagram of your estimated cash flows for each decision. The line with the *black* dots shows your estimated yearly cash flows if you decide *not* to attend business school. The line with the *white* dots shows your estimated yearly cash flows if you *do* choose to pursue an MBA degree.

Table 5.1 shows your yearly income if you decide not to get an MBA (the numbers are the same as those for the line with the black dots in Figure 5.1). In the year before you would have started for your MBA (Year 0), your income is assumed to be $35,000. If you don't get an MBA, it is assumed that your salary will grow at 5% per year to $49,248 by Year 7.

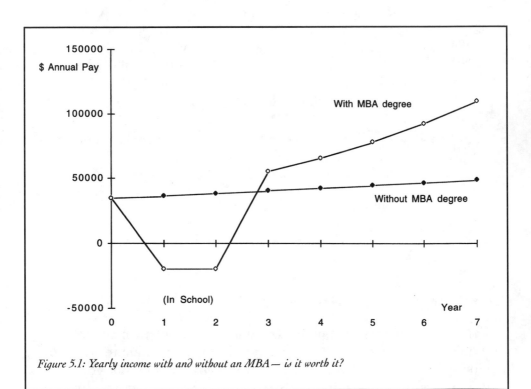

Figure 5.1: Yearly income with and without an MBA— is it worth it?

TABLE 5.1: YEARLY INCOME WITHOUT AN MBA	
	Column A **Pay without MBA**
Year 0	$35,000
Year 1	36,750
Year 2	38,588
Year 3	40,517
Year 4	42,543
Year 5	44,670
Year 6	46,903
Year 7	49,248

Let's assume that you are thinking about attending the Johnson Graduate School of Management at Cornell University, where the tuition is $19,500 per year. After consulting a number of books about MBA programs, you find that starting salaries for graduates of the Cornell MBA program have averaged a 58.5% increase above pre-MBA pay.[3]

In Figure 5.1, the line with the white dots shows your estimated yearly income if you choose to attend business school. Again, in Year 0, your income is $35,000. In the two years while attending school (Years 1 and 2), you will have no salary, but there will be tuition costs of $19,500 per year, so your cash flow for each of these two years is shown as –$19,500. (Note that I have not included the cost of room and board at Cornell, because I assume you will have about the same living costs whether or not you go to business school.)

In the first year following receipt of your MBA (Year 3), your estimated annual income is $55,475, which is 58.5% higher than your pre-MBA pay of $35,000. Furthermore, based on the historical growth of the post-MBA pay of Cornell graduates, this amount will grow over the next five years to $109,907.[4]

	Column A Pay without MBA	Column B Pay with MBA
	TABLE 5.2: YEARLY INCOME WITH OR WITHOUT AN MBA	
Year 0	$35,000	$35,000
Year 1*	36,750	-19,500 (tuition and no salary)
Year 2*	38,588	-19,500 (tuition and no salary)
Year 3	40,517	55,475 (starting salary is 58.5% above pre-MBA pay)
Year 4	42,543	65,816
Year 5	44,670	78,084
Year 6	46,903	92,639
Year 7	49,248	109,907

* = *years in school*

Table 5.2 adds a column for your annual pay with a Cornell MBA degree.

In Table 5.3, column C shows the yearly *increase* in income if you earned a Cornell MBA. This is calculated by subtracting Column A from Column B to get the difference between these two alternatives.

Note that in Years 1 and 2, this difference is negative. This occurs for two reasons: You are paying tuition of $19,500 per year and you are foregoing your annual salary, which would have grown to more than $38,000 by Year 2 if you had stayed in your old job. In fact, this analysis shows rather dramatically that *the major cost of attending a full-time MBA program is not the tuition. Rather, it is the foregone salary during the two years in school.* This is a very important insight that is not obvious until you actually analyze the numbers.

	Column A Pay without MBA	Column B Pay with MBA	Column C Difference (B - A)
TABLE 5.3: THE DIFFERENCE IN ANNUAL PAY DUE TO EARNING AN MBA			
Year 0	$35,000	$35,000	$0
Year 1*	36,750	-19,500	-56,250
Year 2*	38,588	-19,500	-58,087
Year 3	40,517	55,475	14,958
Year 4	42,543	65,816	23,273
Year 5	44,670	78,084	33,414
Year 6	46,903	92,639	45,736
Year 7	49,248	109,907	60,659

* = years in school

Finally, Table 5.4 shows the time it will take to recover your investment in the MBA program by calculating the *cumulative* value of Column C for each year. Note that at the end of Year 2, immediately after graduating with an MBA, you are $114,337 "in the hole" on your investment. (This is what I was referring to when I said that you will invest more than $100,000 to pursue a full-time MBA program.)

Also, note that the values in Column D finally turn positive in Year 6, which is the fourth year of work following graduation. This means that from the time you actually start investing in your MBA (Year 1), it takes six years to recover your investment and start to show a profit. (In reality, you probably would do better than this. In our conservative example, we assumed the worst case—that you would receive no scholarships to reduce the tuition cost and would earn no income from your summer internship.)

By Year 7, you are really starting to pull ahead. You have recovered all of your investment and are ahead by nearly $64,000 as the result of going to business school, and this amount will continue to grow rapidly from here on.

	Column A Pay without MBA	Column B Pay with MBA	Column C Difference (B-A)	Column D Cum Difference
TABLE 5.4: IT TAKES SIX YEARS TO BREAKEVEN ON AN INVESTMENT IN AN MBA				
Year 0	$35,000	$35,000	$0	$0
Year 1*	36,750	-19,500	-56,250	-56,250
Year 2*	38,588	-19,500	-58,087	-114,337
Year 3	40,517	55,475	14,958	-99,379
Year 4	42,543	65,816	23,273	-76,106
Year 5	44,670	78,084	33,414	-42,692
Year 6	46,903	92,639	45,736	3,044
Year 7	49,248	109,907	60,659	63,703

* = *years in school*

THE POWERFUL CONCEPT OF PRESENT VALUE

Suppose you do some work for me, and I ask you whether you would prefer for me to pay you $100 in cash today, or give you my written promise to pay you $100 a year from today. Which would you prefer to have?

Most people would prefer to receive the $100 today, for several reasons:

- A year from now, I might change my mind about paying you, or you might not be able to find me to get me to pay up, so there is some risk in waiting a year before getting paid.

- If inflation is running about 3% a year, the $100 paid to you a year from now might have a purchasing power of only $97.

- If I pay you $100 today, you might be able to invest it safely at 6% in a government-insured bank account, so that a year from now you would have $106.

While all three of these are good reasons for your insistence on getting paid today, to keep things simple, let's just deal with the third reason. Again, to keep things simple, let's assume that I am completely trustworthy, that you see me every day, and that there is no risk that I won't pay you a year from now. Let's also assume that there is no inflation. Under these special circumstances, you should be indifferent to my paying you $100 now or $106 in a year.

In other words, $100 received today is worth the same to you as $106 received a year from now. Or, in financial terms, the *present value* (that is, the value right now) of $106 received a year from now is $100, if the interest rate (which is called the *discount* rate when talking about present value) is 6%. Then, what would be the present value of $100 that you would receive a year from now, at 6%? It would clearly be less than $100. It would be an amount, that when invested at 6%, will equal $100 a year from now. That amount turns out to be $94.34, because $94.34 increased by 6% equals $100. (This is calculated by dividing $100 by 1.06, which equals $94.34.) Therefore, we can multiply $100 to be received a year from now, by a *present value discount factor* of 0.9434 to get its present value of $94.34.

What, then, is the present value of $100 received two years from now? Because we are receiving compound interest on our savings account, we apply the one-year present value discount factor twice. So the present value of $100 received two years from now is 0.9434 times 0.9434 times $100, which is $89.00. Putting it another way, if we received $89.00 today and invested it for two years at 6% per year, we would have $100 two years from today. So, the present value discount factor for two years at 6% is 0.8900.

If we continue this process, we will find that the present value discount factor for three years is 0.840, for four years it is 0.792, and so on. If you have to wait to receive your money, you lose the opportunity to invest your $100 and earn interest. Therefore, the longer you have to wait, the less valuable that future payment is.

These discount factors are listed in Column E of Table 5.5.

Applying Present Value to Your Personal Investment Decision

The concept of present value is one of the most useful analytical techniques for assessing major investment opportunities where the benefits may not be received until several years in the future. Consider, for example, your decision about whether to invest in an MBA degree. From Column C in Table 5.4, we see that once you graduate, you would earn a lot more each year than if you did not have your MBA degree—$14,958 more in Year 3, $23,273 more in Year 4, and so on. But to do this, from Column D, you will have to invest $114,337 in tuition and foregone salary to generate this flow of increased earnings. Is it worth it?

To get an accurate assessment of whether it is worth it to invest over $100,000 in an MBA, we need to discount those future costs and benefits by the present value discount factors for the years in which they occur. Once again, the longer you have to wait to receive the benefits from your investment in an MBA degree, the less valuable that investment.

In Table 5.5, Column C is copied over from Table 5.4. Next, these values are multiplied by the present value discount factors in Column E to get the present value of the costs and benefits of earning an MBA, as shown in Column F. Note that the discounted values in Column F are always smaller than the *undiscounted* values in Column C.

Finally, in Column G, we find the *cumulative* present value (called the *net* present value) of the numbers in Column F, just as we did in Column D of Table 5.4. Note that it now takes until Year 7 to breakeven. The final value at the bottom of Column G, $23,798, shows how much more money you would have at the end of seven years by investing in an MBA, versus putting your investment in the bank at 6% interest. But this analysis really understates the present value of earning an MBA because it is cut off at the end of 7 years. In fact, if you were to extend this analysis for the 20 to 30 years you expect to work, you would find that the present value of an MBA degree would be worth many hundreds of thousands of dollars over the course of your career.

TABLE 5.5: IT TAKES SEVEN YEARS TO BREAKEVEN ON A NET PRESENT VALUE BASIS				
	Column C Difference (B-A)	Column E Present Value Factor @ 6%	Column F Present Value	Column G Net Present Value
Year 0	$0	1.000	$0	$0
Year 1*	-56,250	0.943	-53,044	-53,044
Year 2*	-58,087	0.890	-51,697	-104,741
Year 3	14,958	0.840	12,565	-92,176
Year 4	23,273	0.792	18,432	-73,744
Year 5	33,414	0.747	24,960	-48,784
Year 6	45,736	0.705	32,244	-16,540
Year 7	60,659	0.665	40,338	23,798

* = years in school

Comparing Alternative Business Schools

Let's assume that based on this preliminary analysis, you are seriously interested in pursuing an MBA degree. But from which business school?

By using published data on pre-MBA pay, post-MBA starting salaries, post-MBA pay growth in the years following graduation, and tuition costs, it is possible to construct a net present value table for the top business schools.[5] Note that in Table 5.6 these net present values are calculated at the end of *seven* years of post-MBA salary, rather than at the end of the five years of post-MBA salary used in Table 5.5.[6]

As we noted previously, the value of the MBA accrues over the remaining 20 to 30 years of your career, so in theory the analysis should be extended over this longer time horizon. But making forecasts of income for 20 to 30 years is risky. So we will truncate the cash flows at the end of seven years post-MBA and recognize that the true net present value of degrees from these top schools is likely to be much higher than the figures shown. It is generally better to err in the direction of conservatism when making these kinds of analyses.

TABLE 5.6: THE TOP BUSINESS SCHOOLS
(Pretax Net Present Value @ 6% through Year 7 post-MBA)

Rank	Business school	Net present value of the MBA degree
1	Harvard	$267,727
2	Stanford	203,582
3	Chicago	200,681
4	Columbia	193,956
5	MIT	177,561
6	Yale	169,880
7	Wharton	144,608
8	Northwestern	134,433
9	UCLA	129,579
10	Berkeley	127,534
11	Dartmouth	100,425
12	Cornell	97,550
13	Virginia	97,113
14	Michigan	83,602
15	Carnegie Mellon	79,051
16	Texas	65,572
17	NYU	52,351
18	Rochester	51,100
19	North Carolina	44,572
20	Indiana	41,657
21	Duke	32,994

The present value discounted at 6% of the amount typical graduates of each school earn in the first seven years on the job after paying business school tuition, less what they would have made foregoing business school and staying in their old job. These amounts are, of course, only a fraction of the true lifetime value of earning an MBA. Salary data is for the Class of 1992, and was published in A Business Week Guide: The Best Business Schools, *third edition, McGraw-Hill, 1993. Unpublished data for Columbia's salaries was provided to Columbia by* Business Week *in a private communication dated August 19, 1994.*

THE VALUE OF ANALYSIS

Is it worth doing all this analytical work? Think about it this way. Suppose you were admitted to the MBA programs at Yale and Indiana. The tuition at Indiana, a state school, is much lower. Would it be worth it to calculate the net present values of the degrees from these two schools, as shown in Table 5.6? The difference is more than $140,000. You might still choose Indiana, but you will have made a much more informed decision than if you had just used your intuition to choose between these two fine schools.

WHY DOES THE NET PRESENT VALUE VARY SO MUCH FROM SCHOOL TO SCHOOL?

The results of analysis are usually easier to understand if they are presented in graphical form. Suppose, for example, you wanted to get a better understanding of why the net present value of MBA degrees from the schools shown in Table 5.6 varies so much.

One possibility—let's call it a hypothesis—is that some business schools are able to attract better quality students than others.[7] They start with better raw material. If this is the case, then we should be able to plot a graph of each school's net present value (NPV) from Table 5.6 versus the quality of its incoming students. And, if our hypothesis is correct, a line fitted to this data should slope upward. In other words, if a school has a higher quality of incoming students, the NPV of the school's MBA degree will be higher.

But how do we measure incoming student quality? There are at least two possible methods:

1. GMAT scores: The measure of student quality used by most business schools is the prospective students' score on the Graduate Management Admission Test (GMAT). The GMAT is a good measure of the ability to do well on tests, and it has been shown to have value in predicting first year grades in business school. If our hypothesis is correct, then the higher a school's average GMAT, the higher the NPV of its MBA degree.

2. <u>Pre-MBA pay</u>: Because almost all students admitted to the top business schools typically have had three or four years of work experience, another measure of student quality would be their pay in the final year before they enter business school. Average pre-MBA pay should be an unbiased, market-based measure of incoming student quality that is influenced not only by intelligence but also by motivation, personal skills, undergraduate education, the ability to communicate, years of work experience, and whatever else it takes to succeed in the real world. Again, if our hypothesis is correct, the higher a school's average pre-MBA pay, the higher should be the NPV of its MBA degree.

To see whether either of these measures of student quality is associated with the NPV of the schools' MBA degrees, let's begin by plotting the data for each case.

Figure 5.2 shows a graph of NPV (from Table 5.6) versus average GMAT for each of the top business schools.[8] Although there seems to be some upward slope to the data, the data

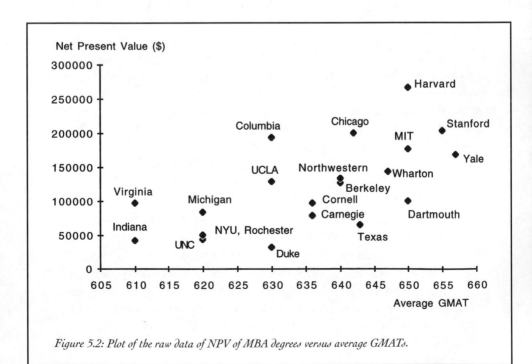

Figure 5.2: Plot of the raw data of NPV of MBA degrees versus average GMATs.

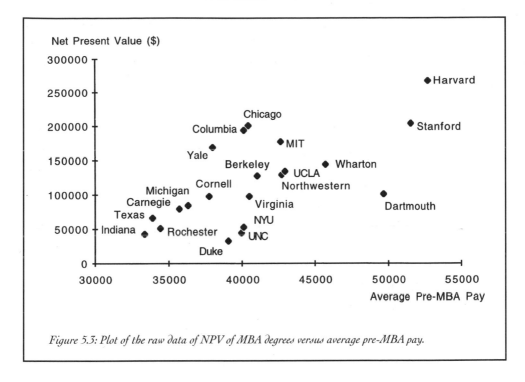

Figure 5.3: Plot of the raw data of NPV of MBA degrees versus average pre-MBA pay.

points are so scattered that it is not clear whether there is a meaningful relationship between NPV and GMAT.

Similarly, when we plot NPV versus pre-MBA pay in Figure 5.3, there is so much scatter that again it is difficult to tell whether there is really a meaningful relationship here.

REGRESSION ANALYSIS

Fortunately, there is a technique, known as *regression analysis*, that will fit a line through data like this, and that will also give us a number that indicates the "goodness of fit" to provide us with an indication of whether the relationship is really meaningful.

In Figure 5.4, the data from Figure 5.2 have been plotted again, but this time we have used regression analysis to fit a line through the data. This regression line is drawn to give the best fit of all the points relating the NPVs of the various schools to this measure of student quality. The line shows how the "average" business school's NPV increases as GMAT scores increase. Note that only a few of the schools are approximately "average." Most are above or below the line.

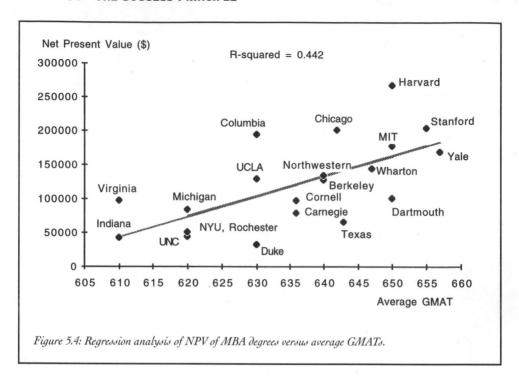

Figure 5.4: Regression analysis of NPV of MBA degrees versus average GMATs.

This line shows that for schools where the average GMAT scores are around 610, the NPV of their MBA degrees is about $50,000; whereas for schools with average GMATs of 650, the NPV tends to be about $170,000—a very sizable difference.

But how do we know that this relationship is "real?" Maybe this is all random, all due to chance. There are two indications that this association is not random:

- Statistically, the slope of the line in Figure 5.4 is "significantly different from zero at the 0.001 level." This means that it is very unlikely that we would have observed this positive slope if the true correlation were zero.

- The "R-squared" of 0.442 shown at the top of the plot is a measure of the "goodness of fit" of the line to the data, and indicates in this case that 44.2% of the variation in NPV can be explained by the variation in GMAT scores. It's not 100%, but 44% is not bad, either.

Similarly, in Figure 5.5, the addition of a regression line shows that for schools where the average pre-MBA pay is around $35,000, the NPV of the MBA degree is about $75,000;

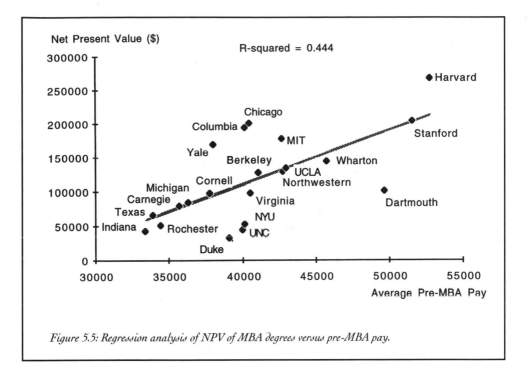

Figure 5.5: Regression analysis of NPV of MBA degrees versus pre-MBA pay.

whereas for schools with pre-MBA pay of $50,000, the NPV is typically about $200,000.

Interestingly, the strength of the association between NPV and pre-MBA pay is almost identical to the association between NPV and GMATs. The slope of the line is again significant at the 0.001 level, and the R-squared of 0.444 means that 44.4% of the variation in NPV can be explained by the variation in pre-MBA pay across schools.

Are these two measures of incoming student quality, GMATs and pre-MBA pay, just measures of the same thing? They do overlap to some extent. The correlation between these two variables is 0.568 (where 0.000 would be no correlation, and 1.000 would be perfect correlation). We cannot just add the 44.2% R-squared from GMATs and the 44.4% from pre-MBA pay to claim that we can explain 88.6% of the variation in NPV.

Cause and Effect?

It is important to caution you that these regression results, although statistically significant, do not by themselves prove cause and effect. Sometimes two things co-vary because they are both being caused by a third variable. For example, it is colder in the winter and the days are shorter, although it is not colder *because* the days are shorter. In the Northern Hemisphere, it is colder *and* the days are shorter in the winter, and *both* are caused by a third variable, the earth's axis being tipped away from the sun in the winter.

Let's look at another example. One of my graduate students found in a study of 169 MBA students that those who had summer internships had post-MBA starting salaries that averaged $6,000 higher than those who didn't.[9] But this doesn't prove that getting the internships caused the higher starting salaries. Most likely, the internships did help the students get a head start with their future employers. But it also may be that only the best (i.e., the most employable) students got summer internships, and they would have gotten higher starting salaries with or without the internships.

Although it seems reasonable that higher student quality, as measured by GMATs and by pre-MBA pay, is an important factor in explaining why the NPVs of degrees from some schools are higher than others, there could be other factors that are also affecting the value of these degrees, such as the cost of living in those areas where most of a school's graduates locate.

Above and Below the Line

What is the significance of schools lying above or below the regression line? The vertical distance from the school to the line is called a *residual*, and it is a measure of whether an individual school is outperforming or underperforming the 'average' *school for a given level of student quality*. For example, in both plots, Chicago, Columbia, and Harvard are well above the line, meaning that their NPV is higher than would be expected given the quality of their students. On the other hand, Duke and Dartmouth are well below the line in both plots, indicating that the NPV of their degrees is below what would be expected, again given the quality of their students. This suggests that there are other factors, such as the geographic location of the school or the content of the courses, that are affecting the NPV of the degrees from these schools.[10]

To recap our discussion of regression analysis:

1. We found that the value (i.e., the NPV) of the MBA degree from the top schools varies greatly across schools.

2. From this, we developed a hypothesis that this variation in value might be caused at least in part by the average quality of the incoming students for each school.

3. We were able to obtain two sets of data on the quality of incoming students for these schools: average GMAT scores and average pre-MBA salaries.

4. When we plotted the raw data in Figures 5.2 and 5.3, there was so much scatter in the data that we could not tell by inspection whether there is a significant relationship between the NPVs of the degrees and either of these measures of student quality.

5. But when we used regression analysis, we learned that:

   • There is a statistically significant association between incoming student quality and the value of the MBA degrees that is very unlikely to be due to chance.

   • Incoming student quality explains roughly 40% to 50% of the variation in the value of the MBA across these schools, which means that it is probably the largest single factor affecting the value of the MBA degree.

   • Pre-MBA pay is virtually identical to GMAT scores as a means of measuring incoming student quality for this purpose.

   • For a given level of student quality, some schools — those well above the regression line — are doing a superior job of preparing their students, while those well below the line are underperforming.

Is it worth it to do this kind of quantitative analysis? Clearly yes. *There is no way that intuition alone will provide you with this kind of insight.* This is a very important investment decision. You are considering investing $100,000 and two years of your life in getting an MBA degree. You don't want to make a mistake.

DECISION ANALYSIS

Let's assume that, after all this analysis, you have decided to go for an MBA. Furthermore, you have studied the catalogs of all the top schools listed in Table 5.6 and you have decided that you would be interested in attending any one of the following three schools: Rochester, Carnegie Mellon or MIT.

Assume also that each school has a non-refundable application fee of $100, and that you can only afford to apply to one of the schools.[11] To which one should you apply?

If your chances for being accepted were equal at all three schools, the answer is easy—you would pick the one with the highest NPV, which would be MIT in this case. But you know that your chances of getting in are not the same at all schools. After talking with the Admissions Office at each school, you estimate that the probability of your being accepted at each school is:

School	Probability of acceptance
Rochester	80%
Carnegie Mellon	40%
MIT	10%

Using these probabilities of acceptance and the NPVs of each school from Table 5.6, we can compute the *expected value* of applying to each school by multiplying each NPV by the estimated probability of acceptance:

School	Probability of acceptance	NPV	Expected value
Rochester	80%	$51,100	$40,880
Carnegie Mellon	40%	$79,051	$31,620
MIT	10%	$177,561	$17,756

Since you can only afford to apply to one school, the best choice would be to apply to Rochester, because this choice has the highest expected value.

Comparing alternative courses of action based on their expected values is called *decision analysis*. A complex management decision can be set up as a *decision tree*, in which each branch represents the expected value of one possible outcome.

In reality, managers do not always choose the alternative with the highest expected value. Sometimes there are nonfinancial reasons for choosing another alternative. For example, if your heart is really set on attending MIT, you might apply there first, doing this early enough so that if you are turned down, you will still have enough time to apply to one of the other schools—if you can find someone to lend you another $100.

The value of decision analysis is that it provides a rational way for you to consider the economic outcomes when you choose among alternatives where there is uncertainty introduced by factors that you cannot control, in this case the decisions of the school's Admissions Offices. Even though you might ultimately make a different choice than the one having the highest expected value, you will benefit by having a much better understanding of the consequences of your decision.

Ann Langley, a professor at the University of Quebec at Montreal, has noted that formal analysis, in addition to providing "the best answer," is often used in organizations as a means of persuasion. A fancy report with plenty of graphs and charts can be a very effective selling tool, inside and outside the company. And a requirement for formal analysis is also a way to exert control over subordinates. You can always say, "Go back and analyze your proposal once more."[12]

PARALYSIS BY ANALYSIS?

In this chapter, we have introduced several analytical methods to show how they can shed light on an important investment decision, in this case, the decision of whether or not to pursue an MBA degree. Yet some managers complain that such formal analysis is too abstract and too slow. When Ross Perot was on the board of directors of General Motors Corporation, he was appalled at the tendency of the board to value analysis over action:

> *"I come from an environment where, if you see a snake, you kill it. At GM, if you see a snake, the first thing you do is go hire a consultant on snakes. Then you get a committee*

*on snakes, and then you discuss it for a couple of years.
The most likely course of action is—nothing. You figure
the snake hasn't bitten anybody yet, so you just let him
crawl around on the factory floor."13*

Perot has a good point. Analysis can be overdone.

THE IMPORTANT ROLES OF INTUITION AND EXPERIENCE

Formal analysis is *not* a substitute for intuition and experience in the management of organizations. Intuition includes the ability to discern complex patterns that are too subtle for formal analysis. Seeing such patterns is the result of many years of experience. The novice, lacking such experience, laboriously grinds through the problem analytically, whereas the experienced person sees a possible solution immediately—not the best solution, perhaps, but one that works. Such people draw on years of experience to discern complex patterns that mean nothing to the novice.

Gary Klein, who studies how military officers make decisions on the battlefield, often under extreme time pressure, notes that the best decision-makers are those with the most experience. "The secret of better decision-making under such circumstances," says Klein, "is to gain more relevant experience." He continues, "An employee who wants to sharpen her decision-making should ask, for example, to be rotated through a variety of jobs within her specialty and to serve on task forces, and should try to soak up as much secondhand experience as she can from old-timers in the office."14

In his best selling book, *Emotional Intelligence*, Daniel Goleman argues that the old paradigm of always subordinating the emotions to purely rational thinking is hazardous when making the most important decisions in life—where to work, whether to quit your job, or whom to marry. The emotional wisdom from past experiences—the gut feeling about these important matters—more often than not puts up a red flag that steers us away from potentially dangerous courses of action. (Gut feelings seem to be more likely to warn us about losers than to alert us to winners.) We may not understand or remember the experiences that trigger these warnings, but we should pay attention to them.[15]

Successful managers rely heavily on their experience. Hewlett-Packard co-founder David Packard, in one of his first jobs at General Electric after graduating with his engineering degree from Stanford, was given a challenging assignment to improve the manufacturing quality of a high-power industrial vacuum tube called an ignitron:

> "... [GE] was having problems manufacturing ignitrons, and I was given the job of finding out why so many were failing during testing. I learned everything I could about the causes of failure and decided to spend most of my time on the factory floor, making sure every step in the manufacturing process was done correctly. I found several instances where the written instructions provided the manufacturing people were inadequate, and I worked with them on each step in the process to make sure there were no mistakes. This painstaking attention to detail paid off, and every tube in the next batch passed its final test.

> "As I look back, my decision to work on that ignitron problem with the people in the factory had a profound influence on the management policies we developed for the Hewlett-Packard Company. That was the genesis of what has been called MBWA [Management by Walking Around]. I learned that quality requires minute attention to every detail, that everyone in an organization wants to do a good job, that written instructions are seldom adequate, and that personal involvement is essential."[16]

THE BOTTOM LINE

Formal analysis has become important because business has become too complex for managers to wing it on intuition and experience alone. As we add Analytical Skills to the organization chart of your "company of one" in Figure 5.6, we recognize

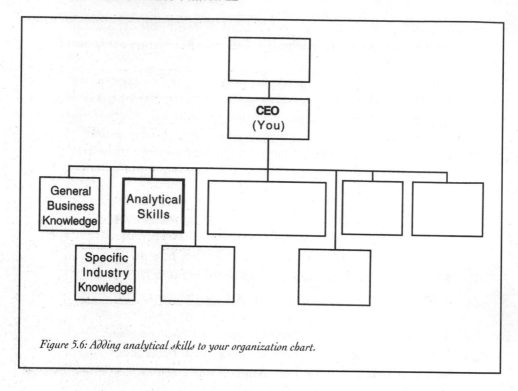

Figure 5.6: Adding analytical skills to your organization chart.

that the best managers are those who have learned to combine the hard science of formal analysis and the softer skills of management intuition and experience.

1   This illustration is from *Snapshots from Hell* by Peter Robinson, Warner Books, 1994, p. 24. The solution is easy. A piece of typing paper is 0.004 inches thick. If we fold it once on itself, it will be twice as thick, or 0.008 inches thick. If we fold it a second time, it will be 0.016 inches thick, and so on. The general formula is "thickness = 0.004 times 2 to the nth power," where n = the number of folds. Using a hand calculator, we can set this up as a table:

Number of folds (n)	2 to the nth power	Thickness
0	1	0.004
1	2	0.008
2	4	0.016
3	8	0.032
.	.	.
.	.	.
32	4294967296	17179869 inches (which – 271 miles)

2   See Yeaple, R., *The MBA Advantage: Why It Pays to Get an MBA*, Bob Adams Inc., 1994, pp. 264 - 273.

3   See Yeaple, *The MBA Advantage: Why It Pays to Get an MBA*, 1994, p. 37, or Byrne, J., *A Business Week Guide: The Best Business Schools*, 3rd ed., McGraw-Hill, 1993, p. 58. Note that in the 4th edition of the *Business Week Guide*, the post-MBA stepup in pay for Cornell has risen to 77% (Byrne, 1995, p. 57), so our analysis of the financial value of a Cornell MBA degree may be on the conservative side.

4   The assumptions for this example are explained in Yeaple, 1994, Appendix C, pp. 288 - 291.

5   The assumptions for this table are explained in Yeaple, 1994, Appendix B, pp. 268 - 270.

6   Note that in Table 5.6, the NPV of a Cornell MBA degree is shown to be $97,550, which is much higher than the $23,798 shown in Column G of Table 5.5. The reason is that in calculating Table 5.6, the analysis was

extended out for seven years post-MBA, rather than the five years used to calculate Table 5.5. This was done so that all of the schools in the table would show a positive net present value. The post-MBA salary growth rates, both with and without the MBA, were assumed in years 6 and 7 to be half of the growth rates in years 1 through 5 post-MBA, to simulate the eventual slowdown in salary growth that typically occurs. Also, a different assumption was made about how fast pay would grow *without* an MBA. In Table 5.5, it was assumed that pay without the degree would grow at 5% per year. In Table 5.6, it was assumed that pay without the degree would grow faster—at 9.3%, which is half the rate of growth *with* a Cornell MBA. This is a more conservative assumption which tends to reduce the calculated marginal value of earning an MBA degree. Similar assumptions were made for all of the schools in Table 5.6. (See Yeaple, 1994, p. 32, for further discussion of these assumptions.)

7   If prospective students are somewhat aware of the differences in the NPV of the MBA degree across the various schools, these candidates would be expected to apply to the best schools (i.e., those with the highest NPVs) that they believe will admit them. (It costs time and money to apply to a business school, so prospective students are unlikely to apply to schools where they feel they have no chance of being admitted.) If the schools aggressively pursue the best candidates who apply to them by means of generous financial aid and other incentives, then given that each school has a limited number of seats in its first year class, the highest quality candidates would be expected to be found in the schools with the highest NPVs. Therefore, we would expect to see a positive correlation between the average NPV of a school's MBA degree and the average quality of its incoming students. Causality could also flow the other way—high quality students ought to be more successful after graduation, so attracting a larger percentage of high quality students in the incoming class would tend to drive up

the average NPV of a school's MBA degree. These two factors would tend to reinforce each other, keeping the positive correlation across schools between NPV and student quality stable over time.

8   The data point for each school is the average of 50 to 250 student responses from that school and is for the graduating class of 1992. See Yeaple, 1994, for a detailed discussion of how the data was obtained.

9   Daum, M., "Predictors of MBA Starting Salaries," MBA summer research project, William E. Simon Graduate School of Business Administration, August, 1993.

10 For an in-depth analysis of factors that seem to affect the value of MBA degrees from various schools, see Yeaple, 1994, pp. 273 - 287.

11 As one of my colleagues pointed out, this example is a bit contrived. If you were about to invest more than $100,000 (including foregone salary) in an MBA degree, you would probably find a way to raise the money to apply to more than one school.

12 Langley, A., "Between 'Paralysis by Analysis' and 'Extinction by Instinct,'" *Engineering Management Review*, Fall 1995, pp. 14 - 24.

13 Perot, R., "The GM System is Like a Blanket of Fog," *Fortune*, February 15, 1988, pp. 48 - 49.

14 Farnham, A., "Are You Smart Enough to Keep Your Job?" *Fortune*, January 15, 1996, pp. 42 - 48.

15 Goleman, D., *Emotional Intelligence: Why It Can Matter More Than IQ*, Bantam Books, 1995, p. 53.

16 Packard, D., *The HP Way*, HarperCollins 1995, pp. 155 - 156.

BUILDING COMPUTER COMPETENCE

'Robert' is one of many success stories of the computer revolution. At 38 and living in suburban Chicago, he runs his own consulting and software development company with 15 employees. For the past five years, his total pay has averaged $700,000 per year (that's right, *$700,000 per year*).

In 1978, Robert graduated with a degree in computer science, and without the usual two- or three-year pause to gain work experience, plunged directly into an MBA, majoring in Marketing and Information Systems Management. After completing his MBA in 1980, he accepted an entry-level position as a systems analyst with a major office equipment company for $21,000 a year. But his dream was to start his own company.

Today, as head of his own firm, Robert works an average of 45 hours a week in the office and another five hours or so at client locations. His advice to aspiring young professionals: "Learn the practical application of theory and technology, and take risks while you're young." Like many young managers today, Robert has used the Strategic Skill of Computer Competence to turbocharge his career.

Because young managers like Robert have grown up with computers, computer proficiency offers youth a huge advantage in the competition for good jobs. Fred Moody, who spent a year with a product development team at Microsoft Corporation, describes the culture of youth at Microsoft as one of "youngsters suddenly being turned into managers and supervisors." Often, the oldest person at a meeting would be thirty, with the others in their early twenties. A key project leader who supervised eight software developers was only twenty-five. None had previous management experience.[1]

COMPUTER COMPETENCY AS A DEFENSIVE STRATEGY

Computer proficiency is one of the best areas where the ambitious manager can leverage change. But computer competency can also be the basis for a strong defensive strategy for keeping your job. While middle managers continue to bear the brunt of job cuts, those with technical and professional skills are still being hired.[2]

Fifty-year-old managers are losing out, less because of age than because of obsolescence, according to Eric Greenberg, director of management studies for the American Management Association. Those that consider touching a keyboard to be mere clerical work are most at risk, says Greenberg.[3]

COMPUTER USE BY MANAGERS IS WIDESPREAD

One of the surprises from our survey research of business school graduates was the nearly universal use of computers by managers at *every* age and salary level. Ninety-five percent of the responding managers reported using a computer in their office (Figure 6.1). Among younger managers (age 38 and younger), computer use in the office was reported by 97%. But older managers are also keeping up; of those 45 and older, 91% reported using a computer in their office.

WORD PROCESSING AND SPREADSHEET APPLICATIONS

According to the survey, word processing and spreadsheet analysis are the most frequent applications that managers use on their own personal computers (Figure 6.2).

Learning these and other computer applications has paid off for a number of our survey respondents:

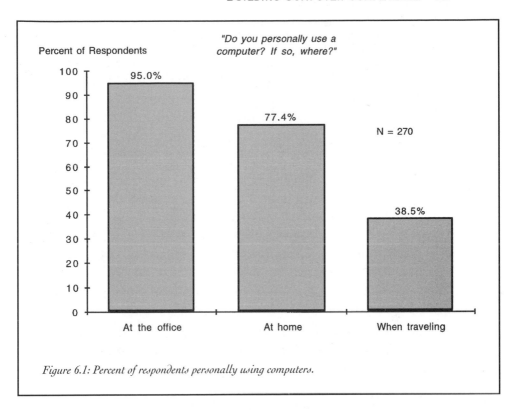

Figure 6.1: Percent of respondents personally using computers.

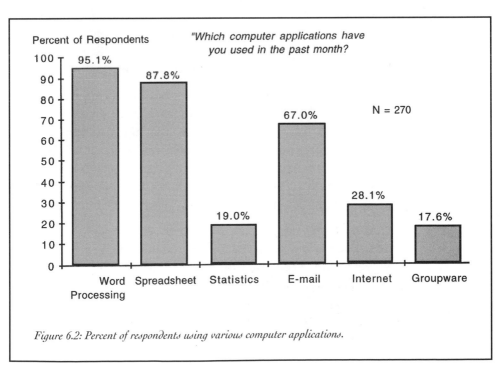

Figure 6.2: Percent of respondents using various computer applications.

- 'Paul' is 29 and works for a major computer company as a Senior Financial Analyst, at $58,000 a year. He graduated in 1988 with a bachelor's degree in Economics and continued on for his MBA in Finance in 1991. Spreadsheet analysis for accounting, net present value, and pricing studies were the most valuable skills he acquired in business school, according to his survey response. His five year objective: to start his own company.

- Graduating in 1985 with a degree in Journalism, 'John,' 35, took a job for five years as a Financial Consultant at a mutual funds company before returning to school for his MBA. Today he is an Assistant Vice President for a commercial bank and earns $71,000 a year. He credits the computer skills he gained in word processing, spreadsheet analysis, and in business school as being important factors in his professional success.

- 'Rick,' also an officer of a bank, is 29 and earns $57,000 per year. He graduated in 1988 with a degree in English, and worked for three years as an office manager for a cash management firm before beginning his MBA studies. In 1993, he received his MBA with a triple concentration, in Accounting, Finance, and Information Systems Management. His advice to other young managers: "Take Information Systems courses even if you are not interested. Every job depends on Information Systems."

- As CEO and publisher of a medium-sized charitable periodical, 'Allen,' age 49, earns $134,000 a year. He graduated in 1967 with a bachelor's degree in Management Science, and continued on for his MBA in Finance and Applied Economics. His advice to others in management: "Number one is to emphasize information technology."

- Finally, meet 'Ross,' 34, Senior Vice President of an investment bank, with an undergraduate degree in Chemistry and an MBA in Finance and Marketing. Currently he earns $225,000 a year. He reports that the most valuable training he received in business school was to become proficient in the use of the personal computer.

These case histories dramatize how alert managers have been successful in leveraging their Strategic Skills with computers to achieve their professional objectives.

CHANGE FAVORS THE PREPARED MIND

For some, a rapidly changing professional environment is a source of anxiety; for others, it is recognized as a source of opportunity. There is no area in management that is changing faster than that of computer information systems, and for the alert manager, there are few areas that offer more opportunities for innovation and professional growth.

"One of the great things about this industry is that every decade or so, you get a chance to redefine the playing field," says IBM's CEO Louis V. Gerstner, Jr.[4] When computers first emerged on the business scene in the 1950s and '60s, the mainframes were isolated in secure, air-conditioned rooms from all but a few technicians. In the 1970s, time-shared mainframes became common, with dozens or hundreds of remote terminals on users' desks communicating with the mainframes. This technology revolutionized airline reservations and banking, where each person who communicated with the public had a remote terminal that gave near-instantaneous responses.

The introduction of the personal computer in the 1980s changed everything. Initially introduced as substitutes for typewriters in word processing, today's PCs, as Figure 6.2 shows, are also heavily used *as computers* by nearly 90% of the managers surveyed to calculate spreadsheets, and increasingly to provide communications service as an e-mail terminal.

In the mid-1990s, the Internet has brought in a new wave of innovation, linking millions of personal computers around the world to communicate and share information. "The Internet is the most important single development to come along since the IBM PC was introduced in 1981," wrote Microsoft CEO Bill Gates in an internal memo that was published in *The Wall Street Journal*.[5] Dominant companies, such as Microsoft and Intel, suddenly recognized that the Internet could greatly change their markets. Some industry experts now believe that in the future, the Internet will be tapped by inexpensive "dumb" terminals that draw their operating system and application programs from the network each time they are used, rather than storing them internally. The demand for complex and expensive PC operating systems, such as Windows 95, and for high capacity PC microprocessors, such as the Pentium, could whither in the face of such innovation.

Whether such changes will in fact occur remains to be seen. But one thing is crystal clear: Rapid changes in computer-based information services will continue to transform the very nature of business—and this means outstanding opportunities for those managers who are alert enough to capitalize on these innovations. More than ever, in today's environment, change favors the prepared mind.

AVOID BEING CLASSIFIED AS OBSOLETE

Whatever else you do in developing a strategy for your "company of one," don't back away from computers. Add Computer Competence to the organization chart of your "company of

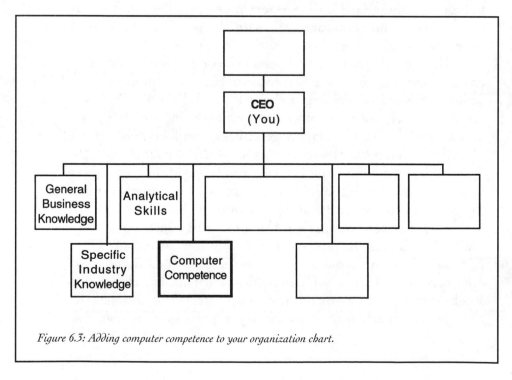

Figure 6.3: Adding computer competence to your organization chart.

one," as shown in Figure 6.3. Keep up with the applications of computer technology in your firm. Learn to use new software that could help you in your job by taking short courses if necessary. Or better yet, learn from your computer-literate spouse, son or daughter. Know how to run spreadsheets and make professional-looking presentations. Learn the jargon so you can keep up with the discussion at the lunchtable. You don't have to become a computer nerd, but it is vital to avoid being classified as obsolete. Remember, it is the obsolete managers who get the pink slips in a corporate downsizing.

SELF ASSESSMENT OF COMPUTER COMPETENCE

Are you keeping up with other managers in terms of your ability to understand and work with computers?

1. Where do you use computers? (Check all that apply.)

    ☐ At the office

    ☐ At home

    ☐ When traveling

2. How frequently do you use each of the following computer applications?

	Never	Once or twice per year	Once or twice per month	Weekly	Daily
Word processing					
Spreadsheets					
Statistics					
E-mail					
Internet					
Groupware					

3. Now compare your answers to Questions 1 and 2 to those of other managers, as shown in Figures 6.1 and 6.2. Are

you keeping up? If not, get busy. Remember, in today's fast-moving corporate environment, the cost of obsolescence is a pink slip.

1   Moody, F., *I Sing the Body Electronic*, Viking, 1995, pp. 3, 29.

2   Lublin, J., "Corporate Survey Finds Fewer Layoffs, Increase in New Jobs to Balance Cuts," *The Wall Street Journal*, October 23, 1995, p. A2.

3   Graham, E., "Their Careers: Count on Nothing and Work Like a Demon," *The Wall Street Journal*, October 31, 1995, p. B1.

4   "The View from IBM," *Business Week*, October 30, 1995, p. 142.

5   "Stripped Down PCs Will Be Talk of Comdex," *The Wall Street Journal*, November 10, 1995, p. B1.

LEARNING TO MANAGE INNOVATION

Let's begin with a short quiz.

Q: What do these individuals have in common?

	Value of stock holdings[1]
Bill Gates	$13.8 billion
Paul Allen	$5.3 billion
Larry Ellison	$4.2 billion
Ted Waitt	$1.1 billion
Jan and Bob Davidson	$691 million
Michael Dell	$651 million

A: They are all founders of high tech companies, and they made all of this money in less than 20 years.

Economists have found that the single most important factor in the economic growth of many companies is the development of new technology.

Yet many practicing managers find the new product development process mysterious and confusing. Currently, improving the new product development area is a hotbed of strategic development in companies, with emphasis on accelerating time-to-market and on making sure that the new product meets customer requirements. In fact, Hewlett-Packard has found that in its high-tech businesses, getting to market six months ahead of the competition can double or triple the profitability of a new product program.

INNOVATION: THE DRIVING ENGINE OF OUR ECONOMY

The concept of technological innovation historically has caused problems for economists. It is unpredictable and difficult to incorporate in mathematical models of the economy. Because of its mathematical intractability, many economists in the past simply assumed that innovation was "outside the system" and therefore didn't exist.

But Joseph Schumpeter, an economist who did his work in the first half of this century, strongly disagreed with his colleagues about the importance of innovation in the economy. He argued that innovation could not be ignored in any analysis of economic growth. In fact, said Schumpeter, innovation was the great driving engine of a capitalistic free enterprise system. Innovation was not outside the economic system; it was central to the system. More recently, economist Paul Romer, who divides his time between the University of California at Berkeley and the Hoover Institution at Stanford University, has shown that technological innovation is basic to our economy, a third fundamental factor of production to be added to the traditional factors of capital and labor.[2]

Today, everyone can see the immense effect that technological innovation has had on individual companies, and on the economy as a whole. Huge personal fortunes have been built by innovators, such as Microsoft founder Bill Gates, and the investors in such companies have also grown wealthy. As our survey showed, today over 90% of managers have a PC in their office and yet the PC is barely a decade old. Medicine is being revolutionized by innovations such as MRI machines and genetic engineering. Automobiles have been transformed by dozens of imbedded microprocessors, home entertainment by satellite broadcasting, and telecommunications by cellular telephones and the Internet.

Innovations are not always the result of breakthrough technologies. Consider, for example, innovations in the field of retailing. Sam Walton, in creating Wal-Mart, envisioned a new approach to distribution featuring quality merchandise, low prices, and friendly and knowledgeable personal service. Michael Dell saw the potential for mail-order distribution of personal computers that bypassed traditional PC dealers, and built a multibillion dollar company. In the field of innovative services, Fred Smith conceived an overnight package delivery service that became FedEx.

Similar revolutions had occurred during Schumpeter's lifetime. Edison's electric power generators brought light and power to homes and factories at the flip of a switch, while Henry Ford's automobile introduced new freedom in personal transportation. The Bell telephone opened new horizons in communications, and Sears, Roebuck & Co. pioneered new channels of distribution of consumer products for a largely rural America.

Schumpeter argued that innovative entrepreneurs such as Edison and Ford (and, today, Gates and Dell) are the creators of true economic profits in the economy. When an innovation is new, unique, and often protected by patents or manufacturing trade secrets, the entrepreneur rides the wave of surging demand, charging high prices and making large profits. The free enterprise system encourages innovation and rewards successful creative risk-taking with high profits.

THE INNOVATION CYCLE

But Schumpeter also saw that innovations typically go through a distinctive product life cycle. When an innovation is new, there is usually only one supplier. Production cannot keep up with demand, prices are high, and profits soar. These high profits attract competitors who bring out copies of the innovation, sometimes with improvements of their own. While overall demand for the innovation may continue to climb, competition becomes more aggressive, prices soften, and profits begin to fall. An example is the PC business in the mid-1990s. Eventually, late in the product life cycle, so many competitors crowd in that industry capacity greatly exceeds demand. Full-scale price wars erupt, profits disappear, and sooner or later, some of the competitors go bankrupt.

It is the liquidation of these bankrupt competitors that inspired Schumpeter's most widely-quoted phrase, "the creative destruction of capital." He saw that the tendency of an industry to overbuild capacity was the natural consequence of competition. Only the strongest producers would survive, and the others would be liquidated and their assets recycled by the capital markets to invest in the next wave of innovation. From the wreckage of these liquidated firms would emerge the venture capital for the next generation of emerging entrepreneurs. And it is this dynamic cycle, powered by the search to find and develop profitable new innovations, that fuels the driving engine of the free enterprise system.

THE ADVANTAGE OF BEING FIRST

Common sense supports Schumpeter's view of how the market rewards innovative companies, and in recent years, many economists have confirmed the advantage of being first with major innovations. Research by Professor William Robinson, who teaches in the business school at Purdue University, has shown that the firms that pioneer a new product concept typically maintain the largest market share even late in the product life cycle, after the competitive shakeout has occurred.[3] In consumer products, for example, Campbell Soup pioneered condensed canned soup and still dominates the category, and Procter & Gamble, innovators with Ivory Soap, continues to dominate the soap and detergent business. In general, Robinson found that the average *long-run* market share of pioneers—measured 20 years or more after product introduction—was 29%, substantially larger than that of "early follower" and "late entrant" companies that came into the market later (see Figure 7.1). This was found to be true for both consumer goods and industrial goods companies. Robinson found that being first conveys sustainable competitive advantages. Innovation pays.

In a similar study of innovative consumer non-durables, MIT's Professor Glen Urban found that over the long run—after a number of competitors have entered the market—the

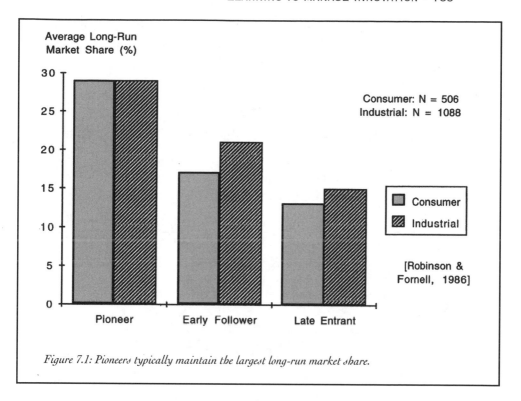

Figure 7.1: Pioneers typically maintain the largest long-run market share.

pioneer typically still maintains the largest market share, at 27%.[4] (Note that this 27% is close to Robinson's finding of a 29% long-run market share for pioneers, even though Urban's study was done independently using a different methodology and data base. The closeness of these two results increases our confidence that these findings are valid.)

Both Robinson and Urban provide empirical evidence that Schumpeter was right: It pays to innovate. In his study, Robinson found that there were two major reasons why pioneers are able to hold onto a larger market share than their late-to-enter competitors:[5]

- The pioneering company, being first into the market, has the advantage of being free to target the largest and most profitable market segment. Those that follow may find that they have to settle for smaller, less profitable niche markets in order to get a foothold.

- Successful pioneers tend to compete on product quality rather than low price. Any cost savings they achieve in manufacturing costs due to economies of scale and learning curve effects are plowed back into continuing product improvement.

On the other hand, contrary to some of the folklore of management, Robinson found that patents and heavy introductory advertising are not necessarily essential for *long-term* success:

- Although some innovations are protected by patents and trade secrets, on average, pioneering firms succeed without having the advantage of strong patent protection.

- Similarly, although intensive introductory advertising is often used to launch an innovative new product, such heavy introductory advertising does not appear to provide any long-term market share advantages to the pioneering company.

INNOVATION AS A STRATEGY FOR YOUR "COMPANY OF ONE"

Throughout this book, we have sought to apply strategies that have proved successful for major corporations to your "company of one." If innovation is a good strategy for corporations, would it not also be a good strategy for your "company of one?"

The answer is a qualified "yes." Do you work for a large firm? There is a saying among corporate old timers that you can always identify the pioneers in an organization by the arrows sticking out of their backs. While this is a rather cynical view, it makes the valid point that there are risks as well as rewards for individuals who try to innovate. This is due to the reward structure for innovators working in large companies.

Suppose you are a young product engineer working for a large company and you come up with what you believe is a terrific idea for a new product. You tell your boss about it and he encourages you to think more about it, but then gently reminds you that your current project is behind schedule. You, on the other hand, would like to drop what you are doing and develop your new idea. You work over the weekend to write up your ideas in a report, you submit it to your boss on Monday morning—and nothing happens. Days pass, the weeks come and go, and you get no response. Why?

WHY BIG COMPANIES DON'T INNOVATE

Why doesn't your boss respond? Why aren't large companies more innovative? The fact is, most large companies are not very receptive to new ideas. The reasons are complex and subtle:[6]

- *Change is risky:* First of all, a large company has a big stake in keeping things the way they are. One of the reasons that large companies are successful is that they develop huge learning curve cost advantages. They produce so much of a product that they can drive the manufacturing cost of the product down far below what it would cost a smaller company to produce the same product.

  But this learning curve cost advantage continues only so long as the product remains unchanged. If substantial innovations are made to the product, the company may lose its learning curve cost advantage, thus becoming more vulnerable to competition. So large firms have a big incentive to avoid change.

- *Not invented here:* Secondly, the *people* within the large company have an incentive to resist change. For some, unless the idea is theirs, it can't be very good (this is the 'NIH' *factor*—'Not Invented Here'). For others, who made their reputation with the current line of products, the concept of change is threatening. And for still others who are buried in day-to-day tasks, there just isn't any time to look at new ideas.

- *Dependence on formal marketing research:* In large firms, there is more reliance on formal marketing research, which, believe it or not, can work against the adoption of an innovation. Unlike small firms, where product designers are likely to work directly with prospective customers, in large companies cautious managers may commission one market study after another before proceeding. When Hal Sperlich, the father of the minivan, tried to sell his superiors at Ford on developing the minivan concept, he was turned down repeatedly, because Ford's marketing research did not show that there was a market for the minivan. Finally, Sperlich gave up trying and took his concept from Ford to Chrysler, where it was developed and became a huge success. But until the product was launched, some senior managers in the automotive industry remained skeptical. Says Sperlich:

> *"In 10 years of developing the minivan, we never once got a letter from a housewife asking us to invent one. To the skeptics, that proved there wasn't a market out there."*[7]

- *It doesn't pay individuals in big companies to innovate:* Finally, there are limited financial incentives for an individual in a large company to take the personal risk of pushing an

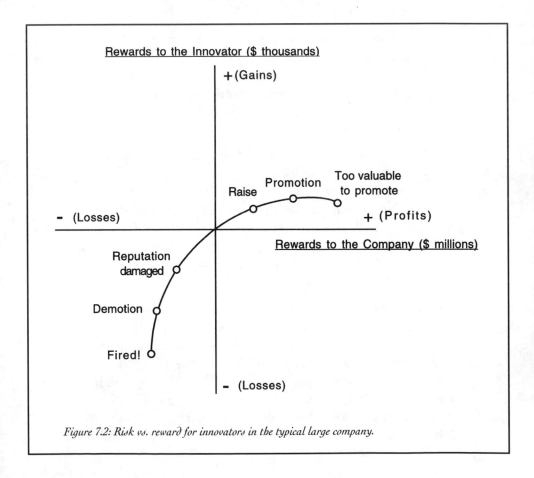

Figure 7.2: *Risk vs. reward for innovators in the typical large company.*

innovation. Referring to Figure 7.2, suppose you have an idea for a great new product. You stand at the crossroads in the middle of the diagram, trying to decide whether to push it through the bureaucracy.

If you push the idea and it fails, your reputation will be damaged, you could be shoved aside in the organization or demoted, and if it turns out to be a real money loser for the company, you could get fired (lower left quadrant of the diagram). There is considerable downside risk to you for pushing the innovation.

But if, as you expect, the new product is a big hit and makes millions of dollars of profit for the company, the rewards to you will be modest (upper right quadrant). You might get a raise and even a promotion. Moreover, if the idea is a smashing success, there is even some possibility that your rewards will be reduced because management will decide you are too valuable in your present position to promote.

So pushing an innovation in the typical large company involves considerable downside risk for failure and not much in the way of upside rewards if the innovation succeeds. Therefore, it follows that most large companies are not very innovative.

Fortunately, some large companies do realize that occasional failure is part of the price of progress. George Fisher, who left Motorola to assume the position of CEO of Kodak, had this to say in an interview shortly after joining Kodak:

> *"The nice thing about Motorola . . . [is that] there's nothing wrong with failure. There's something wrong if you don't try a lot of things. I don't know many people [at Motorola] who haven't failed. And I hope that at Kodak we can get to the point where people don't fear failure, that the sin is not trying, that we're measured on our batting average, and if our batting average is 1000, we probably haven't tried enough things."*[8]

Regrettably, in large companies, not every boss is as wise as George Fisher.

- *It does pay to innovate in very small companies:* Unlike in the giant corporation, in a very small firm there can be a powerful upside potential for large personal gains for innovating (see Figure 7.3). Although the downside risks for failure are about the same as in a large company, the upside reward for success does not flatten out in a small company as it does in a large firm—like the Energizer bunny, the rewards just keep going up, up, up. If you own 10% of the stock in a small company and your idea adds $1 million to the total value of the firm's equity, the value of your stock will increase by $100,000. If your innovation adds $10 million to the value of your firm's equity, your stock will go up by $1 million. In a very small firm,

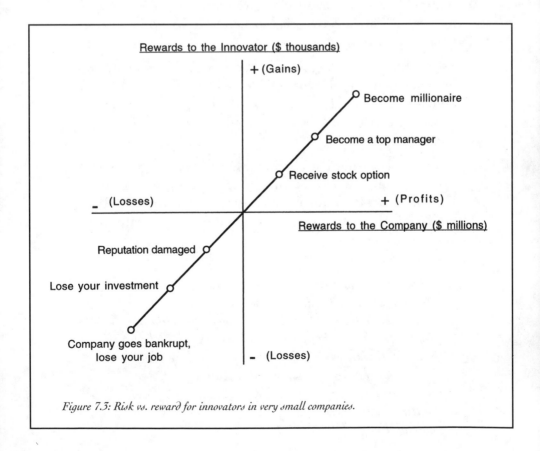

Figure 7.3: Risk vs. reward for innovators in very small companies.

your success is directly proportional to the company's success.

Are small companies more innovative? There is evidence that small firms are highly efficient at developing new products. In 1964, Arnold Cooper described a series of interviews with R&D managers in both large and small companies in which the consensus was that a large company typically spends from *three to ten times* as much as a small company to develop a particular product.[9] More recently, a large-scale study by Acs and Audretsch of more than 2600 innovations found that small firms (those with fewer than 500 employees) have an innovation-per-employee ratio *6.6 times* that of large firms (500 or more employees).[10]

Small firms have to be more efficient at innovation if they are to survive. Large companies have the learning curve advantage of low manufacturing cost of standardized products, the power of established channels of distribution, and the benefit of recognized brand names, so the only way small firms can compete is to offer innovations that large firms cannot manage. Another way to look at it is that only the *innovative* small firms survive; those that are not innovative are soon gone.

HOW DOES YOUR EMPLOYER TREAT INNOVATORS?

The decision of whether to innovate as a strategy for your "company of one" is very much dependent on how your employer rewards innovation. Pay particular attention to how your company treats innovators, not only those whose innovations succeed, but also those whose innovations fail. Not everything that a company tries will pay off, and if those who try and fail are punished by exile or termination, the rest of the organization will quickly get the message that it doesn't pay to even try.[11]

If, however, your firm recognizes and rewards successful innovation, and if it works with those who fail to help them learn from their mistakes, then innovation could be an important strategy for your "company of one." Innovation is one of the most powerful strategies by which firms grow and prosper, and in the right environment it can help turbocharge your "company of one."

HOW YOUR "COMPANY OF ONE" CAN PROSPER BY MANAGING INNOVATION

Let's begin by assuming that your firm encourages and rewards innovation. If it doesn't, you could find yourself in the situation illustrated in Figure 7.2: plenty of downside risk for innovators and not much upside potential for reward. If your firm discourages innovation, then innovation will *not* be a successful strategy for your "company of one," and you should make plans to change firms, because eventually every company must innovate to survive. For Hal Sperlich, the champion of the minivan, trying to sell the minivan concept to his bosses at Ford was a long, frustrating ordeal:

> *"You're walking a very lonely road. Life in a large corporation is easier if you go with the flow and don't support major change. People who propose things that are different make more conservative people nervous, and the corporate environment just doesn't reward people for challenging the status quo."[12]*

Unable to sell the minivan concept to Ford, Sperlich abandoned a 20-year career and moved to Chrysler where he convinced CEO Lee Iacocca of the minivan's potential. Chrysler, which was near bankruptcy and desperate for new products to sell, introduced the minivan in the mid-1980s. It was an instant success, and Sperlich believes the minivan saved the company. Says Sperlich, "If we hadn't done minivans, Chrysler would be gone, no question."[13]

What follows is a blueprint for turbocharging your "company of one" by managing innovation.

1. Be realistic about challenging the paradigms.

   More than 30 years ago, Thomas Kuhn, now a professor emeritus at MIT, published a book, *The Structure of Scientific Revolutions*, in which he introduced the concept of the paradigm (pronounced 'pair-a-dime'), which means "a constellation of beliefs," a term that has become a management buzzword signifying the accepted way of thinking about a subject.

In the field of finance, for example, a central paradigm is the Efficient Market Hypothesis, which states that stock prices instantly adjust to reflect all publicly available information about a company. The implication is that it is impossible to systematically outperform the market by buying or selling shares based on information in *The Wall Street Journal* and similar public sources. (This doesn't keep people from trying, but one piece of supporting evidence for the Efficient Market Hypothesis is the finding that over the long term, most actively-managed mutual funds, which have to deduct their trading expenses from the returns on their market portfolios, underperform stock market averages such as the *Standard & Poor's 500*. This was true even in the strong stock market of 1995, when the S&P 500 index surged 37.5%, beating more than 85% of the actively-managed domestic stock mutual funds for the year.[14])

Paradigms are very powerful mechanisms for maintaining the status quo. They work against innovation. For example, although the Efficient Market Hypothesis is a useful paradigm, there are a few anomalies—such as Peter Lynch's long streak of outperforming the market with the Magellan Fund, or the sudden catastrophic drop in stock prices in 1987—that are difficult to explain in terms of efficient markets. But in most universities it would be politically unwise for a young assistant professor seeking tenure in the field of Finance to try to disprove the Efficient Market Hypothesis.

The reason is that most of the prominent people in any field are totally committed to their paradigms; indeed, they may have helped create them. They will not change. Many years ago, Max Planck, a world-renowned physicist, wrote:

> "An important scientific innovation rarely makes its
> way by gradually winning over and converting its

opponents: It rarely happens that Saul becomes Paul.
What does happen is that its opponents gradually die
out and that the growing generation is familiarized
with the idea from the beginning."[15]

Chances are that certain paradigms dominate the thinking in your company and your industry. They may have to do with the way you design your products or the way you market them to your customers. At Ford in the mid-1980s, the accepted paradigm was that the big Ford station wagon with its leather seats and simulated wood siding was the perfect vehicle for the suburban housewife. Ford was completely unable to see the potential for the minivan.

As Planck said, the opponents of change are seldom converted. You have to wait for them to die or retire, and this can be a long wait.

If your "company of one" is to follow a strategy of innovation, you should begin by realistically assessing the likelihood that your employer will accept—indeed, will welcome—the challenge to its paradigms. If it will not, your choices are the same as those faced by Hal Sperlich: either go with the flow and don't innovate, or be prepared to leave.

If, however, you are associated with an innovative firm that competes in an industry with large firms that wear the paradigm blinders, the payoff for innovation can be very high. In the mid- and late-1970s, Xerox's Palo Alto Research Center (PARC) invented or refined most of the elements of the modern personal computer: the "bit-mapped" screen that provides fine-grained images, the concept of "windows" that allows several pieces of work to be displayed simultaneously on the screen, an early text processing program called Bravo that became the foundation for Microsoft Word, the Ethernet for communicating on a network, the mouse pointing device, and the "icon" that allows applications and documents to be opened by pointing and clicking with the mouse.

With such a technological head start, Xerox should have dominated the personal computer business in the 1980s.

But Xerox's management was mentally locked into a paradigm called "the office of the future," in which Xerox copiers, workstations, printers, storage devices, and other office machines would all be linked together on a proprietary network. There was no room in Xerox's office-of-the-future paradigm for a stand-alone, un-networked personal computer.

Blocked from commercialization by Xerox's office-of-the-future paradigm, PARC's technological breakthroughs might have languished for years, but for a chance visit by one of the founders of a then-small company, Apple Computer. In December, 1979, Steve Jobs, Apple's Vice Chairman, visited PARC with some colleagues to poke around.

"Their eyes bugged out," recalls Lawrence Tesler, at that time a PARC researcher. "They understood the significance [of these innovations] better than anyone else who had visited." Seven months later Jobs hired Tesler to commercialize many of these innovations for the Lisa computer, which was the predecessor of the very successful Macintosh.[16]

The lesson to be learned here is that the same paradigms that cause major companies like Xerox to overlook important innovations such as the personal computer provide the opportunities for small, flexible companies (in this example, Apple) to enter the market and thrive without fear of competition from the larger firms. Putting it another way, it may be a more effective strategy to challenge entrenched corporate paradigms from *outside* the large company than to try to change the company's thinking from the inside.

There is a direct analogy here for your "company of one." As *individuals*, senior managers and even distinguished scientists often resemble large, successful companies in terms of their resistance to new ideas. They have their own paradigms and their own views of the world based on principles and strategies that have worked for them in the past. Don't be discouraged if they are slow to see the potential of your proposed innovation. Consider these examples:[17]

"Radio has no future. Heavier-than-air machines are impossible. X-rays will prove to be a hoax."

... William Thomson, Lord Kelvin, English scientist (1824-1907)

"Space travel is utter bilge."

... Sir Richard van der Riet Wooley, *The Astronomer Royal* (1956)

"While theoretically and technically, television may be feasible, commercially and financially I consider it an impossibility ... "

... Lee DeForest, American inventor of the vacuum tube (1873-1961)

"Rail travel at high speeds is not possible, because passengers, unable to breathe, would die of asphyxia."

... Dionysius Lardner, English scientist (1793-1859)

"Who the hell wants to hear actors talk?"

... Harry M. Warner, founder, Warner Bros. Studio (1927)

Sometimes firms resist innovation because they have a massive investment in the current technology. They may be well down the learning curve with the current technology, they may be the lowest cost producer in the industry, and they have no incentive to change. Innovation means giving up these advantages and starting over. Because such companies are so committed to their current technologies, they are particularly vulnerable to being overthrown in the quest for market leadership by innovative newcomers to the industry.

Consider, for example, the situation that Eastman Kodak faces with conventional film-based photography. In terms of excellence of image quality at a low cost, nothing can match modern color film. Nor are any of the new electronic imaging processes as potentially profitable to Kodak as continuing to make color film. Yet gradually, segment by segment, electronic photography is replacing color film because of its convenience. First to go was television news, which used to shoot all of its remote footage on film. Today it is shot on videotape. Next was the home movie business, which lost out to camcorders. The concern now is that high-quality electronic still cameras will begin to win away the huge amateur photography market.

Yet even within a mature field like film-based photography, there are opportunities for innovation. The single-use, disposable cameras introduced by Kodak have revitalized film-based amateur photography through a combination of convenience and low price. More recently, Kodak has led a consortium of photographic companies in the development of a new, more convenient color film format that may replace 35mm color film.

Kodak has struggled mightily with the challenge of electronic imaging. For more than a decade, the company went through a succession of home-grown CEOs as it sought to prepare itself for the age of electronic photography. Finally, the Board of Directors went to the outside to hire George Fisher away from the presidency of Motorola. Fisher, an innovator who built his reputation at Motorola by creating a world-class pager business that dominates even the low-cost electronics producers of the Far East, came to the job free of the historical paradigms of the film business. While Fisher sees conventional silver halide film as still the highest quality storage medium for images, he is also beginning to move the company aggressively into the field of electronic photography. Kodak no longer sees itself as a chemical company. Today it is fully committed to being the world leader in imaging, whatever the technology.[18]

2. Be skeptical of marketing research about proposed innovations.

For more than ten years, I have taught MBA courses in marketing research. As part of these courses, my students are required to develop and carry out a comprehensive marketing research project for a local company or charitable organization. I am a strong believer in the value of marketing research, provided that it is used within its limitations.

A properly done marketing research study can provide valuable facts and insights about a market *as it currently exists*. If you want to know how many cans of Diet Pepsi were sold in Cedar Rapids, Iowa, last week and at what prices, marketing research can provide you with an accurate answer. In fact, in a number of markets, marketing research services such as Information Resources, Inc. or A.C. Nielson can even provide you with demographic information—age, gender, income level, education—about each of the people who bought the Diet Pepsi in Cedar Rapids, and how they differ from the people who bought Diet Coke last week. The sales and pricing information is collected by supermarket checkout scanners and the demographic information about the purchasers is picked up when they identify themselves at the checkout with a card that entitles them to a store discount on some other item.

Marketing research can also measure more subtle things, such as how effective television advertising is for stimulating sales of a grocery item. This is done by wiring up certain test market areas with split-cable TV systems, so that half the residents see the ad for Alpo dog food and the other half, which serves as a control group, do not see the ad. Again, by using scanner data it is possible to see how much more Alpo was purchased by those households who were exposed to the ad. This gives a direct measure of the effectiveness of the ad in increasing sales.

If a new product is similar to one that consumers are currently using, marketing research methods are fairly successful in predicting the sales of that new product. However, marketing research fails when it attempts to predict the sales of a totally new product, one that prospective customers are not familiar with.

In large firms, risk averse managers may commission study after study before authorizing the start of product development for an unfamiliar new innovation. But as Chambers et al. point out, for truly new (i.e., discontinuous) product concepts, the quantitative market research techniques that work so well for variations of familiar products prove difficult to apply in the absence of historical data.[19] Edward Tauber notes that for these discontinuous products, formal market research is inherently biased against innovation, and tends to systematically *understate* the true size of the potential market.[20] This is because when people are asked whether they would consider buying a totally new product concept such as a personal computer, they are unable to envision how they could possibly use it. (Originally, the developers of personal computers thought that PCs would be used mainly to store recipes and balance the checkbook.)

Similarly, when the Japanese introduced the VCR, it was thought that these new machines would be used primarily to save off-the-air television programs. The designers did not envision the benefit of time-shifting (being able to program your VCR to record your favorite soap opera while you are away at work). Furthermore, they did not see the potential for home viewing of Hollywood movies. In fact, when the VCR first entered the market, the Hollywood studios vigorously fought the idea of distributing movies as home videos, charging that home videos would wipe out the neighborhood theaters and destroy the industry. Nor did the VCR manufacturers anticipate the development of small, inexpensive camcorders for consumers that would ultimately allow videotape to replace home movies. This underscores how difficult it is to anticipate the many creative ways customers will find to use a new product, once it is on the market.

New product adoption is partly a social process.[21] According to Tauber, many of those surveyed about a discontinuous new product concept that is totally unfamiliar are likely to say they wouldn't buy it. Yet after the product is on the market for a while and their friends and associates have bought it, they become avid consumers. The folklore of new product development includes accounts of many discontinuous new products that failed the test of formal market research, yet went on to become immensely successful. For example, just before product introduction, total U.S. sales of the first Xerox copier, the Model 914, were forecasted by Arthur D. Little, Inc., an internationally-respected consulting firm, to be 5,000 units. In fact, over 200,000 units were placed worldwide.[22]

Small firms may not be able to afford formal market research. Instead, the R&D organizations in small firms use their close relationships with the market to work very closely with a few potential customers, developing prototypes and making modifications until the product is satisfactory before designing production versions. The quality of such information for discontinuous products is better than that provided by formal market research studies. Because the product designers in a small firm work very closely with potential customers, they turn out products that are "just right" and that create greater customer satisfaction than those developed by larger firms.

An example of a fast-growing company that believes in working very closely with its customers is Silicon Graphics, Inc., which has specialized in the development of hardware and software for creating super-realistic computer-generated three-dimensional images that move, such as the dinosaurs *in Jurassic Park*. Rather than dictating product strategy from the top, senior management has organized the company so that the brightest scientists and engineers maintain close working relationships with customers. Says Silicon Graphics' CEO, Edward R. McCracken:

> *"We put a project team in each market segment and let those teams decide what to design in cooperation with their customers. As long as the teams have bright ideas and are really excited about them, our top managers stay out of the way."*[23]

Large corporations often find it difficult to compete head-on with smaller, more agile companies in getting the product "just right." For example, the giant General Electric Company, despite its enormous financial and technical resources, found in the mid-1980s that it could no longer compete profitably with smaller, more specialized companies in small electrical appliances such as coffee makers and hair curlers. The GE Housewares Division frequently lost money while its small competitors, such as Con-Air, stayed ahead in product design and features.[24]

In many markets, particularly those involving high technology, success is achieved not by developing exhaustive long-term marketing research studies to determine what products to build, but rather by staying close to the customer and building a very fast-reaction R&D capability as ideas bubble up, to get new products to the market faster than the competition. Says Silicon Graphics' McCracken:

> *"Long-term product planning is dangerous in our industry and many others because it forces companies to make wild guesses about what our customers might want. We don't believe in planting flags way out ahead and then trying to reach them. Long-term planning weds companies to approaches and technologies too early, which is deadly in our marketplace and many others. No one can plan the future. Three years is long-term. Even two years may be. Five years is laughable."*[25]

Hamel and Prahalad extend McCracken's ideas even further, using a process they call "expeditionary marketing." They compare the idea of launching a new product with trying to hit the center of a target with a bow and arrow. You may be lucky and hit the bullseye with the first arrow, but more likely you will have to shoot a number of arrows—getting feedback from each shot—before you hit the center of the target. The same with new products; you may have to *quickly* launch three or four versions before you get it exactly right.[26]

For some products, of course, expeditionary marketing may not be practical. If you are building jet aircraft, you obviously want to get it right the first time. And unless your first product is pretty close to the mark, you may turn off buyers from even considering your second or third versions. But, for other products it is possible to quickly offer a number of variations built around a standard "platform," and then see which ones sell. For example, the hugely successful Sony Walkman personal tape player has been offered in over 100 different plastic case shapes and colors, but inside there are only three different electromechanical platforms.

To summarize, as you develop your capability to manage innovation, be cautious about depending on marketing research studies for assessing the potential of truly innovative new products. Marketing research can give you an accurate fix on the market as it exists now. But, in most cases, a better approach is to stay very close to your customers and develop a fast-cycle new product development capability to quickly turn the ideas that emerge into new products and services.

3. Learn how to speed up the new product development process.

In our continuing search for successful corporate strategies that you can apply to your "company of one," we will begin by reviewing a succession of successful competitive strategies that Japanese companies followed, from immediately after World War II to the present time.[27]

In 1945, at the end of World War II, Japanese factories were in ruins and the economy was devastated. At the time, Japanese wages were very low compared with those of the West, and Japan began to rebuild her economy by concentrating on industrial export products with high labor content, such as steel and shipbuilding.

During this time, a number of today's giant Japanese consumer products companies emerged from the ashes as entrepreneurial startups. Honda set up shop to build its first light-weight motorcycles, and Sony founders Masaru Ibuka and Akio Morita experimented with the company's first consumer products: an electric rice cooker that didn't sell and a tape recorder that did.

As Japan's economy began to pick up speed in the early 1960s, labor costs rose rapidly and manufacturing companies were forced to invest in labor-saving capital equipment to remain competitive. During the decade of the '60s, Japanese engineers became experts at designing labor costs out of the product. For example, they created complex molded parts that snapped together to eliminate the need for screws. By concentrating on high volume products such as radios and television sets to take advantage of economies of scale and manufacturing cost reductions from the learning curve, Japanese labor productivity soared.

Simultaneously, Japan began its drive for unexcelled product quality. On occasion, Japanese manufacturers employed new technology to gain an advantage in product quality. For example, while U.S. manufacturers continued to build television sets with vacuum tubes that burned out, the Japanese introduced TVs that were all solid-state and much more reliable. By refining both the engineering designs and the manufacturing processes, Japanese automobiles arrived at dealers with doors that fit, radios that worked, engines that were tuned, and wheels that were balanced. And the Toyotas and Hondas ran and ran, for years and years after they were delivered. It took more than a decade for domestic auto makers to catch up, and even today, many U.S. drivers continue to insist that Japanese cars are more refined in design and assembly.

In the 1990s, the competition has shifted again, this time to speed-of-response in bringing out new products. Previously, Japanese auto companies developed new models in about half the time—and with half as many people—as their U.S. and German competitors.[28] In the mid-1980s, Toyota developed new cars in 3 years, whereas Detroit typically required 5 years or more.[29] But in the 1990s, U.S. companies are catching up and even surpassing their Japanese competitors. Chrysler's Neon was brought out in the 1990s for a fraction of the resources required by Detroit in the past.[30] Similarly, Motorola's U.S.-based computer-controlled pager manufacturing line—code-named 'Bandit' because the engineers were directed to look around and swipe the best manufacturing ideas from anywhere and anyone—was designed and running in less than two years. The Bandit project regained the market for the U.S. in this high volume consumer electronics field, an area that traditionally has been dominated by Far East manufacturers.

Moreover, the Bandit pager line provides customers with an added value they would find difficult to obtain from a Far East mass producer: the ability to get fast delivery while being able to choose from among more than 21 million different combinations of product features. Pagers are assembled quickly and automatically on Motorola's state-of-the-art line, with the appropriate sets of parts selected by computer control directly from the customer's order.

Fast response time in conceiving, developing, and bringing new products to the market has become a competitive advantage of an increasing number of U.S. firms. As noted previously, Hewlett-Packard has found that in their high-tech businesses, getting to the market six months ahead of the competition can double or triple the profitability of a new product program.

How do you achieve fast-cycle new product development? There are a number of ways:

- **Emulate the speed of decision making in small companies.** Organize the new product effort into small multifunctional product development teams made up of people from Engineering, Marketing, Manufacturing, Finance, and any other functional areas of the organization that will be involved with the launch of the new product. Chapter 8 will have more to say about multifunctional teams.

  Amar Bhide, a professor at the Harvard Business School, analyzed more than 200 entrepreneurial ventures and found that successful small companies have a bias toward speed and a tendency to do their planning on the fly. They quickly weed out unpromising ideas and race ahead to get prototypes of the surviving innovations in the hands of customers, so they can get fast feedback to improve the product as early as possible in the development cycle.[31]

  Successful entrepreneurs typically learn the business with someone else's money. According to Bhide, nearly three-quarters of their concepts for successful new ventures are based on ideas encountered in a previous job. To compete effectively with their previous employers, an important part of their entrepreneurial strategy is "hustle," the ability to seize short-term opportunities in the industry and execute them brilliantly before their larger competitors are able to get organized.

  In startup companies, where the penalty for error can be bankruptcy, planning is important, but the emphasis tends to be on short-term cash flow and on a rough analysis of the size of potential markets. Completeness of planning is less valuable than flexibility of planning. For these small firms, detailed long-term NPV spreadsheet analyses of opportunities are less useful than the flexibility to quickly change the plan to pursue new opportunities as they arise.

- **Make sure that people who have to work together sit close to each other.** This sounds simplistic, but it isn't. Years ago, when I was working as a manufacturing program manager for Xerox, I was responsible for getting a new product with lots of innovative technology into production. This was the first production Xerox copier to incorporate such advanced features as xenon flash lamps to expose the document, a flat photoconductive belt instead of a drum, and high-resolution toner to improve the sharpness of the image. Because there was so much new technology, we had enormous problems building this new machine on a production line and getting it to work reliably.

The new machine had been designed by a product design engineering group, who were now in the process of handing off the project to a group of manufacturing engineers who reported to me. The two groups were located on opposite sides of the plant, about a five minute walk. Problems were thrashed out in a large conference room midway between, where as many as 30 engineers would sit around a large table drinking coffee and staring into space while two engineers, a design engineer and a manufacturing engineer, argued about the location of a hole in a casting. And every dispute had to be documented with a series of memos. It was a slow and painful process.

One day I was having lunch with my counterpart, the design engineering program manager, and we were bemoaning the slow progress of the project. Over coffee, we decided to try an experiment. The desks of all of my manufacturing engineers would be moved out of the manufacturing engineering area and across the plant to the design engineering area, where they would be located in the cubicles of the design engineers. Instead of massive meetings, problems would be ironed out on a one-to-one basis between individual design and manufacturing engineers, working together in their cubicles.

The experiment worked beautifully. Within a week, there were no more big meetings in the conference room, and the number of finger-pointing memos fell off sharply. People were too busy working together in the cubicles to bother with meetings and memos. Before long, the first machines were rolling down the production line.

After several weeks, the line was up and running, and I brought all my manufacturing engineers back over to my side of the plant. But within a week, we were back in trouble, with meetings in the big conference room again, and a blizzard of memos between the two organizations. There were still some major technical problems to be resolved. This time, I didn't hesitate. Once again, my manufacturing engineers moved back over to the design area, and this time they stayed for several months until the line was running smoothly and we could handle most of the problems without the help of the design group.

A few years later, when I began teaching, I ran across an article by MIT's Thomas Allen in which he described how rapidly the frequency of communications in R&D organizations drops off with increasing distance. People tend to communicate most frequently with those in the next office or just down the hall, but if the distance is more than a hundred feet or so, they might as well be located in different buildings.[32] What I had discovered at Xerox was generally true: If you want people to communicate with each other, then keep their offices close together.

- <u>Focus on customer wants, not on organizational tasks.</u> Customers are the best source of successful new product ideas. As shown in Figure 7.4, Haeffner found, in a study of the origins of ideas for 597 commercially-successful innovations, that 75% of these ideas came from customers (45% from outside customers, and another 30% from in-house customers, such as Production looking for a new machine for in-house use, which the company later added to its regular product line and sold to outside customers).[33]

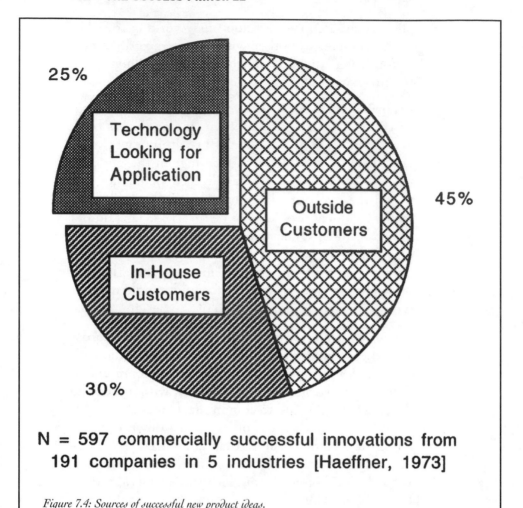

25%

Technology
Looking for
Application

45%

Outside
Customers

In-House
Customers

30%

N = 597 commercially successful innovations from
191 companies in 5 industries [Haeffner, 1973]

Figure 7.4: Sources of successful new product ideas.

In large companies, it is easy to become so immersed
in the day-to-day demands of the bureaucracy that
the customer is ignored. For example, in the late
1970s GE had nine layers of management who spent
most of their time in meetings with each other. The
nine layers filtered information that was passing up
and down the chain of command, often selectively
editing or distorting it. Top executives were over-
whelmed with useless information. It became impossible for senior managers to find out what was going
on in the divisions. According to one GE consultant:

"Briefing books [for senior executives to take to meetings] grew to such dense impenetrability that top managers simply skipped reading them. Instead, they relied on staffers to feed them 'gotchas' (GE lingo for tough questions designed to make people sweat) with which to intimidate subordinates at meetings."[34]

Bureaucracy also occurs in R&D organizations, driving out time to talk with customers. In my own research on new product development, I found that although product development engineers rated customers as having the most accurate information about market needs, 65% of those engineers surveyed reported that they seldom talk with customers—either once or twice a year, or not at all.[35]

- Involve senior management early. In Chapter 4, we told the story of 'Ed,' a young research engineer who was frustrated with his inability to convince his company to develop his idea for available light home movies—until the chairman of the board learned of the project and quietly opened a few doors and the idea became a successful new product. Similarly, nothing happened with the minivan at Chrysler until CEO Lee Iaccoca became enthusiastic.

  In the early stages of a new product concept, senior managers can have a powerful effect on the encouragement of innovation in the organization, even though ultimately they may have to kill the project. David Packard told how his close friend and cofounder of Hewlett-Packard, Bill Hewlett, interacted with innovators and inventors at HP, a process known as Bill's "hat-wearing process."

  When Bill was first approached by a creative inventor, he would put on a hat called "enthusiasm," expressing interest and appreciation, while asking a few gentle questions. A few days later, he would meet again with the inventor, this time wearing his "inquisition" hat as he asked very pointed, tough questions. Shortly thereafter, Bill would meet once more with the inventor, but now wearing his "decision" hat. With logic and sensitivity, Bill would render judgment and make a decision about the project. Whatever the outcome, whether the project was to proceed or be halted, the inventor was left with the satisfaction that his idea was given fair and thoughtful consideration by top management—a process that encouraged continuing enthusiasm and creativity from the technical staff at HP.[36]

Sometimes it is necessary for senior managers to cut their enthusiastic innovators enough slack so that they can pursue their dreams, even without official approval. Such unsanctioned development efforts are known as "bootleg projects." David Packard cites an example. A bright, energetic HP engineer was told to stop working on a new computer display monitor. Shortly thereafter, he left for a vacation trip, taking a prototype of the monitor along to show to potential customers. When he returned, filled with enthusiasm from the response of prospective customers to the prototype, he convinced his boss to rush the monitor into production, despite senior management's previous order to discontinue development of the product. Subsequently, HP sold more than 17,000 of the monitors, generating sales revenues of $35 million.[37]

- Make sure that you have thought about an alternative approach. This is good advice for any kind of planning, and it is particularly important in the new product development process. Don't bet your project (and your job) on one technical approach. Think about what you will do if your preferred alternative doesn't work or is too costly or too unreliable. Because of the high uncertainty where new technology is involved, it always pays to think about Plan B. Whenever possible, run parallel development projects with competing approaches.

When Sony was developing its video recorder technology, the company pursued 10 major technology options with the hope that at least one would result in a successful product. (It did. One of the options, the helical scan approach, became the fundamental technology for the home VCR).

Where parallel approaches are undertaken, eventually one approach will be chosen and the others will be discontinued. At Sony, the company is very careful not to penalize the losing teams whose technical approaches are not adopted. Says one Sony senior R&D executive:

> *"We never talk badly about these people. [Sony founder] Ibuka's principle is that doing something, even if it fails, is better than doing nothing. A strike-out at Sony is OK, but you must not just stand there. You must swing at the ball as best you can."*[38]

Even after you have made your final choice, it is wise to keep a few alternatives going as smaller scale options, just in case the planned option fails.

- Recognize that developing a new product in a large firm is like raising a child. A new product idea is very fragile when first conceived and must be carefully nurtured. Even after the concept is born as an approved project, the new product development process is still like raising a child. It needs a mother who loves it (a product champion), a father with resources (a senior manager who supports it), and pediatricians (functional specialists in Marketing, Manufacturing, etc.) who will get it through difficult times.

Some companies try to develop new products by just assigning 'pediatricians' to the project. Without the mother and the father, the chances of success are slim.[39]

4. Protect your intellectual property.

The output of the innovation process is intellectual property, which may be in the form of patents, copyrights, trade secrets, or trademarks, all of which are subject to legal protection. As CEO of your "company of one," you should have a working knowledge of how to protect your own intellectual property and that of your employer.

Patents When most people think about intellectual property they think of patents. The U.S. patent system, which was authorized by the Constitution in one of the first laws enacted by the new republic, is designed to create a balance between the incentives to promote innovation and the dangers of monopoly that reduce competition. A patent can be thought of as a contract between the inventor and the people of the United States. The inventor gives the public a full disclosure of the invention from which new innovations will follow, in return for which the public gives the inventor exclusive use of the invention for a limited time, after which it can be used by anyone.

Copyrights Whereas patents are for protecting intellectual property in the form of inventions, copyrights protect intellectual property in the form of original works of authorship. This book, like others on the market, is protected by a copyright that prohibits others from making and selling copies of parts or all of the book without my publisher's permission, except for brief quotes that are properly credited to the author with a footnote. Scientific papers, works of art, sheet music, and most software can be protected by copyrights from being copied. The duration of an individually-owned copyright is for the life of the author plus fifty years.

It is much easier to secure a copyright than a patent. All original works of authorship are protected from the moment they are recorded in a tangible medium of expression. A statement that the work is copyrighted and the name of the copyright owner printed at the beginning of the book or article enhances the author's rights. You no longer even have to display the "©" symbol, and you only have to register your work with the Copyright Office if you expect to engage in a lawsuit.

Trade secrets A third classification of intellectual property subject to legal protection is the trade secret. These typically are secret information (for example, the formula for Coca-Cola) or manufacturing processes that provide a company with an economic advantage over its competitors. They also may include sensitive business information, such as a Rolodex file of the company's customer list, an engineering drawing, or a confidential marketing plan for an unannounced new product.

Unlike patents and copyrights, trade secrets are not protected by federal statute. Instead, they fall under the protection of common law and case law. The basic rule is that the owner must take steps to protect the trade secret. There are a number of steps you should take to gain protection for a trade secret:

- As a condition of employment, every employee who has access to trade secrets should sign an agreement to maintain the confidentiality of the trade secret and to not disclose it to others inside or outside the company without the permission of the owner.

- Suppliers, consultants, partners, and other outsiders who are provided with trade secrets in order to serve the company should also sign confidentiality and nondisclosure agreements.

- Documents containing trade secrets should be clearly marked "Confidential Trade Secret Material" and stored in locked files.

- Employees should be reminded periodically that they have a legal obligation to protect the company's trade secrets, and that the future success of the company depends on their acceptance of this responsibility.

In some cases, companies prefer to protect their manufacturing processes as trade secrets, even though they might be eligible for patenting. The reason is that a patent requires full disclosure of the process, and it is always possible that a competitor could find ways to make changes to get around the patent while still capturing most of the benefits. Furthermore, a patent has a limited life, whereas trade secrets can be maintained as such indefinitely.

<u>Trademarks and service marks</u> Trademarks, brand names, and company logos are among the most valuable assets a company can have, because they assure a certain level of quality to a prospective customer. It takes decades to establish the value of a trademark like 'Coca-Cola' or 'McDonald's.' And it is this assurance of quality that motivates imposters to copy the trademarks of leading companies.

The right to a trademark is established by its use in commerce or by applying for a registration based on an intention to use the mark, followed by its actual use. Legal protection can be enhanced by registering the trademark with the U.S. Patent and Trademark Office.

Ironically, the very success of a product or service can endanger the legal right to prohibit others from using its trademark. Familiar words like "aspirin" and "cellophane" were once trademarks, but through lack of diligence on the part of the owners to insist that these were valuable brand names, the terms became generic. This is why Xerox Corporation continues to remind everyone that the word "Xerox" is a registered brand name, and that it is a violation of its trademark to use the word as a verb, as in "I am going to xerox this memo." Unless Xerox Corporation continues to aggressively protect its trademark, someday their valuable brand name could become a generic synonym for the phrase "to copy."

Patents for Your "Company of One": a Personal Case History

Let me return to the subject of patents by relating one of my own experiences with patents. The message of this story is that patents can be of great value to your "company of one." A number of years ago, I invented a new dental instrument that was designed to improve the early diagnosis of periodontal disease, a gum disorder that is the leading cause of tooth loss in adults. (With periodontal disease, the teeth are lost when the gums are no longer able to mechanically support the teeth, which then become loose.)

The invention came about after I was contacted by a leading dental research organization that was looking for a way to improve the quantitative assessment of periodontal disease. (Prior to becoming a business school professor, I was Executive Vice President of the Ritter Company, at that time the world's leading manufacturer of dental equipment, so I knew quite a bit about dental instrumentation.) This research organization was running clinical trials of a new treatment for periodontal problems with a large group of patients who already had periodontal disease. Half the patients in the study were given the new treatment, and the other half were untreated and served as a control. The scientific question was whether the patients who were treated experienced significant improvement, compared to the control group.

At the time, the accepted way to measure the condition of a patient's periodontal health was to probe the gums along the side of each tooth with a blunt metal probe that had a millimeter scale engraved on its tip. For patients with periodontal disease, the gums pull away from the side of the teeth, forming little "pockets," and the probing examination is known as "measuring the pocket depth." The deeper the probe went, the deeper the pocket, and the worse the periodontal problem.

The difficulty with this method is that the gum tissue is soft. If you press lightly on the probe, it doesn't go very deep, but if you press hard, it will go deeper. Some dental examiners press very lightly while others press very hard. This made it very difficult to interpret the results of the clinical study, because there was so much variation in measured pocket depth due to differences in examiner probing technique that the effect of the new treatment was hidden in the noisy data. Attempts to train the examiners to probe at a specified force were not very successful.

After spending some time with the clinical researchers, I agreed to try to develop an instrument that would ensure that the probing would be done at a known standardized probing force, irrespective of who was doing the examination. The research institution signed a letter agreeing that if the design turned out to be patentable, I would have all the patent rights. After several months of part-time work, I invented a small handpiece with a built-in miniature magnetic torsional balance that would register any probing force between 10 and 100 grams, that was not subject to errors due to gravity (it had to be equally accurate whether you were probing around the upper teeth or the lower teeth), that was lightweight and rugged, and that had interchangeable removable sterilizable tips. The handpiece was connected by a lightweight cable to a small battery-operated control box with a knob that adjusted the probing force.

I built two prototypes of this electronic force-sensing probe and presented them to the research institution, where they were used in the clinic. It immediately became clear that standardizing the probing force was producing much higher quality data. Shortly thereafter, I received inquiries from other dental researchers who had visited the clinic and, having seen the new instruments in use, wondered if I would build instruments for them as well.

At this point, I decided that before too many more people had a chance to look at my new invention, I would try to get a patent. In the U.S., you must file for a patent within one year of "public use" of the invention, which in my case could be interpreted as the date that researchers from outside the clinic were first allowed to see the instrument. Commercial use of the invention, even if secret, also starts the one year period. Furthermore, if the instrument were to be described in a published research paper, this clearly would be public disclosure, which is the same as public use. So the clock was running.

In order to be granted a U.S. patent, an invention must meet three tests:

It must be *new*, compared to the "prior art" (previously developed periodontal instruments, in my case) in the field.

It must be *functional* (the Patent Office is not supposed to issue patents on inventions that clearly violate the laws of physics, such as perpetual motion machines).

It must be *non-obvious* to "someone skilled in the art" (an invention is supposed to be made in a flash of insight like the little light bulb that comes on over peoples' heads in the comic strips).

To find out if my invention was *new*, I hired a patent attorney to do a search of existing patents. A search is usually done by having your patent attorney send an informal description of your invention to one of several firms that specialize in searching the patent office files. This step typically costs about $750. The search firm runs copies of all the existing patents they find that seem to resemble your invention. If the search uncovers "prior art" that is identical to your invention, there is no point in going further, because the invention does not meet the test of being new. But it is up to you and your patent attorney to judge whether your invention is new and different from the inventions in the stack of "prior art" patents provided by the search firm.

I was not concerned about whether my invention was *functional,* because there were research clinicians who were using it every day, and it would soon appear in research articles in the dental journals as an essential instrument for certain kinds of clinical research.

The question of being *non-obvious* was more subtle. Since it took me several months to figure out how to do it, I did not feel that the invention was obvious, and because the search of prior art uncovered nothing that was even close to my concept, I felt that it was not obvious to anyone else either. But there was always the possibility that the Patent Office might disagree.

My invention passed these first hurdles, so I authorized my patent attorney to prepare a patent application for submission to the U.S. Patent and Trademark Office. The Patent Office is very particular about the form of an application. Even the drawings have to be made in a certain style that meets their requirements. A patent application contains a listing of "prior art" uncovered in the search, together with arguments as to why they are not the same as the invention being submitted. (You should know that you and your patent attorney are required by law to bring all relevant "prior art" that your search uncovers to the attention of the Patent Office, even if it might hurt your case. Otherwise, the patent will be invalid, even if the invention might have been patentable over the "prior art" that you concealed.)

The application also includes arguments as to why the invention is useful, as well as a lengthy formal verbal description of the invention that is keyed to the drawings. The most important part of the invention is the section at the end that contains the specific claims, because it is on these claims that patent protection will be granted. Preparing the patent application can easily cost several thousand dollars. When the application is received by the Patent Office, you receive a form that gives the date on which your application was officially filed, and a unique serial number.

As previously noted, the inventor is required to give the public a full disclosure of the invention (through copies of the published patent, which are available to anyone after the patent issues), in return for the rights to exclusive use of the invention for a limited period. The test of full disclosure is whether the patent is sufficiently clear and complete that someone else who is "skilled in the art" could build a working model based on what is disclosed, without engaging in undue experimentation.

As I noted earlier, the date of application has to be within one year of your first public use or disclosure of the invention. (There is nothing to prevent you from working on your invention for years in the privacy of your home or company, as long as you are diligent in your efforts to try to perfect the invention and you don't disclose it to the public and don't use it commercially, even in secret. The one-year clock starts running only when you make public or commercial use or disclosure of your invention.)

Under current U.S. law, patents are granted to those who are first to *invent* rather than those who are first to *file* at the patent office. Under our current first-to-invent system, it is essential that an inventor keep a signed, dated, and witnessed notebook of ideas that might become inventions, because the burden of proof is on the inventor to show that he or she was in fact the first to invent.

Most of the rest of the world grants patents to those who are the first to *file*, and there is increasing pressure on the U.S. to change to this approach. A first-to-file system is much easier to administer, since you only have to look at the Patent Office's date stamp on the application to determine who was first. But a first-to-file system may discriminate against small companies and individual inventors, who—because filing for patents is expensive—may hold off filing until they are pretty sure they have a viable invention.

Note that I did not have to submit a working model of my invention to the Patent Office. Reduction to practice, in the sense that you have to be able to show a working prototype, is not required in order to get a patent. But the Patent Office is always on the lookout for submissions that look like perpetual motion machines, so you must be prepared to show that your invention does not violate any of the laws of physics and *could* be made to work.

About a year after my filing date, I received word from my patent attorney that the patent examiner assigned to my invention had rejected the application on the basis that the invention was not new. This was upsetting, but I had been through this with other patent applications, which were eventually granted.

The examiner had included a stack of patents that he claimed were "prior art" that was sufficiently close to my invention to cast doubt on my claim of newness. Some of these were patents that were found in our initial search, but there were others that I had not seen before.

The next step was to go through this new stack of "prior art" and meticulously answer each of the patent examiner's objections. If changes in the application are necessary to skirt around the claims of one or more of these "prior art" patents, this is the time to make them. After doing this, I resubmitted the entire package to the Patent Office.

Finally, nearly three years after the initial application, the patent was issued on July 20, 1982. My total investment was about $3500. For the next 17 years, I would have exclusive rights to this invention. (In 1994, the rules changed. Now protection is granted for 20 years from the date of *application*, rather than 17 years from the date the patent is issued. Furthermore, this change was retroactive, so now my patent will expire in 20 years from the date it was filed. The Patent Office is now processing applications faster, so the average time from application to issuance is about 18 months.)

My patent prevents anyone else from *making, using*, or *selling* this instrument in the United States without my permission. Most people think that a patent only controls who can manufacture a patented invention. But a patent also applies to the sale and even the use of a patented invention. If someone were to copy my instrument overseas and bring it into the U.S. to use in a clinical study, this would be an infringement of my patent. Similarly, if an overseas manufacturer were to copy the instrument and then import it for sale in the U.S., the seller would be infringing. Because I applied only for a U.S. patent, however, I have no recourse if an overseas company makes and sells copies of the instrument outside the U.S.

In retrospect, the investment in this patent was money well spent. Through published research articles and word-of-mouth in the research community, the instrument became well-known internationally as a necessary component for several kinds of clinical studies. Building and selling these instruments has been an interesting and profitable home business to complement my teaching and research as a business school professor, and today there are hundreds of instruments in use in laboratories and universities all over the world.

A few years after the first instruments were purchased for periodontal research, I received a call from a scientist doing research on toothpastes for teeth that are unusually sensitive to heat, cold, and pressure. By making a small modification to fit the instrument with a sharp dental explorer tip instead of a blunt periodontal tip, this researcher had succeeded in making quantitatively reproducible measurements of tooth sensitivity. Using the force measuring capability of the handpiece, he gently increased the force of the explorer tip against the side of the tooth until it was just perceptible to the patient. Then he repeated the measurements after the patient had brushed for several weeks with a sensitivity-reducing toothpaste, to measure the effectiveness of various toothpaste formulations.

This unexpected new application for measuring tooth sensitivity with the instrument is a perfect example of how customers will find new, unforeseen uses for a product once it is on the market. It turned out to be a major new market. Because the Food and Drug Administration requires advertising claims for clinical effectiveness of sensitivity-reducing toothpastes to be backed up by clinical research, all the companies that make these toothpastes have become my customers. Today when I watch an ad for a sensitivity-reducing toothpaste on television, I have the satisfaction of knowing that my invention was used to help develop that product.

Protection of inventions by patents provides a critical advantage that allows creative small companies and individual inventors to compete with large corporations. I doubt that I would have spent the time to develop the electronic probe if there had been no such thing as patent protection. Over the years, the electronic probe has been a source of income and also of personal satisfaction, because I know that there are millions of people around the world who are benefiting from periodontal medications and sensitivity-reducing toothpastes that are more effective because the research was done with the help of my invention.

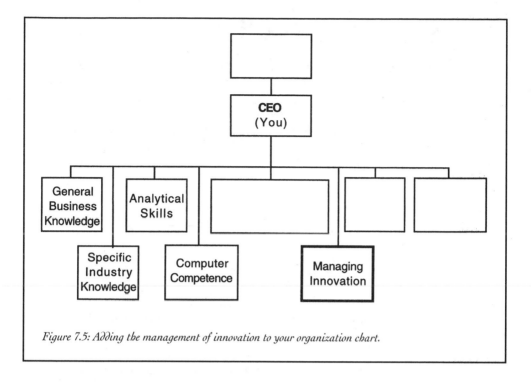

Figure 7.5: Adding the management of innovation to your organization chart.

THE BOTTOM LINE

Innovation is the most powerful source of economic growth for both companies and individuals. But there are many barriers to innovation, particularly in large companies. In this chapter, we have examined a number of ways to stimulate the flow of innovations in your firm, and to protect the intellectual property rights that result from your innovations. In Figure 7.5, the Strategic Skill of Managing Innovation has been added to the organization chart of your "company of one."

In the final analysis, as CEO of your "company of one," it is your responsibility to make sure that the innovations you create are developed in such a way as to make you personally better off. If you properly manage these innovations, both you and your employer will benefit greatly from your creativity.

A CHALLENGE TO INNOVATE

Create an idea for innovation. It can be for your employer or for your "company of one," or as the basis for a part-time business or even an entrepreneurial startup.

1. Compared to existing products or services, describe how your innovation provides any or all of the following advantages:

    ☐ Better

    ☐ Faster

    ☐ Cheaper

2. What is your strategy for making your "company of one" (not just your employer) more successful by developing this innovation?

3. How will you test the market acceptability of your innovation?

4. How will you protect your intellectual property rights in this innovation?

....

1   As reported in *Forbes ASAP*, October 9, 1995, p. 95.

2   Robinson, P., "Paul Romer in the Shrine of the Gods," *Forbes ASAP*, June 5, 1995, pp. 67 - 72.

3   Robinson, W. and Fornell, C., (1985), "Sources of Market Pioneer Advantages in Consumer Goods Industries," *Journal of Marketing Research*, XXII, pp. 305-317.

4   Urban, G., Carter, T., Gaskin, S., and Mucha, Z. (1986), "Market Share Rewards to Pioneering Brands: An Empirical Analysis and Strategic Implications," *Management Science*, 32, No. 6, pp. 645-659.

5   Robinson, W. and Fornell, C. (1985).

6   For a more comprehensive discussion of the reasons for differences in receptivity to innovation in large and small firms, see Yeaple, R., "Why Are Small R&D Organizations More Productive," *IEEE Transactions on Engineering Management*, November, 1992.

7   Huey, J., "Nothing is Impossible," *Fortune*, September 23, 1991, p. 92.

8   "George Fisher's Vision for Kodak," *Rochester Business Journal*, May 27, 1994, p. 7.

9   Cooper, A., "R&D is More Efficient in Small Companies," *Harvard Business Review*, May/June 1964, pp. 75 - 83.

10 Acs, Z. and Audretsch, D., "Innovation in Large and Small Firms: An Empirical Analysis," *The American Economic Review*, 78, No. 4, pp. 680 - 681.

11 Many years ago, when someone asked Dr. Edwin Land, the famous inventor and founder of Polaroid Corporation, for his secret of success, he responded, "Fail, fail, fail, fail . . . and eventually you will succeed."

12 Huey, p. 135.

13 Huey, p. 136.

14 McGough, R., "It's Strange . . . ," *The Wall Street Journal*, January 5, 1996, p. R4.

15 Planck, M., *The Philosophy of Physics*, 1936.

16 Uttal, B., "The Lab that Ran Away from Xerox," *Fortune*, September 5, 1983, p. 99.

17 From an advertisement by Electronic Data Systems Corp. in *Fortune*, December 11, 1995, p. 196.

18   "George Fisher's Vision for Kodak," *Rochester Business Journal*, May 27, 1994, pp. 5 - 7.

19   Chambers, J., Mullick, S., and Smith, D., "How to Choose the Right Forecasting Technique," *Harvard Business Review*, July/August 1971, pp. 45 - 74.

20   Tauber, E., "How Market Research Discourages Major Innovation," *Business Horizons*, June, 1974, pp. 22 - 26.

21   Rogers, E., *Diffusion of Innovations*, Free Press, 1962.

22   Jacobson, G. and Hillkirk, J., *Xerox: American Samurai*, Macmillan & Company, 1986, pp. 60, 64.

23   Prokesch, S., "Mastering Chaos at the High-Tech Frontier," *Harvard Business Review*, Nov-Dec 1993, pp. 137 - 138.

24   Tichy, N. and Sherman, S., *Control Your Destiny or Someone Else Will*, HarperBusiness, 1994, p. 106.

25   Prokesch, pp. 137 - 138.

26   Hamel, G. and Prahalad, C., "Corporate Imagination and Expeditionary Marketing, *Harvard Business Review*, July-August 1991, pp. 81 - 92.

27   See Stalk, G., "Time — The Next Source of Competitive Advantage," *Harvard Business Review*, July-August 1988, pp. 41 - 51.

28   Ibid. p. 49.

29   Bower, J. and Hout, T., Fast-Cycle Capability for Competitive Power, *Harvard Business Review*, November-December 1988, p. 113.

30   Hamel, G. and Prahalad, C., Competing for the Future, *Harvard Business School Press*, 1994, p. 158.

31   Bhide, A., "How Entrepreneurs Craft Strategies that

Work," *Harvard Business Review*, March-April 1994, pp. 150 - 161.

32 Allen, T., and Fusfeld, A., "Design for Communication in the Research and Development Labs," *Technology Review*, 1976, pp. 65 - 71.

33 Haeffner, E., "The Innovation Process," *Technology Review*, March/April 1973, pp. 18 - 25.

34 Tichy and Sherman, p. 48 - 49.

35 Yeaple, R., "Why are Small R&D Organizations More Productive?" *IEEE Transactions on Engineering Management*, 39, No. 4, November 1992, p. 340 - 341.

36 Packard, D., *The HP Way*, HarperBusiness, 1995, pp. 100 - 101.

37 Ibid. pp. 107 - 108.

38 Quinn, J., "Managing Innovation: Controlled Chaos," *Harvard Business Review*, May/June 1985, p. 79.

39 Ibid. p. 79.

DEVELOPING SKILLS FOR WORKING WITH PEOPLE

P eople skills—the ability to get things done through other people—are what distinguish managers from individual contributors. People skills include leadership, teamwork, and the ability to persuade others through written and oral communications.

The star loner is of little value in today's organizations. A manager's value is directly tied to how much he or she can accomplish in cooperation with others. Team players are sought and networking is encouraged.

Learning to lead and manage people are perhaps the most difficult of the Strategic Skills to acquire. In our survey of business school graduates, the respondents agreed that while MBA programs do a great job of teaching analytical skills, they are weak in teaching people skills. Yet people skills may be more important. As one plant engineer, who graduated with an MBA in 1983, wrote on his survey: "Technical knowledge is good, but people and managerial skills make the executive."

With the decline of organizational hierarchy, interpersonal relationships are based less on authority of command and more on cooperative associations of peers—task forces, multidisciplinary new product development teams—that are much like strategic alliances between companies. In today's organizations, with the relaxing of formal organizational structures, people skills are more important for the success of your "company of one" than ever before.

LEARNING TO LEAD

Every company says that it wants to hire and promote leaders. Is it possible to teach men and women how to lead?

As Harvard Professor John Kotter has pointed out, leadership and management are not the same. In times of peace, armies are managed; in times of war, armies are led. Management is about coping with complexity; leadership is about coping with change. Both are necessary in today's organizations. Managers deal with complexity by planning and budgeting, using the tools of analysis and problem-solving that business schools are well-equipped to teach. Leaders lead by setting direction, by motivating and by inspiring an organization. Leadership does not produce plans; it creates vision and strategies. Leaders do not organize people; they align them.[1]

One can learn how to manage by taking business courses or pursuing an MBA degree, but how does one learn to lead? Leaders create visions of what the company can become. The challenge for the leader is to get the organization:

- To *understand* the vision (by developing written and oral communications skills),

- To *accept* the vision (by developing a track record for success and a reputation for integrity), and

- To empower subordinates to *internalize* the vision (by working to ensure that supervisors throughout the organization are aligned with the vision).

Based on his research on the development of leaders and leadership, Kotter offers this career path advice for those who would be leaders:[2]

- Take on significant challenges with real risk and reward potential early in your career, in your twenties or thirties. Take chances and learn from your triumphs and your mistakes. Build a track record. Learn to lead by leading.

In his first job at General Electric as a young plastics engineer in his twenties, future CEO Jack Welch jump-started the sales of an unknown engineering plastic, Noryl, by going against the conventional wisdom at GE of selling bulk plastic on the basis of engineering specifications. Instead, Welch made prototypes of parts—such as automobile taillight lenses for customers—out of Noryl at GE's expense, and usually got the production order. At thirty-three, Welch was rewarded for his leadership by becoming GE's youngest general manager, his first step on the road to becoming CEO.[3]

- Broaden your knowledge beyond the area of your functional specialty. Be willing to take lateral career moves if they will give you the chance to learn skills that could be useful later in your career. Volunteer for task force assignments, particularly those that will help you build a network of colleagues outside of your immediate functional area. Although trained as an engineer, Jack Welch made his early reputation in sales and marketing.

- Look for employers that push decision-making authority and accountability deep in the organization, to create more challenging jobs at lower levels. Companies such as Johnson & Johnson, Hewlett-Packard, 3M, and GE are well-known for such decentralization, which gives potential young leaders the chance to show what they can do early in their careers.

HOW SENIOR MANAGERS LEAD

One of the best ways to understand the concept of leadership is to see how it is actually practiced by successful top executives. How do senior managers lead an organization? In a classic article, Edward Wrapp describes what life at the top is really like, and how senior managers get things done in their organizations.[4]

Wrapp begins by listing some of the common myths about top management:

- "Life gets less complicated as a manager reaches the top of the pyramid."

- "The manager at the top level knows everything that's going on in the organization, can command whatever resources he or she may need, and therefore can be more decisive."

- "The general manager's day is taken up with making broad policy decisions and formulating precise objectives."

- "The top executive's primary activity is conceptualizing long-range plans."

These myths are nonsense, says Wrapp. They do not give an accurate portrayal of what a general manager actually does. He observes that in reality, successful executives have five skills that seem especially noteworthy in getting the job done:

- The successful executive *keeps well-informed* by maintaining a network with nodes at many levels in the organization. Senior managers often reach deep into the organization to keep track of what is happening, making phone calls or dropping in unexpectedly at a subordinate's office. At Hewlett-Packard, they even have a term for it: "Management By Walking Around" (MBWA).[5]

  GE's Welch has a voracious appetite for information. When he wants to find out something, he ignores the chain of command and calls people several layers down in the organization. As a result, he often knows more about a particular business than the people who run it. In a meeting, he might have better numbers than the division managers, and he has no tolerance for ill-informed managers who try to make up stories to cover their ignorance. Says one member of GE's Executive Management Staff, "The one thing you can never do with Jack is wing it. If he ever catches you winging it, you're in trouble. Real trouble. You have to go in with in-depth information."[6]

  Experienced executives know that depending on the formal communications channels in the organization leaves the choice of what the senior manager hears and sees in the hands of subordinates, who may choose to modify and distort it for their own purposes. As Wrapp says, "The very purpose of a hierarchy is to prevent information from reaching higher levels. It operates as an information filter, and there are little wastebaskets all along the way."

- A good manager knows that he or she has limited time and energy, and that it is necessary to *maintain focus on those things that will have the greatest long-term impact on the company*. For other problems brought to his or her attention, the manager simply acknowledges the receipt of the information. On occasion, the manager nudges one of these peripheral problems along a desired path, not by giving direct orders, but by asking a few perceptive questions.

- The successful manager is *politically astute*, taking time to assess both support and opposition in the organization. An experienced senior manager knows that the organization will tolerate only a limited number of proposals from the top, and that an idea from the corporate office is likely to solidify opposition from the divisions. Instead, he or she will stimulate the release of the idea in the form of a trial balloon from someone else in the organization, and then study the reactions of key individuals.

The effective manager develops a good sense of timing, knowing that a new concept requires a certain amount of "soak time" while people get used to the idea, and that pushing too early can lead to defeat.

For many top managers, patience and steady pressure from the top toward the desired outcome are more effective than sharp confrontations. HP's David Packard tells how he learned this management technique by herding cattle on his ranch:

> "I have enjoyed many pleasures as the result of my experiences as a rancher; I've also learned a thing or two. Every season we would round up cattle from the range and drive them to the corral. Along the way, we'd come to a gate. The trick was to get them through the gate and not stampede them. I found, after much trial and error, that applying steady, gentle pressure from the rear worked best. Eventually, one would decide to pass through the gate; the rest

would soon follow. Press them too hard, and they'd panic, scattering in all directions. Slack off entirely, and they'd just head back to their old grazing spots. This insight was useful throughout my management career."[7]

Yet other CEOs, such as GE's Welch, are highly confrontational:

According to former employees, Welch conducts meetings so aggressively that people tremble. He attacks almost physically with his intellect—criticizing, demeaning, ridiculing, humiliating. "Jack comes on like a herd of elephants," says a GE employee. "If you have a contradictory idea you have to be willing to take the guff to put it forward."[8]

- Although the successful senior manager has a clear vision for the organization, the *specific means and methods to get there remain imprecise.* The wise subordinate welcomes this imprecision of methods from the top because it opens a much wider range of options for implementation. Jack Welch has communicated a clear vision for GE to his managers: GE will be Number One or Number Two in every market the company serves. He tells his managers that if they are not Number One or Number Two in their market, they should "either fix it, sell it, or close it down."[9]

The goal is explicit. The choice of methods is up to the managers.

- The successful executive is talented as a conceptualizer; analytical, but more than an analyst. He or she *welcomes change and knows how to exploit it,* how to ride the waves of new technologies and fresh innovations. The senior manager sees relationships and subtle patterns within the company and in the surrounding environment that lead to new opportunities for the organization—because above all else, the successful executive is a leader.

IDENTIFYING POTENTIAL LEADERS

How do people become leaders? Is it a learned skill, or is it programmed in the genes? Or is it some of both?

The consensus is that leadership is a natural talent, like musical talent, that can be developed and honed by lessons, similar to learning to play the piano. And, like piano lessons, leadership is developed by a combination of coaching and practicing. Leadership is not a pure intellectual concept like Net Present Value. One does not become a skilled corporate leader by reading books about leadership or by sitting in a classroom or working on a computer. Skill in leadership comes about through *practice.*

Leadership comes in many forms. Although most would characterize the leader of an organization to be like the captain of a great ship, Peter Senge sees the real leader of an organization to be the *designer* of the organization, as influential as the designer of the ship. In Senge's view, it does no good for the captain of the ship to order a thirty degree turn to starboard if the designer of the ship has built a rudder that will turn the ship only to port:

> Although "leader as designer" is neglected today, it touches a chord that goes back thousands of years. To paraphrase Lao-tzu, the bad leader is he who the people despise. The good leader is he who the people praise. The great leader is he who the people say, "We did it ourselves."[10]

Learning about leadership is not time wasted. Those who take lessons in leadership, like those who take piano lessons, will have a greater appreciation of the art of leadership of HP's David Packard or GE's Jack Welch, just as those who study the piano as children have a better appreciation of the artistry of Vladimir Horowitz as adults. They will better understand what Packard, Welch and Kodak's George Fisher have accomplished, and as a minimum they will be better followers. And for many, lessons in leadership may help them be more effective in small organizational units and charitable groups, just as those who study piano in their youth play for family get-togethers and for their own enjoyment.

To succeed in today's dynamic markets, good management is necessary but not sufficient. With the demise of organizational hierarchy and the formal authority of command, decisions are being delegated further down in the organization, and leadership is vital at all levels if the company is to survive and prosper.

For organizations, the development of leaders has two components:

- Identifying those with natural talent for leadership.

- For those who are identified with having the talent for leadership, finding the right method to provide the "piano lessons" to develop the potential of that talent.

Like musical talent, the talent for leadership usually shows up early. For example, Procter & Gamble, which places a high value on leadership, asks 28-year old graduating MBAs searching questions about how they showed leadership in sports or extracurricular activities when they were in *high school*. P & G also asks professors to describe specific instances where a candidate showed leadership in the classroom. As one P&G interviewer said to me over lunch at the Faculty Club, "We want more than just team players. We want evidence of team *leadership*."

Jack Welch's vigorous leadership style emerged in high school, where he was involved in activities of all kinds, particularly sports, as captain of the hockey team and the golf team. His class voted him the "'most talkative and noisiest boy.'"[11]

THE IMPORTANCE OF INTEGRITY

To teach the methods of leadership to those with potential, you have to understand what leadership is. Frances Hesselbein, former CEO of the Girl Scouts and now head of the nonprofit Drucker Foundation, sees leadership as the ability to sense people's emotional needs and to match those needs with the needs of the organization, a process she calls "brokering." To Hesselbein, the brokering function of a leader requires consistency and integrity:

> *"My definition of leadership was very hard to arrive at, very painful. Leadership is not a basket of tricks or skills.*

It is the quality and character and courage of the person who is the leader. It's a matter of ethics and moral compass, the willingness to remain highly vulnerable. You can't talk about developing every person to his or her highest potential and then treat those people in ways that diminish and limit and contain. The only way we achieve high performance is through the work of others."[12]

In response to a journalist's question, Kodak CEO George Fisher had this to say about the need for integrity in today's complex business environment:

Q: "You've stressed a value system for Kodak . . . for example, 'uncompromising integrity.' How does that translate into action, how the company operates?"

Fisher: "In a world that has become increasingly complex, that particular value is becoming one of the most important . . . . In business today, if you don't have uncompromising integrity — the minute you show the slightest deviation from complete integrity in any of your dealings, whether it's with competitors, customers, employees, anybody — then it's a slippery slope and you are on your way out. Integrity is something you practice every day."[13]

Like Fisher, GE's Welch sees integrity as a business essential:

"On the question of integrity and company policy, the message is very clear. You are responsible for your organization's behavior. We will not shoot the Indians and let the chiefs go. There's no place in this company for any behavior by anyone that could condone or give the implication of condoning any violation."[14]

TEACHING LEADERSHIP

Can leadership be taught? Prior to his promotion to CEO, PepsiCo's Roger Enrico headed an in-house executive leadership training program to help develop the next generation of

PepsiCo's top management. Classes were small—typically nine participants—and the course was structured so that each participant focused on a major new business opportunity for his or her division. Enrico found that there are three essential ingredients in successful leadership courses:

1. For credibility, the program was headed up by a proven leader, in this case, himself.

2. Enrico spent the first five days of the program leading an off-site seminar of presentations by Pepsi executives, instruction on problem-solving skills, workshops, and one-on-one mentoring sessions between Enrico and each of the nine participants.

3. The centerpiece of the program was a 90-day project that each participant was required to create and lead, to launch a major new business opportunity for his or her division. This was a high profile assignment, and participants were exposed to real risk if the project failed. Although the participants returned to their home divisions to direct these projects, Enrico stayed in close contact every step of the way—mentoring, offering advice, and keeping each project on track. A number of very successful new business innovations for PepsiCo were launched as part of Enrico's course.[15]

The keys to Enrico's successful approach to teaching leadership were *mentoring* and *hands-on practice* by launching real new business opportunities that put the participants at risk as they applied what they had learned. As Harvard's Kotter said, you learn to lead by taking on challenges with real risk and reward potential. Take chances, learn from your triumphs and mistakes, and build a track record.

THE DECLINE OF HIERARCHY

Personal leadership is becoming more important because the old command-and-control model of management—"do it because I'm the boss"—is on the way out. Some organizations have taken out entire layers of managers, and in doing so have sped up the decision-making process, reducing the time to get new products to the market.

GE's Jack Welch removed an entire layer of executive vice presidents, the sector chiefs who intervened between the CEO and the thirteen major businesses of the company. He found that the sector chiefs had no real power, that their role was to transmit information up and down the hierarchy, often selectively filtering it in the process. They had no first-hand knowledge of their businesses. When he asked them a question, he wouldn't get an answer. They would have to check with someone who knew, who was actually running one of the businesses—and this often took days.

By removing this layer of senior executives, Welch accelerated the flow and improved the accuracy of information between the businesses and corporate headquarters. The results were improved leadership, better understanding of markets, and faster decisions on new products.[16]

In recent years, Hewlett-Packard has also found it necessary to shed layers of bureaucracy to remain competitive. HP began as an electronic instrument company; a company of engineers designing and building instrumentation for use by other engineers. Often a successful new product was created when an HP engineer had a particular measurement problem and designed a new measuring instrument—say, a new digital voltmeter—just for his own use. But then another HP engineer working nearby in the same lab would see the new instrument and would ask to have one built for him too. Soon, there would be a number of these new instruments in various labs in the company, and before long the new digital voltmeter would appear in the HP catalog as a new product to be offered to customers. This phenomenon was so common at HP that it became known as "the next bench syndrome," because new instruments tended to proliferate and to be added to the HP product catalog depending on their appeal to the engineers at the next bench.

In those early days at HP, decisions to create new instruments and add them to the catalog were made at the lowest organizational level, close to the customer. There was little interference from a management hierarchy. The creators of these new instruments understood their customers needs, because the customers were engineers very much like themselves. The company was highly decentralized and decisions were made quickly. Most of the new products were successful, and the company grew rapidly.

But by the late 1980s, computers had become a major part of HP's business, and because the computer business is a systems business that also requires coordinated software development, it seemed wise at the time to centralize decision-making about new product development to ensure coordination of all of the various system components and the software. This led to task forces, councils, and committees intended to improve coordination, and many levels of management who had to sign off on new product developments. Critical decisions were delayed for weeks or even months.

By 1990, the company faced a major crisis. Committees had taken over the decision-making process at HP. While competitors in the fast-moving computer business surged ahead, HP's new product programs slowed to a crawl. And the virus of decision-by-committee began to spread to other parts of HP that were unrelated to the computer business. Thanks to the company's open door policy, founders Bill Hewlett and David Packard began to receive visits from deeply-concerned managers. After listening and touring a number of HP facilities, the two founders finally stepped in and dismantled the committees and the bureaucracy, returning decision-making authority back to the individual operating units.[17]

The new organizational strategy worked—brilliantly. In its cover story recognizing Hewlett-Packard as its "Performer of the Year" for 1995, *Forbes* reported the following:

> *Products introduced within the last two years account for 70% of HP's orders . . . . [In 1995], HP's earnings per share rose 51%, and its share price gained 90%—both extraordinary accomplishments considering that both increases came from a high base . . . . For a very large company—HP's revenues were $31.5 billion—its sales growth, too, was extraordinary: 26% last year, up from a five-year average of 22%. In 1995, HP added more than $6 billion to its revenues.*

[HP] creates jobs as well as wealth. Unlike most of the other outstanding companies, HP has achieved superior profitability without massive layoffs and painful restructurings . . . . HP has never had major layoffs . . . . [The company] employs almost 20,000 more people worldwide than it did ten years ago; in the same period IBM has shed half of its workforce. For those who entrusted their careers to it as well as those who entrusted their investment, HP has delivered.[18]

THE CHANGING ROLE OF MANAGERS

With the decline of hierarchy, the role of management is changing. While the world of commerce will always need leaders, it may not need as many managers. At the limit, *Fortune's* Walter Kiechel foresees the possibility that in a future dominated by computerized information systems and multifunctional teams, management as we know it may disappear:

"Managers will command no premium in status or compensation over the people whose work they coordinate. If [managers] no longer have a lock on the information of most value to the company [because the company's computerized information system will provide multifunctional teams with whatever information they need to do their jobs], and if they bring no special expertise comparable to that of other team members, why should they be paid more?"[19]

A few management gurus even predict that the company itself will disappear, to be replaced by temporary affiliations of networked specialists, so-called "virtual corporations" without formal corporate structures. Advocates point to ad-hoc motion picture production companies—consisting of a producer, a director, screenwriters, actors, and financiers who pool their resources temporarily to produce a movie and then disband—as present day examples of the virtual corporation of the future.[20] They see, as the first step in the process of dismantling the traditional corporation, the trend toward widespread outsourcing of data processing and other support functions that previously were done in-house. Reportedly more than 40% of the Fortune 500 companies recently have outsourced some department or service, such as data processing, legal services, human resources, public relations, or accounting.[21]

But while the decline of hierarchy and the changing role of management are well-established trends, the concept of a completely "virtual" corporation has not been widely accepted and the very idea generates a number of unanswered questions. After it disbands, who will own the intellectual property (patents, trade secrets) created by the virtual corporation? Without a boss in charge of the project, who will make the decisions when there is no consensus? And because the virtual corporation has a short life, will participants spend most of their workday lining up their next job? Will there be a tendency for the participants to cheat each other ("take the money and run") because they foresee having no long-term professional relationship with each other?

A more probable scenario for the organization of the future will be similar to what law firms and management consulting companies currently follow. These organizations typically hire the best and brightest young talent in their field and allow them five to ten years to make partner, or they are out. McKinsey and Company, a top-rated global consulting firm with more than 3,000 professional employees and annual revenues in excess of $1 billion, has only four layers of professionals:

- At the bottom are the Associates—often hired right out of business school at salaries ranging from $70,000 to $100,000 or more—who travel constantly, work very long hours, and do most of the analytical work for the firm. Associates are under extreme pressure to produce. They have six years to make Partner or be asked to leave, and because only one out of five makes it, the turnover at this level is high.

- At the next level, McKinsey has about 450 Partners, who typically make $250,000 per year.

- The most senior professionals are the Directors, who earn from $800,000 to $2,500,000 annually. There are about 150 Directors at McKinsey.

- At the top is the Managing Director, the CEO of the firm, who is elected by the Directors every three years and is paid $3,500,000.

Much of the work at McKinsey is carried out by their version of multifunctional project teams, which for a typical assignment might consist of:

- A Partner from the local office who acts as the senior sponsor on the project.

- An "engagement manager," typically an Associate with an MBA and three or four years of experience, who serves as project leader.

- A "quant jock," a computer science graduate or MBA from a "quantitative school" such as Carnegie Mellon, to crunch the numbers.

- A "business analyst," most likely a newly-hired Associate, and

- An "industry specialist," someone in the firm who has chosen to specialize in problems of one industry, such as the auto industry.[22]

This flat organizational form with relatively little hierarchy works well for law firms and for consulting firms like McKinsey, both of which are in the knowledge business. The Darwinian up-or-out policy for Associates and the high pay levels for Partners ensure that only the best talent stays. But the absence of multiple levels of hierarchy also means that over the course of one's career, there are few promotions to strive for. Individual productivity of McKinsey Partners tends to peak at age 45, after which they settle into a reduced role, retiring around age 60.[23]

Whether the McKinsey form of organization will prove to be the prototype for the organization of the future in industries such as manufacturing remains to be seen. If, in the future, companies will compete more on the basis of their human capital—on knowledge and innovation rather than on capital investment and economies of scale—even manufacturing companies may begin to take on a McKinsey-like form. One attempt to reorganize a major manufacturing company, Xerox Corporation, around horizontal work flows rather than functional hierarchies has been underway since 1992. Yet insiders report that the changeover is far from complete, and some senior executives who are at the top of the current hierarchies are said to be resisting.

But individual business units *within* large manufacturing firms—for example, the $2 billion per year black-and-white film manufacturing operation at Kodak—have successfully dismantled their hierarchies and have constructed team-oriented flat organizations that are built around work flows and are far more efficient. In two years, the black-and-white film operation went from being 15% over budgeted cost to 15% under budgeted cost, while simultaneously chopping its response time to customer orders from 42 days to about 21 days. Furthermore, at the end of this two-year transition, morale in the organization had zoomed from one of the lowest in Kodak to one of the highest.[24]

Seek Cross-functional Experience and Learn to Work in Teams

'Mark,' age 31, is Manager of Internal Audit for a major manufacturing company. He received his undergraduate degree in Accounting in 1986 and worked as a financial analyst for three years before beginning a part-time MBA program with concentrations in Accounting and Finance. At the time he began his MBA studies, Mark was earning $35,000 a year, and when he graduated three years later, he was promoted to Plant Controller at a salary of $48,000. Last year he earned $80,000, up 9% from the prior year.

Mark has two pieces of advice for aspiring managers: 1) Be sure to get a broad business education, seeking cross-functional experience rather than staying in one field, and 2) Learn to work in teams, and concentrate on developing teamwork skills.

MULTIFUNCTIONAL TEAMS

Survey respondents were in agreement about the importance of learning to work in multifunctional teams, as illustrated by the advice of the successful alum at the left.

With the decline of the hierarchy of multiple layers of management, the multifunctional team has become the new organizational unit of performance. A multifunctional team is a small group drawn from the company's various functional areas—Engineering, Marketing, Finance, and Manufacturing—for the purpose of accomplishing a defined task, such as the creation and launching of a new product.

Business schools have been quick to incorporate team learning in their MBA programs:

> *Companies have lobbied for courses that teach the "team" management techniques that have swept Corporate America, and now many schools embrace the team concept in nearly every discipline. Even in finance, USC Dean [Randolph] Westerfield says, "We now recognize that to be a leader, it takes a whole new set of communications skills. And those can only be taught in a team environment."*[25]

What is so special about using teams to get the work done? According to Peter Senge, the fundamental characteristic of truly effective teams is *alignment*. Senge describes an aligned team as having a resonance or synergy, where the individuals' energies harmonize in a commonality of purpose, a shared vision, and an understanding of how to complement one another's efforts. The experience is similar to that of a jazz ensemble that is "in the groove"—a state of playing as one.[26]

In research for their bestseller, *The Wisdom of Teams*, Jon Katzenbach and Douglas Smith clarified the difference between a *team* and a *committee*.

- A *committee* (or a task force) may be just a group of people working together. The emphasis is on the individual performance of the team members, on what each member can contribute as an individual.

- A *team*, on the other hand, is distinguished by the joint work that the members do together, what Katzenbach and Smith call *collective work-products*, such as surveys, experiments, and new product specifications. It is this joint work that distinguishes the team from the committee.[27]

In a committee, the focus is on individual contributions. Committee members do not take responsibility for results other than their own contributions. In contrast, team members are committed to the collective output of the whole team, not just their individual contributions.

For example, if you are appointed as the Marketing representative on a new product *committee*, your responsibility is to provide the committee with marketing input—sales forecasts, customer requirements, pricing recommendations, and so on—and to ensure that the resulting new product is satisfactory to the Marketing organization. But if you are appointed to a new product *team*, your responsibility is to use your marketing expertise to work jointly with your colleagues from Engineering, Manufacturing, and Finance to make sure that the new product is a winner for the whole company. You wear your company hat, not your Marketing hat.

The leadership of a committee is a chairperson, usually appointed by senior management. But the leadership of a team is dynamic, and may change as the project moves from one phase to another. For example, at the outset the Marketing person may be the unofficial leader as he or she clearly defines the status of the market for this new product and the features that customers require. Later, the leadership role may pass to Engineering as the various design tradeoffs are explored and debated. Near the conclusion of the project, Manufacturing may assume leadership as the time for product launch approaches.

How do you maximize the performance of teams? In their research, Katzenbach and Smith observed a number of approaches shared by many successful teams:

- <u>Establish urgency and direction</u>: The more urgent and worthwhile the goal as understood by the participants, the better the performance. Getting everyone's buy-in at the beginning is critical. This is consistent with Senge's observation that the defining characteristic of successful teams is the alignment of the participants.

- <u>Assemble a complementary skills mix</u>: The team members should be chosen, not for their personality or their position in the company, but for the mix of skills needed to accomplish the goal.

- <u>The first meeting sets the tone</u>: First impressions count. What the team leaders do is more important than what they say. If a senior executive leaves after ten minutes to take a phone call and does not return, participants will get the message that the project is not very important.

- Establish ground rules at the outset: At the beginning of the project, the team should agree on a set of ground rules, such as "no interruptions to take phone calls," "all disagreements stay within this room," and "everybody will be called upon to report on their assignments at the start of each meeting."

- Set a few initial goals that can be accomplished quickly: Teams work better when they feel they are making progress, and a few early victories will boost morale.

- Challenge the group with new information: Maintain a flow of fresh information from the outside to the team to keep the project from getting stale. Teams are more likely to err when the members assume that they know all they need to know about a subject.

- Spend lots of time together: Much of the success of the team is based on trust. Spending time together, not only in formal team sessions but also over lunch and dinner and on trips and social outings, helps build trust.

- Recognize and reward performance: Occasional notes or visits from senior management and a few "gold stars" handed out for exceptional efforts help keep the team focused on the importance of performance.[28]

POLITICS AND PROMOTIONS

My MBA students often say to me that they didn't like their previous job "because of the politics." But whenever there are more than two people in an organization, there are "politics." Alan Schoonmaker explains why every company has politics:[29]

> *The term [politics] refers to the distribution of power. If we use the term in this sense it becomes obvious that politics is unavoidable. Since power exists in every group or organization, politics must necessarily exist in every firm. You can therefore get away from politics only by becoming a hermit. As long as you live and work in groups and organizations, politics will influence your career—whether you like it or not!*

Schoonmaker then goes on to explain why MBAs are particularly vulnerable to politics:

Politics is particularly important for an MBA, because you work at jobs which are very hard to evaluate objectively. A [production line] worker's performance can usually be measured by fairly objective criteria such as number of units produced or amount of scrap. Your performance can rarely be measured accurately and objectively, and the standard 'measurement' is usually some form of performance rating [i.e., an opinion]. Since ratings are notoriously subject to bias, your performance record depends on politics . . . whether you like it or not, your career is very dependent on politics.

The question is not, then, whether you should play politics, but what kind of politics you should play. And to answer this question you must learn who has the power in your firm and how he or she uses it. You should do three things:

1. *Understand the rules of the political games in your firm.*

2. *Decide which game you want to play, [and] whether you want to play the games in your firm at all. [The alternative is to] go someplace where the game is more to your liking.*

3. *Learn to play the game you do select more efficiently.*

I advise my students that it is unrealistic to expect that getting an MBA will lead to a job without politics. But having an MBA from a good school gives you more bargaining chips because it raises your market value, as a result of the Strategic Skills you learn and the additional academic credentials on your resume. Sooner or later, the politics in your organization may get so destructive that you may be faced with the choice of staying or leaving. Your investment in mastering the Strategic Skills demanded in today's workplace will give you more bargaining power to get what you want if you stay, and it will give you more employment options if you decide to leave.

STRATEGIC ALLIANCES AND NETWORKING

As CEO of your "company of one," you recognize that your effectiveness is determined in large part by your ability to get things done with and through other people. In the past, these relationships were defined by the management hierarchy of the organization. Status was clearly defined by title and office size. Business and social interactions tended to be with peers; Grade 10 managers did not have lunch with Grade 8s. Information flows were vertical, and decision-making was centralized.

As we have seen, in the emerging organizational forms of the late 1990s, decisions are being decentralized to the lowest practical levels of the organization, and information flows are horizontal as well as vertical. With less management hierarchy, relationships among professional people in the company are less well-structured. The old command-and-control model of management—"do it because I'm the boss"—is becoming less prevalent, and managers are increasingly dependent on their own personal leadership skills to get things done.

In the absence of structured relationships, skill in building informal strategic alliances with other professionals inside and outside the organization is becoming more valuable. The old saying that "It's not what you know, it's *who* you know that counts" isn't exactly right—you still have to know *what* to do— but knowing *who* to work with to get it done is more important than ever before.

Throughout this book we have searched for successful corporate strategies that can be applied to your "company of one." Strategic alliances between companies have been studied by Harvard professor Rosabeth Moss Kanter for many years, and as we will see, many of the principles for successful strategic alliances that she has uncovered can be applied to individuals as well. Think of this as a sophisticated approach to networking.

In recent years, companies have formed strategic alliances as an alternative to formal acquisitions or mergers between firms. Strategic alliances avoid the organizational rigidities and legal complexities of a formal acquisition, in which two corporate entities are merged into one. In a strategic alliance, each firm keeps its own identity and legal structure. As an example, in the early 1990s, IBM, Apple Computer, and Motorola set up a strategic alliance to work together to develop a new microprocessor chip, the PowerPC, to lessen their dependence on Intel Corporation for microprocessors.

Furthermore, a strategic alliance can have a limited life. The two partners work together on a specific project until complete, and then the alliance can be dissolved. For example, in 1991, when Apple Computer realized that it did not have the manufacturing capacity to produce its new line of PowerBook notebook computers, it established a strategic alliance with Sony Corporation to have Sony produce the least expensive version. A year later, after selling more than 100,000 Sony-made models, Apple ended the alliance.[30]

If the strategic alliance is expected to have a long life, the two partners may create a new corporation that they jointly own. For example, to exploit new opportunities in glass fibers, Owens-Illinois and Corning Glass Works joined forces more than 50 years ago to create a new corporation, Owens-Corning Fiberglass, that is still in existence. In the late 1980s, about 50% of Corning Glass Works' net income came from more than twenty partnerships, most with fifty-fifty ownership.[31]

One of the difficulties in forming and managing strategic alliances is that they are inherently unstable—like riding a bicycle—because such voluntary associations between companies are formed without the benefit of an overarching management structure between the two partners to hold things together. Like riding a bike, it takes continual attention, in the form of ongoing management commitment and goodwill on the part of each partner, to create and maintain a productive strategic alliance.

Many of the lessons that have been learned by Kanter and others about strategies for successful strategic alliances between companies can be applied to developing successful strategic alliances between your "company of one" and your peers, both within and outside of your firm. In her best-selling book, *When Giants Learn to Dance*, Kanter describes a number of requirements for successful strategic alliances that are also appropriate for your "company of one":

- The relationship has to be *important* to both partners. Where the strategic alliance includes companies, it should be important enough to command the attention of the CEO of each firm. To overcome the inherent instability of the strategic alliance, it has to fit the major strategies of each partner, so that they each have an incentive to make it work successfully.

- There should be *interdependence* between the partners, so that they continue to need each other for the life of the strategic alliance. Like the members of multidisciplinary product development teams, the partners should have complementary skills, and they should depend on each other. Both should benefit from the relationship, and it should not be easy for one of the partners to simply walk away from the alliance.

- If there is money involved, there should be a written *agreement* upfront, before there is any money on the table, on how any rewards from the alliance are to be distributed. The responsibilities and decision rights of the partners should also be spelled out.

- A mechanism is needed to ensure *information* flows between the participants. This usually involves a schedule of periodic meetings to keep the communications flowing.

- Finally, there should be opportunities for the partners to get together *informally*, over lunches, dinners, and at parties and picnics, to build trust and linkages between the partners in areas of common interest outside of the workplace, such as sports or favorite charities. Ultimately, given the absence of an overarching management structure to bind the partners together, mutual trust is an important factor in making strategic alliances work.[32]

How does all of this work on a personal level? How can strategic alliances be of value to your "company of one?" Let me tell you about two examples of successful personal strategic alliances from my own experience.

CASE HISTORIES: TWO EXAMPLES OF SUCCESSFUL PERSONAL STRATEGIC ALLIANCES

A number of years ago, when I was working on my thesis for my Ph.D. in electrical engineering—specifically in the field of biomedical engineering—I came up against a difficult measurement problem that eventually led to my inventing a new kind of distance measuring device. Subsequently, I entered into a personal strategic alliance with a major aerospace company with the goal of commercializing this new technology.

My thesis involved doing research on a new treatment for strabismus, a medical condition in which the eyes are out of alignment. Strabismus is a fairly common congenital disorder; about 2% of children in the U.S. are born with eyes that are not straight. Strabismus can also arise later in life, often as the result of a severe blow to the head (the depiction of a comic strip character exhibiting crossed eyes as he is hit over the head has some basis in fact). In addition to the cosmetic hardship to someone with misaligned eyes, there is also a functional concern, since misaligned eyes often cause double vision.

The traditional ways to treat strabismus are through eye exercises (by patching the eye of a young child, for example) and, in more stubborn cases, by surgery to straighten the turned eye by repositioning one or more of the six tiny muscles that control the movement of each eye. When this surgery is done, it requires general anesthesia and a hospital stay of two or three days.

In the late 1980s, a researcher in San Francisco developed a new way to straighten the eyes, by injecting a highly diluted sterile solution of botulism toxin into one of the eye muscles under a local anesthetic, to paralyze that muscle for a period of about eight weeks. As the paralysis then gradually wore off over the next several weeks, the turned eye often (but not always) slowly drifted into perfect alignment with the other eye. This new outpatient treatment took about 20 minutes and was done in the ophthalmologist's office. The procedure was fast, painless, relatively inexpensive, and avoided the medical risks of general anesthesia. Patients reported that it was less traumatic than having a tooth filled.

My research was directed at trying to understand the mechanism by which this new procedure worked, and to gain insight into why it worked well for some patients, but not for others. To carry out this research, I found it necessary to invent a new medical instrument that would electronically measure and record the mechanical characteristics of the rotational system made up of those tiny eye muscles, while a patient was under general anesthesia for strabismus surgery. Specifically, it was necessary to simultaneously measure both the force needed to rotate the eye being operated on and the angular distance it rotated, as the surgeon applied gentle rotational force with some sort of instrument handpiece.

Measuring the passive force of the muscle system was not difficult, but measuring the distance turned out to be a major challenge. What I needed was a rugged, nearly frictionless, sterilizable miniature linear transducer, small enough to fit into a compact surgical handpiece, and able to measure a distance of 10 millimeters (roughly half an inch) to an accuracy of 100 microns (about four-thousandths of an inch, the thickness of a sheet of typing paper). At that time, no one made anything even close, at least at a price that I could afford.

After several months of experimentation, I invented a beautifully simple optical linear transducer that did the job. To make a long story short, after I spent more than a year perfecting the transducer in the lab, a nationally-renowned ophthalmologist used the new instrument in a total of 23 surgical procedures. I got the data I needed to complete my Ph.D., and we collaborated on a number of papers for the ophthalmology research journals. The instrument itself, however, was strictly a research device, and there was no appreciable market that made it worth commercializing.

A few years later, I was at a Cornell alumni dinner and I happened to be seated next to the chairman of the board of a major aerospace company. In the course of our conversation, I told him about my optical linear transducer. He wondered if it could be scaled up so that it could be used as part of a new optically-based aircraft control system ('fly-by-light,' a proposed successor to 'fly-by-wire'). To find out, I built some larger models and found that it could easily be scaled up to accurately measure distances of several inches. (Later, I discovered how to build a version that accurately measured distances up to six feet.) He invited me to his plant to put on a demonstration of the scaled-up prototype for a group of his engineers. The transducer worked perfectly, the engineers were impressed, and later we decided that it would be worthwhile to do some research to see if the device could be commercialized.

The next step was to come up with a business arrangement for doing this research that would allow us to work together without my joining his company. I was happy with my teaching job at the Simon School and didn't want to leave, so there was never any discussion about my becoming an employee of his company. Because I had already set up a one-person corporation (me) to manufacture and market the dental instrument I described in the previous chapter, my partner and I decided to structure a strategic alliance between my tiny company and his giant corporation to carry out this research project. As a result of the financial support this alliance provided, I was able to hire four outstanding professional people to work in my company to carry out our part of the project.

Because I had read Rosabeth Kanter's book, my corporate partner and I decided to follow her set of requirements for establishing a successful strategic alliance:

- The relationship was *important* to both companies. It was obviously a wonderful opportunity for my tiny firm, and it was important enough to my large partner that the chairman of the board agreed to attend weekly engineering meetings between the two companies. And despite the pressures of running a major corporation, he kept his word and for the year that this alliance was active, he showed up for every meeting, as did I.

- There was continuing *interdependence* between the two partners. My little company needed the financial support and mechanical engineering expertise of my large partner, and they were looking to us to improve the optical characteristics of the device, pursue various patent opportunities, and do marketing research on possible non-aerospace applications for the new technology.

- We developed a draft *agreement* that reserved all medical applications for my company, while granting industrial and aerospace applications to my partner. The framework for patent licensing fees to be paid to my company was also outlined.

- To ensure maximum *information* flows between the two companies, we agreed that the teams from both companies would meet every Friday morning to review progress and set goals for the next week.

- Finally, to build trust, we always tried to have an *informal* lunch together following each Friday meeting, where we talked about anything and everything.

After more than a year of progress toward our goal, intense financial pressures from a major downturn in the aerospace business eventually forced my corporate partner to abandon this strategic research alliance. We also ran into a stubborn technical problem—electrical drift over extreme temperature ranges—that seemed to indicate that this transducer probably would not be suitable over the very wide range of temperatures encountered in aerospace applications. While, as often happens in research, we stopped short of producing a commercial product, we both look back on this alliance as a very worthwhile and enjoyable experience.

Personal strategic alliances do not necessarily have to be between companies. They can also be between individuals. For example, my thesis work involved a personal strategic alliance with a world-class eye surgeon who was at the time the chairman of the department of ophthalmology of a major medical center. Again, this alliance followed Kanter's guidelines:

- It was *important* to both parties. For me, it was the route to earning my Ph.D. For him, it was the opportunity to engage in and publish articles on the use of a state-of-the-art electronic instrument for measuring the status of the eye muscles during surgery.

- There was *interdependence* between the parties. I was dependent on his comprehensive knowledge of the anatomy of the eye and his ability as a surgeon to use the new instrument in a clinical setting, and he was dependent on my engineering ability to create and operate the new instrument.

- There was no formal written *agreement* in this case, but we did have the discipline of collaborating on research articles to keep our roles and responsibilities in clear focus. The rewards were also clear cut: I would earn my doctorate, and my colleague would have the opportunity to publish articles and give papers at professional conferences on our research.

- Because we worked so closely together, particularly during the clinical trials of the instrument in the operating room, there were more than sufficient opportunities for full and open *information* flows between us.

- Over a period of several years, my colleague and I had many *informal* conversations and we still keep in touch. Not long ago I constructed a simple new surgical instrument for him, and I expect that in the near future it will be the subject of one of his research articles.

THE BOTTOM LINE

With the decline of hierarchy and of formal organizational structures in general, people who get things done in companies will be skilled at building personal strategic alliances with peers and colleagues both within and outside their own firm. Developing and nurturing these strategic alliances is one of your major responsibilities as CEO of your "company of one," and the payoffs can be extraordinary. The addition of People Skills to the organization chart of your "company of one" (Figure 8.1) recognizes the critical importance of developing skills for working with people.

FURTHER READING

Most of the existing literature on the design of organizations comes from the organizational behavior tradition of applied psychology. But many of the critical issues in organizational design can also be analyzed in terms of microeconomic concepts.

The choices in organizational design are complex and there are many tradeoffs to be considered. A new book, *Organizational*

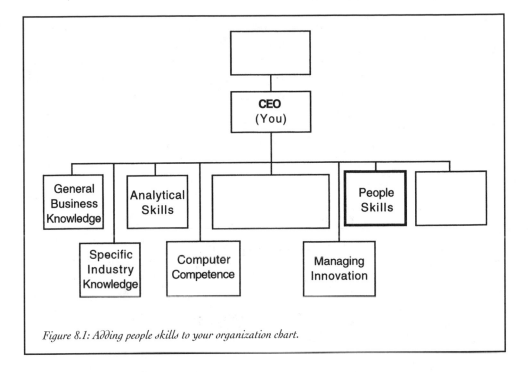

Figure 8.1: Adding people skills to your organization chart.

Architecture: A Managerial Economics Approach, presents an innovative microeconomic framework showing how these tradeoffs can be considered in the context of three broad areas of organizational design:

- The allocation of decision rights.

- The performance evaluation system for individuals and organizational units.

- The method of rewarding individuals.

I recommend *Organizational Architecture* for anyone looking for a fresh, lucid, and cohesive economic analysis of the various facets of organizational design.[33]

1   Kotter, J., "What Leaders Really Do," *Harvard Business Review*, May-June 1990, pp. 103 - 111.

2   Ibid. p. 109.

3   Tichy, N., and Sherman, S., *Control Your Destiny or Someone Else Will*, HarperBusiness, 1994, pp. 60 - 61.

4   Wrapp. E., "Good Managers Don't Make Policy Decisions," *Harvard Business Review*, July-August 1984, pp. 4 - 11.

5   Packard, D., *The HP Way*, HarperBusiness, 1995, p. 155.

6   Tichy and Sherman, p. 98.

7   Packard, pp. 69 - 70.

8   Tichy and Sherman, pp. 103 - 104.

9   Ibid. p. 16.

10   Senge, P., *The Fifth Discipline*, Doubleday Currency, 1990, p. 341, emphasis added.

11   Morris, B., "The Wealth Builders," *Fortune*, December 11, 1995, p. 83.

12   Hadjian, A., "Follow the Leader," *Fortune*, November 27, 1995, p. 96.

13   "George Fisher's Vision for Kodak," *Rochester Business Journal*, May 27, 1994, pp. 6 - 7.

14   Tichy and Sherman, p. 136.

15   Tichy, N. and DeRose, C., "Roger Enrico's Master Class," *Fortune*, November 27, 1995, pp. 105 - 106.

16   Tichy and Sherman, pp. 179 - 180.

17   Packard, pp. 149 - 150.

18   Linden, D. and Upbin, B., "Boy Scouts on a Rampage," *Forbes*, January 1, 1996, pp. 67, 70.

19   Kiechel, W., "A Manager's Career in the New Economy," *Fortune*, April 4, 1994, p. 69.

20 Byrne, J., "The Virtual Corporation," *Business Week*, February 8, 1993, pp. 98 - 103.

21 Lancaster, H., "Managing Your Career," *The Wall Street Journal*, December 12, 1995, p. B1.

22 Huey, J., "How McKinsey Does It," *Fortune*, November 1, 1993, p. 56.

23 Ibid.

24 Stewart, T., "The Search for the Organization of Tomorrow," *Fortune*, May 18, 1992, pp. 93 - 98.

25 Markels, A., "To MBA Candidates, the Top Course Today is to Land a Job," *The Wall Street Journal*, December 5, 1995, p. A1.

26 Senge, pp. 235 - 236.

27 Katzenbach, J. and Smith, D., "The Discipline of Teams," *Harvard Business Review*, March-April 1993, pp. 111 - 120.

28 Katzenbach, J. and Smith, D., "The Wisdom of Teams," *Harvard Business School Press*, 1993, pp. 119 - 127.

29 Schoonmaker, A., "What Price Career Myopia," *MBA Magazine*, April 1968.

30 Byrne, p. 100.

31 Kanter, R., *When Giants Learn to Dance*, Touchstone, 1989, p. 172.

32 Ibid. p. 173.

33 Brickley, J., Smith, C., and Zimmerman, J., *Organizational Design: A Managerial Economics Approach*, Richard D. Irwin, Inc., 1996.

POLISHING YOUR PERSONAL CORE COMPETENCIES

'Joan,' who has a mechanical engineering degree and an MBA in Marketing, is a product manager for a small medical devices manufacturer. Today, she begins work at 7 a.m. in the operating room of a major teaching hospital, where Dr. Henry Metz, Chairman of the Department of Ophthalmology, is about to operate on a three-year-old boy with crossed eyes, a clinical condition known as strabismus. One of the new products that Joan hopes to bring to market in the next year is an electronic instrument that will assist surgeons in measuring the alignment of the eyes before and during the operation, to help bring the eyes into perfect alignment.

This is the fourteenth operation that Joan has observed where a prototype of the new instrument has been used. Clothed in a sterile gown with mask in place, she looks like another member of the medical team as she stands directly behind the surgeon, softly speaking into a miniature tape recorder. The operation begins, and from time to time, Dr. Metz offers a suggestion about how the prototype instrument could be improved.

By 8:30 the operation is over and Joan is in her street clothes and on her way back to the plant for a 9:00 a.m. meeting with Manufacturing to review sterilization procedures for a new disposable medical product that will go into pilot production in about a month. At 10:30, she breaks for another meeting, this time with one of the company's financial analysts to study the financial impact of a number of alternative pricing plans for the new disposable. At noon, she walks over to the Sales Department for a quick lunch with one of the company's salesmen who has heard some rumors about a new product that a major competitor is about to introduce.

Joan admits the job is hectic, but she loves it. As a product manager, she is accountable for the success of a major line of surgical products. This means identifying new market opportunities, assessing the competition, working with R&D on perfecting the right technologies for the product, and developing a marketing plan that includes product specifications, sales forecasts, pricing plans, promotional strategies, and distribution options. "No other job in the company below the level of the CEO has such a broad scope of responsibilities," says Joan. "Next week, I'll be in London to attend a medical conference."

WHAT ARE 'CORE COMPETENCIES'?

Joan is flourishing in her demanding job because she possesses the right mix of core competencies for the responsibilities she carries. Core competencies are the things you do for the company that clearly set you apart from others—skills that make you special and potentially valuable to your employer.

In Joan's case, her core competencies are her knowledge of biomedical engineering, which she acquired by taking electives in this area while pursuing her undergraduate degree; her marketing skills, which came mainly from her MBA courses; her knowledge of production processes (she worked for two years in manufacturing before returning to school to pursue her MBA), and—most important—her comprehensive in-depth clinical knowledge of the field of ophthalmology and the kind of new instrumentation that eye surgeons are looking for to treat disorders such as strabismus.

Joan has developed an excellent working relationship with Dr. Metz, a world-class ophthalmologist, who serves as her mentor. In the past two years, she has appeared as a co-author with Dr. Metz of three clinical papers that were presented at international conferences on ophthalmology. By leveraging her core competencies, Joan is rapidly building her reputation nationally and internationally as an expert in her field. And because ophthalmic instrumentation is a major product line for her company, Joan's value to the firm is skyrocketing. Her investment in building these skills has turbocharged her career.

CORE COMPETENCIES AS THE CORNERSTONE OF CORPORATE AND PERSONAL STRATEGY

To better understand how to apply the concept of core competencies to your "company of one," let's turn to the field of corporate strategy, where the concept was first introduced. Two of the most influential papers to appear on the subject of corporate strategic planning in recent years are Hamel and Prahalad's pair of articles, "Strategic Intent"[1] and "The Core Competence of the Corporation."[2] In these landmark papers, the authors develop the argument that the most successful companies are not those that seek market niches, but those that leverage their core competencies.

How often we hear companies and individuals talk about defending their market niches. Yet Hamel and Prahalad argue that this is the wrong way to think about the problem of competition. Focusing on niches is limiting. It implies finding and defending a little hole in the market that no one else wants, and it argues against challenging an entrenched competitor. Leveraging core competencies, on the other hand, involves becoming so good at some production process that you can dominate your market and sometimes even change the rules of the competitive game to your advantage.

An example of a company's core competency is 3M's ability to coat substances on various kinds of substrates. Although 3M has an extremely broad product line, almost all of its major products involve coatings on substrates. The company's first product was sandpaper (abrasive coatings on paper and cloth). Today, 3M makes magnetic tape, Post-It® Notes, reflective highway signs, masking tape, Scotch® tape, computer diskettes, and photographic film, to list a few of their major product lines, and they all involve coatings on substrates. 3M has leveraged its core competency across a wide variety of products to serve a broadly diversified world market.

Similarly, Honda Motors has leveraged its core competency in gasoline engine technology to enter a wide variety of markets. Beginning with motorcycle engines, Honda expanded into automobiles, outboard motors, portable generators, and lawnmowers, each powered by the most reliable gasoline engines on the market.

CHANGING THE RULES OF THE GAME—TO YOUR ADVANTAGE

Leveraging a core competency can sometimes be such a successful strategy that it changes the rules of the game, even against a large and well-entrenched competitor. An example is Canon's entry into the office copier market. In the 1970s, Xerox dominated the copier business, successfully fighting off competitive challenges from two other giants, Kodak and IBM. But it was Canon, a relatively small Japanese camera company, that revolutionized the copier business. In just six years, from 1976 to 1982, Xerox's share of installed copiers in the U.S. dropped from 80% of the market to 13%, mainly because of inroads by Canon and a few other small Japanese companies.[3]

How did Canon manage to lead this revolution? First, it realized that it could not hope to compete with Xerox head-on. The powerful Xerox marketing organization had built a monolithic fortress around the copier market that looked like a solid brick wall to a tiny potential competitor like Canon. But part way up the wall was a loose brick. And once Canon found the loose brick, it was able to quietly pry out one brick after another until suddenly Canon was inside the copier market, where it swiftly became a formidable competitor.

XEROX'S LOOSE BRICK

Strangely enough, Xerox's loose brick was caused by one of the company's greatest assets, its massive sales and service organization. Xerox had a huge direct sales and service force that was primarily interested in leasing large, high-volume machines. But direct sales calls are expensive, and the Xerox sales force could not afford to bother with small, low-revenue machines—

and this was the loose brick in Xerox's marketing program. So Canon set out to develop a small, low-volume machine that it could sell, not lease, and that it would distribute through office supply dealers rather than selling directly. Such a machine would have to be very reliable, because dealers would not be interested in selling a line of copiers that were constantly breaking down in the field.

The core competency of Canon was its ability to engineer outstanding reliability and serviceability into its small machine. Its breakthrough innovation was the development of a compact, low-cost, replaceable toner cartridge assembly for its small copiers that even an untrained secretary could replace in seconds. Most of the parts of a copier that tend to fail in the field were inside the cartridge, and at the first sign of trouble, the entire cartridge was replaced by a secretary, and the little machine was as good as new. No dealer service call was required.

It was a brilliant strategy. Locked into its own high-cost, high-volume copier strategy, Xerox was unable to respond. Xerox's historical comparative advantages provided by its massive direct sales and service force were suddenly irrelevant in this segment of the market. Canon had changed the rules of the game to its favor, and its market share took off.

But the story gets better. Canon's core competency for manufacturing high-quality replaceable toner cartridges came on line just as Hewlett-Packard was developing its new low-cost laser printer for the personal computer market (high volume laser printers had already been developed, but were the size of a refrigerator and cost upwards of $100,000.)[4] Working with Canon, HP quickly adopted the replaceable toner cartridge for its line of laser printers, and a second huge market for the toner cartridges was launched. Like 3M and Honda, Canon was able to leverage its core competency across multiple markets.

Prahalad and Hamel refer to core competencies as "the collective learning of an organization."[5] They go on to say that unlike physical assets, which deteriorate over time, core competencies can be enhanced and polished through use. Whether it is learning to coat a new material on a substrate or learning how to run a new spreadsheet program on a computer, core competencies improve with use.

DEFINING CHARACTERISTICS OF CORE COMPETENCIES

Prahalad and Hamel show that there are three defining characteristics of core competencies:[6]

1. <u>Core competencies are applicable across a variety of markets and product applications</u>. Certainly this was true in the examples of 3M, Honda, and Canon. The Canon replaceable toner cartridge revolutionized two huge markets, small copiers and laser printers.

2. <u>Core competencies make a significant contribution to the perceived customer benefits of the end product</u>. Clearly, this was the case with Canon's replaceable toner cartridge, which made small copiers much more reliable and thus much more attractive to customers.

3. <u>Core competencies are difficult for competitors to imitate</u>. Because Canon was able to protect its intellectual property through a set of patents on the replaceable toner cartridge, other companies could not use the technology without paying royalties, and Canon made money through patent licensing fees even on the millions of cartridges eventually manufactured by other firms.

YOUR PERSONAL CORE COMPETENCIES

Throughout this book we have been searching for ways to turbocharge your career by applying the most powerful concepts in corporate strategy to your "company of one." Your personal core competencies are the heart of your "company of one," which is why they are shown in the center of the organization chart we have been developing (see Figure 9.1). Think of them as providing high-octane fuel for your personal revenue engine. Your core competencies give you a competitive edge, and it is this that sets you apart from others in today's uncertain job market. And because your core competencies are going to be the focus of your career, they have to involve doing something you truly enjoy.

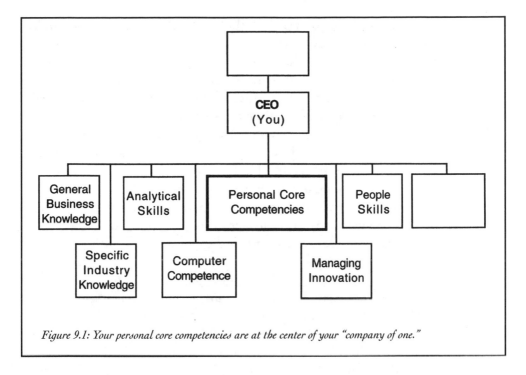

Figure 9.1: Your personal core competencies are at the center of your "company of one."

To develop these core competencies, you will have to invest time and money. Consider this as R&D for your "company of one." In the remainder of this chapter, we will look at some examples of how others have created their personal core competencies and we will show you how to avoid the strategic pitfalls that can occur in selecting your personal core competencies. Finally, we will conclude with a checklist to help you choose and master the personal core competencies that will fuel the revenue engine for your "company of one."

Example 1: Personal core competencies in finance. 'Steven' is 28 and works on Wall Street in sales and trading for an investment bank. He earned his bachelor's degree in computer engineering in 1987, worked for a year as a software engineer at a salary of $30,000, and quit to pursue his MBA full time, which he received in 1990. His first post-MBA job was as a financial associate for a bank, at $55,000 a year. After two years he left to take his current job, where he now earns $100,000 a year. He puts in long hours at the office, typically 60 hours a week, but seldom brings work home.

Although he appreciates the value of what he learned in his MBA courses, Steven feels that the help he has received from senior managers who have served as his mentors has been more valuable. He gives his business school high marks, though, for its ability to open doors of potential employers on Wall Street.

Steven began his career as a software engineer, but he is glad that he made the switch to Finance. The change turbo-charged his career and he now earns three times what he made as an engineer. He credits his business school with developing his core competencies in the understanding of basic finance and accounting theory, and in making professional-quality presentations to customers. His advice to other young managers is to start early and work hard at building a network with peers and prospective employers.

Example 2: Personal core competencies in technical sales. 'Sam,' age 43, earns $250,000 a year. He has a bachelor's degree in electrical engineering but no advanced degrees, and at this point in his life he sees no reason to consider getting either an MS or an MBA degree. Since graduating in 1979, Sam has worked in the field of motion control systems (electronically controlled motors for industrial machinery). His first job was as an applications engineer for Allen-Bradley, the largest and most successful company in the motion control field. Ten years ago, he left Allen-Bradley with two other engineers to start a new independent manufacturers representatives organization. His territory is the Greater Detroit area, and almost all of his customers are in the automotive industry.

Over the years, Sam has invested thousands of hours getting to know the problems his automotive customers face in applying motor control systems in their production equipment. His expertise has become so highly respected that he is frequently called in as a technical consultant by automotive company manufacturing engineers when they are first laying out the design of a new production line. Sam helps the engineers design their new production equipment, and not surprisingly, the purchasing specifications for the motor control systems for the new equipment are often met by the motor control systems that he sells. But in those cases where the equipment he represents doesn't fit the application, Sam helps the engineers find the appropriate equipment from one of his competitors.

Sam's personal core competencies are his comprehensive knowledge of the needs of his automotive company customers and his technical knowledge of how the products he represents can meet these needs. He is exceptionally good at his job, which is why he earns $250,000 a year.

Example 3: Personal core competencies in business communications. 'Carol,' age 35, is Director of Marketing Communications for a very large software company, where she is paid $80,000 a year. She has ten people working for her and puts in long hours at the office, typically working 70 hours a week.

Carol received her undergraduate degree in liberal arts in 1981 and worked for five years as a salesperson for a brokerage firm, earning $20,000 a year, before deciding to pursue an MBA degree full time. After earning her MBA in 1988, she joined a consulting firm at a starting salary of $45,000. She believes that the MBA experience rounded out her general business knowledge, increased her self-confidence, and significantly expanded her earning power, and she feels that her internship experience between the first and second year of the MBA program was invaluable.

She advises young managers to start with a prestigious large company and learn as much as they can, but she is skeptical of the value of the current corporate emphasis on cross-functional training.

Carol's personal core competencies are her professional writing skills and her ability to organize and manage a group of professional people. She credits both her business school education and her mentors with helping her develop her Strategic Skills in teamwork and leadership.

SEARCHING FOR A LOOSE BRICK

As we learned earlier, Canon was able to gain entry into the copier business because Xerox's massive direct sales and service organization could not economically serve the low end of the copier business. This weakness in Xerox's marketing program was the "loose brick" that allowed Canon to enter and eventually dominate the low end of the market.

If you are going to put time and money into the development of personal core competencies, you need to find a loose brick in your company or industry that will allow you to develop personal core competencies that will provide customer value and at the same time be difficult for others to copy. What could you offer that would be very valuable to your employer (which, after all, is the customer of your "company of one"), that would be fun for you to do, and that is not being done very well by anyone else?

As Hamel and Prahalad point out, "The search for loose bricks begins with a careful analysis of the competitor's conventional wisdom."[7] For example, Joan, the product manager for the medical instrument company whom we met at the beginning of this chapter, knew that her most important competitor's traditional strategy was to concentrate on manufacturing complex hardware, in the form of sophisticated electronic instruments. In talking with customers, Joan learned that hospitals often had trouble with the wire leads that attached these instruments to the patient. The leads had to be sterilized before each use, and the sterilization process often caused the wires to break inside the insulation, so that the leads would fail in use. The competitor's response was to introduce heavier wire, which was less flexible and still subject to breakage.

Although her own company had never before offered disposable products, Joan saw this customer problem—the loose brick in her competitor's product line—as an opportunity to add plug-compatible pre-sterilized disposable leads to her own firm's catalog. The disposable leads were introduced and became a big hit with the hospitals—and Joan became the company expert on disposable medical products. Identification of the competitor's loose brick led to the development of a profitable new line of business for her company, and a valuable new personal core competency for Joan.

Sometimes the 'competition' is not another firm, but is another professional person in your own company who is also seeking to get ahead. In cases like this, you should start out by recognizing that competition with others in your company is not necessarily a 'zero-sum game' ("if I win, you lose, and vice versa"). Instead, look for win/win options, where you both can come out ahead.[8]

Friendly competition among the professional staff within the company need not be destructive and can add zest to the job. Members of a company's sales force frequently compete, often for recognition ("first in the Northeast Territory") or for trips and other prizes. Such competition is healthy and the company benefits two ways: first, because the sales force will be more productive, given reasonable incentives; and second, because the company will attract more aggressive sales people, who prefer to work for a place where extra effort is rewarded.

In a situation where the competition is internal rather than with another firm, it still pays to look for the loose brick. Suppose, for example, your company sells financial services such as insurance. In this case, the loose brick might be a small but lucrative segment of the market that no one else has pursued, and where you can become the company expert. Consider the success story on the right.

Finding the Loose Brick

'Michael,' who has an undergraduate degree in accounting, has sold personal health and accident insurance for 20 years. Recently, his state passed a cost-sharing law that would make longterm health care insurance for senior citizens more affordable. But the new law is very complex with many restrictions, and is very confusing to senior citizens. Most insurance salespeople have decided that trying to sell in this new market is more trouble than it is worth. But Michael has studied the new law and has come up with a way to greatly simplify the explanation by means of a computer-generated color graphics presentation. So Michael has found a loose brick—the complexity of the law and the confusion it generates among prospective senior citizen customers. And he has created a valuable personal core competency—his understanding of the new law, as captured by his computerized presentation—that gives him a big competitive edge over the other salespeople he competes against.

BE CAREFUL ABOUT BEING 'HOLLOWED OUT'

One of the defining characteristics of corporate core competencies is that they are difficult to copy. Yet because personal core competencies are intellectual property rather than physical assets, they are fair game to be copied, particularly when your peers realize how valuable they have made you in the organization.

In corporate strategy, the term 'hollowing out' means the company learns everything it can from a partner, and then, when there is nothing more to learn, it dumps the partner and uses the information it learned as if it were its own. Not a nice thing to do, and certainly questionable ethics.

An example from the corporate world of hollowing out occurred a number of years ago when a certain overseas supplier of industrial equipment was trying to gain a foothold in the competitive U.S. market. As an unknown supplier without sales representation in the U.S., the overseas company made little progress in building sales until it formed a marketing partnership with a well-known U.S. manufacturer of complementary products. For several years, the two companies worked harmoniously together, during which time the overseas supplier made a determined effort to learn everything it could about the U.S. market—key customers, distribution channels, U.S. marketing practices. It also developed recognition for its brand name among U.S. industrial purchasing agents.

In the meantime, the overseas company set up its own R&D program to secretly develop a line of new products that would compete with its U.S. partner. Then one day, without prior warning, the overseas supplier announced that the partnership was over, and shortly thereafter it introduced its secretly-developed product line in direct competition with its former partner. Thanks to the education it received from its U.S. partner, the overseas company's new product line took over a sizeable share of the market, causing a substantial drop in the sales of its former U.S. partner. Like a Halloween pumpkin, the U.S. company had been 'hollowed out.' A similar thing can happen to individuals, as the story on the following page illustrates.

Most of your colleagues in your firm are trustworthy and would never engage in such behavior. But with the spread of modern information technology, intellectual property and other sensitive information can travel faster and farther than ever before, and you would be wise to be cautious in sharing everything you know in the areas of your core competencies. Remember that you are the CEO of your "company of one" and it is a competitive world out there. Intellectual property can be at least as valuable as physical assets and is deserving of your protection.

The most effective way to protect your investment in your core competencies from being hollowed out is through continual 'R&D' in your field of expertise to enhance your skills and maintain your competitive edge. You should constantly look for ways to upgrade and polish your core competencies to make them as valuable as possible to your "company of one's" customer, your employer. In this way, if someone is successful in copying your intellectual property, you will already be developing improvements to your personal core competency, and what they have taken from you will soon be obsolete.

Hollowed Out by a 'Friend'

After months of study and analysis, 'Richard,' who has a bachelor's degree in math, perfected a computer program that made highly reliable forecasts of his company's future sales. Management was enthusiastic about the accuracy of the forecasts, and in a short time he became the company guru on sales forecasting. This became his core competency in the firm. One day a 'friend' asked to make a copy of Richard's software, and soon people all over the company were using his forecasting program, usually with poor results because they did not understand the assumptions. His reputation suffered and management no longer called on him. Richard was 'hollowed out.'

MAKE SURE YOUR CORE COMPETENCIES ARE PORTABLE

Core competencies should be applicable across a range of product applications, according to the defining characteristics of core competencies formulated by Hamel and Prahalad. In developing your core competencies, you should guard against the danger of investing in critical skills that are of value to only one employer. With only a single buyer for your skills, the company can exert the power of a monopsonist to dictate terms and prices. (It's like being a defense contractor doing business with the government).

'Sara,' who has a bachelor's degree in economics, has developed a one-person independent consulting business in which she collects and summarizes global sales trends for the world's largest manufacturer of computer desks for home offices and small businesses. This manufacturer, which has a market share of around 70%, does not have its own marketing research department, having been very satisfied with outsourcing this work to Sara for many years.

Over the years, Sara has developed hundreds of useful sources in the office equipment retailing industry who are willing to provide her with the information she needs to produce her statistics and trends.

A few months ago, the computer desk manufacturer was acquired by a major office furniture corporation, and Sara was informed that beginning next year, the corporation's internal marketing research department will take over the work that she has been doing.

Sara is in a difficult position. She has always provided her one customer with valuable information and excellent service, and until recently she thought that she was set for life. But her expertise and her contacts are entirely in the area of equipment for home offices and small businesses, and she has developed no reputation beyond her single customer. Most office equipment manufacturers are now associated with large corporations that have their own in-house marketing research functions, and it will be difficult for Sara to find another manufacturer in her industry that will be interested in what she has to offer. There is a good chance that her tiny consulting company will go out of business.

Although Sara did a fine job of developing personal core competencies as a marketing analyst in the office equipment industry, she made the mistake of working with only one customer. Unfortunately, her core competencies are not portable.

BE ALERT TO SIGNS OF OBSOLESCENCE

'Paul' is an expert in the field of photographic emulsions, the light-sensitive coatings that capture the images in photographic film. With several patents and a string of technical papers to his credit, he is an acknowledged expert in his field. A chemical engineer, Paul has invested more than 20 years in successfully refining and polishing his core competency in developing new photographic emulsion technology.

But today Paul faces a problem. Conventional photography is gradually being overtaken by electronic photography; for example, home movie cameras that use photographic film have been replaced by home video cameras that use magnetic tape to store images. Experts such as Paul who have devoted their entire professional careers to conventional photography are seeing the investment in their core competency lose value, and as the conventional photographic business downsizes, some of these experts have lost their jobs as well. New technology is making their core competencies obsolete.

Obsolescence can also occur as the result of market shifts. In retailing, for example, during the decade of the 1980s, discounters such as K-Mart and Wal-Mart gained market share at the expense of traditional department stores. Consumer goods marketing managers who lived in the past and did not develop personal expertise in the special logistical and billing needs of the major discounters were soon left behind.

As CEO of your "company of one," it is your responsibility to make sure that this doesn't happen to you. New technology and shifts in the market do not change an industry overnight. It usually takes years and sometimes decades for the transition to take place. For those who keep up with their field, there is plenty of warning. But you have to be willing to act on it. Unfortunately, for most people the problem is more likely to be one of denial than a lack of information.

If Paul had faced up earlier to the gradual leveling off of the photographic industry, he might have leveraged his chemical engineering background and his comprehensive knowledge of image quality standards into a leading technical position in the emerging electronic imaging field of inkjet printing. Perhaps it is still not too late.

ARE YOU BEING DISLOYAL TO YOUR EMPLOYER?

By developing your own personal core competencies, are you being disloyal to your employer? Not at all. In fact, the kind of investments in personal core competencies we have been discussing will make you much more valuable to your company, and your employer will share in the benefits from your initiatives.

Furthermore, as we noted earlier, in today's environment, companies are unable to make lifetime commitments to employees. Your boss will be relieved and impressed to learn that you have taken charge of your own career and are not waiting around for him to do something.

Investing in your personal core competencies will provide synergistic benefits to you and your employer, and you will both be the winners.

CHOOSE SOMETHING YOU REALLY ENJOY

Finally—and this is most important—as you narrow your choices in selecting the area for your personal core competencies, look for an area you really enjoy, something that you would like to be able to do, whether you got paid or not.[9]

What you are really looking for is not just a job, but a vocation (literally, a calling). Let me share with you some thoughts about the difference between a job and a vocation, as expressed by Dr. Thomas J. Price, Jr.:[10]

> *A job is something you have or get . . . a vocation is something you respond to.*
>
> *A job is something you decide on . . . a vocation is something that decides on you.*
>
> *A job is something you choose . . . a vocation is something that chooses you.*
>
> *A job is something you do in order to do something else . . . a vocation is something you do for its own sake.*
>
> *A job is a means . . . a vocation is an end to itself.*
>
> *A job is something you go into for what you can get out of it . . . a vocation is something you go into because you can't help it.*
>
> *A job is a responsibility . . . a vocation is a compulsion.*
>
> *A job is an obligation . . . a vocation is a drive.*
>
> *A job is something that when you get enough of it, you quit, or find a new one . . . a vocation is something you can't*

leave, because something bigger than you compels you to stay, and see it through.

A job gives payment . . . a vocation gives satisfaction.

A job gives remuneration . . . a vocation provides fulfillment.

A job offers security . . . a vocation offers risk.

A job is something you do . . . a vocation is something you are.

Choosing your area of personal core competencies and developing the necessary skills may take years. It may involve changing jobs or investing in further education. But as you have seen by the examples of the people in this chapter—some who started out perhaps very much like you—you can turbocharge your career with these new skills, and ultimately transform your life. You *can* do it!

A CHECKLIST FOR CHOOSING THE AREA OF YOUR PERSONAL CORE COMPETENCIES

- ☐ Is the area you are considering merely a job or will it become a vocation for you, as defined above? Explain why this will be a true vocation for you rather than just another job.

- ☐ Have you identified a "loose brick" in the area, that will provide you with an opening for creating real value from developing your core competencies?

- ☐ Will these core competencies be applicable across more than one market? List some of these markets.

- ☐ Will these core competencies provide real benefits to your customers? How will your employer be better off because of your investment in these core competencies?

- ☐ Will these core competencies be difficult for others to copy?

☐ Are these core competencies portable from one employer to another? List a few other employers who would find them to be of value.

☐ Are these core competencies likely to quickly become obsolete from new technology? What are the emerging technologies that could make your newly-acquired skills obsolete? Are you prepared to continue to invest in personal 'R&D' in order to stay ahead in your chosen area of expertise?

☐ Are these core competencies vulnerable to quick shifts in the market?

☐ Do you believe that with hard work and dedication, you have the ability to master the skills to develop these core competencies? Could you become the best in your company? Could you become one of the best, nationally or internationally, in your chosen field? It's a goal worth striving for.

....

1   Hamel, G. and Prahalad, C.K., "Strategic Intent," *Harvard Business Review*, May-June 1989, pp. 63-79.

2   Prahalad, C.K. and Hamel, G., "The Core Competence of the Corporation," *Harvard Business Review*, May-June 1990, pp. 79-91.

3   Kearns, D. and Nadler, D., *Prophets in the Dark*, HarperBusiness, 1992, p. 135.

4   Packard, D., *The HP Way*, HarperBusiness, 1995, p. 114.

5   "The Core Competence of the Corporation," p. 82.

6   Ibid. pp. 83-84.

7   "Strategic Intent," p. 70.

8   For more on developing win/win options, see *Getting to Yes*, by Roger Fisher, William Ury, and Bruce Patton (Penguin Books) and *The 7 Habits of Highly Effective People*, by Steven Covey (Fireside), particularly the chapter on "Principles of Interpersonal Leadership."

9   Richard Nelson Bolles' perennial bestseller, *What Color is Your Parachute?* (Ten Speed Press), offers a number of useful approaches for picking your favorite area, under the heading, "What Skills do You Most Enjoy Using?"

10   From a sermon at the First United Methodist Church of Winter Park, Florida, on January 8, 1995.

10 LEARNING TO MARKET YOUR STRATEGIC SKILLS

'**M**atthew,' age 36, has just been promoted to Manager of Small Business Lending for a large bank in Cleveland and expects to make $96,000 this year, nearly four times what he was making when he began his MBA studies in 1990. Matthew was awarded his bachelor's degree in Economics in 1980 and worked for 10 years as president of his own business, a chain of three gift shops, earning about $25,000 a year. At the time, he says, "I was pigeonholed as being only capable of retail sales."

In 1990, with the support of a merit scholarship that paid 50% of his tuition, he enrolled in a full-time MBA program, concentrating in Finance and Marketing. After graduating with his MBA in 1992, he accepted a position as a loan officer at a commercial bank at $46,000 a year.

Matthew rates his level of job satisfaction as a '5' on a 1-to-5 scale, and his long-term job objective is to get promoted to top management at his bank. He gives much of the credit for his recent success to senior managers who served as his mentors at the bank, and also to the corporate management training programs he has attended since completing his MBA. His advice to aspiring managers: 1) Learn how to sell and promote yourself, 2) Learn how to network, and 3) Learn how to manage your own career, because no one else will.

Learning how to sell and promote yourself is what this chapter is all about. To get the most value from your investment in your personal core competencies, people have to be made aware of them. The premise that you will get promoted if you just do a good job is, unfortunately, naive. As noted in Chapter 2, only 22% of our survey respondents agreed with the statement, "If you do excellent work, you can trust your company to promote you." As CEO of your "company of one," you must learn to market your Strategic Skills within your organization and on the outside, among those in your professional field.

☞ THE "4P'S" OF MARKETING

Marketing your "company of one" is more than just selling yourself. Marketing, broadly defined, is a strategic function involving several key management areas in addition to selling. In marketing courses, it is traditional to introduce the topic of marketing strategy by talking about the "4P's" of marketing: Product, Place, Price, and Promotion. Every decision that a marketing manager makes can be thought about in the context of these four variables:

- *Product* is what you have to sell. For some companies, 'product' is a line of automobiles or computers, for others it is a service such as medical treatment or telecommunications. For your "company of one," your product is the personal expertise and professional service that you can supply your employer. Most of what we have talked about so far in this book has been about how to improve and enhance your product, by acquiring more knowledge about your industry, by improving your computer skills, and by investing in the development of your personal core competencies. But merely having a good product— even an outstanding product—is not enough in today's highly competitive workplace.

- *Place* is the marketing variable that describes the channel through which your product or service is delivered to customers. For an automobile manufacturer, 'place' is its group of franchised car dealerships. In medicine, 'place' is the doctor's office or the hospital. Some companies, such as the local telephone company, sell their product directly to customers. For your "company of one," 'place' is generally an office at your employer's plant or office complex, although 7% of our survey respondents reported spending most of their time working in the offices and plants of their clients or customers, and another 7% work primarily out of their home offices. Unless you plan to start your own company, 'place' for your "company of one" is pretty much dictated by your employer and usually is not a critical variable in the development of a marketing strategy for your "company of one."

- *Price* is what customers are willing to pay for the product. In economic markets, various customers are often willing to pay different amounts for a product or service, depending on the value that product has to *them*. For example, in the economy section of a flight from New York to Los Angeles, a business person on a one-day trip may be sitting next to a vacationer who is willing to stay over the weekend to qualify for a lower fare. They have the same kind of seat, eat the same kind of food, and receive the same level of service from the airline, yet the business traveler may pay twice as much as the vacationer. In establishing the best pricing strategy for your professional services, you must continually monitor the market to find out how much others with your qualifications and experience are being paid. Throughout this book we have seen many individual examples of the salaries of professional men and women with various qualifications. One of the most effective ways to raise your pay, which is the *price* of your professional services in the marketplace, is to get a number of employers to bid for them. But this kind of competition for your services is much more likely to occur if you are proficient at promoting yourself and the value of what you have to offer to potential employers.

- *Promotion* is the method by which you reach out to prospective customers to inform them about what you have to offer. Most large companies depend *on paid advertising* as their primary means of promotion, while startups and small firms are more likely to depend mostly on *publicity* (also known as *public relations*, or *PR*), which can be thought of as advertising that you don't have to pay for. The remainder of this chapter will examine the use of various forms of publicity as the basis for the promotional strategy of your "company of one."

THE POWER OF PUBLICITY

Whereas large companies traditionally use paid advertising to promote their products, they also use publicity, sometimes with outstanding success. A good example was Microsoft's worldwide publicity campaign for the launch of their Windows 95 operating system in August, 1995. Augmented by millions of dollars of paid advertising, the Windows 95 publicity campaign produced extensive coverage on the major television networks and thousands of feature articles in the print media. The Microsoft PR for the launch of Windows 95 filled air time and print space that, at normal paid advertising rates, would have cost the company hundreds of millions of dollars.

I have used publicity on a number of occasions to help small companies launch new products. Several years ago, I helped one small firm get its new audio product on the front covers of the two largest audiophile magazines in the same month, as well as dozens of feature articles in various magazines and newspapers. The estimated value of the advertising space, assuming you could buy a position on the front covers of these magazines, was in excess of $100,000. The out-of-pocket cost of the publicity materials that triggered all this publicity — some photos and a PR release — came to less than $1,000.

REACHING TENS OF MILLIONS OF READERS—FREE

In another example of the power of publicity, when my first book, *The MBA Advantage*, was launched in August, 1994, *The Economist* magazine, which is published in London and has a worldwide circulation of about 550,000, printed a full-page review of my findings about the financial value of the MBA degree from various leading business schools and mentioned the article on their cover. *The Economist* article was then picked up and summarized in leading newspapers all over the world.

The estimated "reach" of the review, including all of the newspaper articles, was in the tens of millions of readers. (The advertising term "reach" refers to the number of subscribers who *could* have read the article. It doesn't mean that they actually read it.) Although I wasn't completely happy with everything that was said in the review (writers of these reviews always feel an obligation to point out any shortcomings of the book as well as the strengths), on balance it was positive, and it gave the book a wonderful introduction to the marketplace. The only cost to me was a sample copy of the book for the writer at *The Economist*.

Publicity can, of course, be negative as well as positive. Unlike paid advertising, where the sponsor controls the content, the content of a publicity article is under the control of the writer and the editor, who are obligated to their readers to present a balanced view. I was once involved in developing a PR piece about a new medical product that made the front page of the newspaper in a large city. To help the writer (and to make sure that he understood all of the medical advantages of the new product), I wrote a two-page description of the product in layman's terms. All of this appeared in the newspaper article, but to provide balance, there was also a paragraph quoting a medical practitioner who admired the product but felt it might be unnecessary in some medical practices.

The electronic media — radio and television — are more hazardous to work with than the print media. Radio talk shows can be fun, but the guest should be ready for unexpected pointed questions from the host that may border on the hostile, in an effort to generate controversy and listener response. Television is even tougher because you have to think about how you look, as well as what you are saying. Worst of all are TV news sound bytes, in which the reporter may edit out all of your half-hour interview except one 30-second remark which, taken out of context, either supports the reporter's point-of-view or is calculated to maximize controversy.

IT MUST BE NEWSWORTHY

The secret of getting good publicity is that the subject must be *newsworthy* for the target audience. Editors and writers are always on the lookout for interesting and provocative articles.

The seeker of favorable publicity must start out with a clear understanding of why this story would be of interest to the viewers of a particular program or the readers of a certain magazine or newspaper. Ask yourself, why would their viewers or readers be interested in this story?

Reporters often cover a wide variety of topics as they go from one story to another, and it is difficult for them to get up to speed with a complete understanding of their topic fast enough to make their deadline. In my experience, anything you can do to help them, such as developing a press release customized for their audience, will be appreciated. If you give them a printed piece, they are more likely to get the story straight.

A good press release is set up so that it is easy for editors to use. (Your local library has books that illustrate how to format a press release.) The secret is to lead off with an intriguing headline and an interesting opening statement—the 'hook' that gets the editor's attention. The first paragraph of the release should be complete enough to serve as a short article by itself, because this may be all the print space that is available in some publications.

THE IMPORTANCE OF CONTENT

The variable that has the most effect on the success of a promotional effort is the *content* of the ads or the publicity material.

A number of years ago I did a consulting study for a small electronics firm in the industrial motor control business to measure the effectiveness of their trade advertising campaign. The company was running two kinds of ads in a trade magazine called *Machine Design* that is read by production engineers who specify the purchase of motor control systems. The first were 'image ads' that talked about the quality of the company's products and the responsiveness of their applications engineers. The second group of ads were 'applications ads' that showed line drawings of typical engineering problems, such as feeding a web of paper through a high-speed machine and cutting it into sheets, and how the company's products could solve these engineering problems. Each ad was keyed to a number on a reader response card in the magazine ("circle the number for more information"), and we could measure the relative effectiveness of each ad by counting the number of inquiries on the reader response cards that each ad generated.

We learned many things from this study, but the most striking was that the applications ads produced *nine times* as many inquiries as the image ads per advertising dollar spent. Apparently, the production engineers who were reading *Machine Design* were much more interested in ads that offered solutions for the specific engineering problems they faced rather than generalities about the company's image. *The content of the ads had a huge impact* on the effectiveness of the company's advertising campaign to generate sales leads through reader response card inquiries.

For your "company of one," the effectiveness of your promotional campaign will depend on the content of your message. Let's turn to the world of advertising to examine some of the major categories of messages that ads carry:

- *Announcement* ads are used where the audience is waiting to find out about the availability of a new product, such as a new microprocessor chip from Intel. People know that the product is coming, and the purpose of the ad is simply to let customers know where and when they can obtain it. Such ads tend to be small, simple, and factual. They succeed because they convey news.

- *Logical argument* ads provide a reasoned set of statements about why customers should buy a product or service. They are often effective for the sale of industrial or professional products (the applications ads described in the above example would fall in this category). They tend to be long on copy, supplemented by graphics to support the claims.

- *Image* ads are often used where the advertiser has nothing factual to say about the product, but wants to paint an image to get the customer emotionally involved. Such ads contain mostly graphics with a minimum of copy. Ads for beer and cosmetics fall into this category.

- *Reminder* ads are effective for keeping the names of familiar products before the public. "Drink Coca-Cola" doesn't tell you anything new; it is simply a reminder.

Not all ads are pure examples of the above categories. For example, an ad for the introduction of a new luxury car might be a combination of an *announcement* ad and an *image* ad.

DESIGNING A PROMOTIONAL CAMPAIGN FOR YOUR "COMPANY OF ONE"

For your "company of one," you are promoting the value of your professional services and the content of your publicity campaign will be *logical argument* messages. (Later, when you are rich and famous, *reminder* messages may be sufficient.) To design your message, you need to address the following questions:

- *What is the goal of your promotional effort?* 'Jean,' age 27, works as a secretary for a large publishing firm. She joined the company five years ago after receiving her two-year associate's degree. By taking courses at night, she recently completed her bachelor's degree in communication arts, and she has taken her first four evening courses towards an MBA degree. Her long-term goal is to become an executive editor in charge of one of the company's many lines of books, and she believes that earning an MBA will help in achieving that goal. She currently works as a secretary to the production manager of her company, and her core competency is in the use of computers to reduce the time it takes to get new books to the market, an area where she has already contributed a number of important innovations.

  Although Jean has gained valuable experience in the publishing industry and has invested heavily in her education, she feels that she will always be looked upon as "just a secretary." *The goal of her promotional effort is to reposition herself as a professional with management potential.* She hopes that she will be offered the chance to advance with her current employer, but if not, she is prepared to leave.

- *Who is your target audience?* Jean has two target audiences: 1) The management of her present company, and 2) The management of other companies that might hire her if she is unsuccessful with her current employer in getting promoted.

- *What is the message you want to deliver to your target audience?* Your message should focus on describing your core competencies and Strategic Skills, and should show why they are valuable to your target audience. In Jean's case, she has developed valuable and rare Strategic Skills in the application of computers in her industry. Specifically, she has become an expert in applying computers to the management of the new product development cycle, to speed up bringing new books to the market. She wants to inform her target audiences about her mastery of these valuable skills.

- *What is the best timing for your message?* Jean estimates that by doubling up on her course load, she can complete her MBA in two years. After looking at the relatively high starting salaries of MBA graduates from her school, she has decided that it would be a mistake to pursue a new job now, particularly if it would require moving away and abandoning her MBA program. Instead, she plans to begin seriously looking around in about 18 months, so that she will be in step with her school's MBA placement program when she graduates. Job offers are typically made three or four months before graduation.

- *What will be the content of your message?* Jean knows that prospective employers look at pre-MBA work experience when making offers, and she feels that merely listing her pre-MBA experience as a secretary will not be very impressive. She feels she needs something additional. She is currently taking a course in Business Process Reengineering, in which she is required to write an original report on the application of computers and information systems technology to significantly improve a business production process.

  After talking with her instructor, she has decided to write her report on the use of computers to accelerate the process of getting new books to market, a subject she knows well. But after she gets credit for this report toward her course, she intends to rewrite the report as an article to be submitted to a major trade magazine in the publishing industry, after clearing it with her boss to make sure it contains no trade secrets. It will take about a year to get the article published, so it will appear a few months before the recruiting season starts. Having a published article to her credit will look good on her resume and may generate some interest among potential employers. She also intends to make sure that a finished draft of the article is circulated to senior managers at her own company.

- *What are the best media choices to deliver your message?* The perceived value of a published article is influenced by the prestige of the journal or periodical in which it appears. Jean knows that her boss is friends with an editor at one of the top trade magazines in the publishing industry, and she intends to ask him to introduce her to this editor so that she can discuss her proposed article with him before she rewrites her business school report. Most journals and periodicals that accept articles from outside authors are happy to provide a brief 'instructions to authors' pamphlet that describes their editorial requirements for submitted articles.

Jean also plans to volunteer to present a summary of her article at a regional conference on the use of computers in publishing, which will be attended by many of the top publishers in the industry.

She knows that one article by itself is only a start. If she intends to build her professional reputation in her field, she will be expected to attend future conferences and to write additional articles to maintain and strengthen her stature as an expert.

Will Jean's promotional campaign work? As a minimum, she will be motivated to refine and package her new skills in a way that will reveal her new core competencies both inside and outside the company. She won't be known as "just a secretary" anymore. She will graduate and perhaps receive a fine job offer from another company, beginning the career path that will lead to realizing her goal of becoming an executive editor. More likely, the management of her present company will wake up to the fact that they have a rising star on the payroll, and will give her the opportunities she deserves to move ahead.

IT TAKES TIME TO GET RESULTS

The response to an advertising or PR campaign is not instantaneous. It takes time to get going. Sales lag behind the advertising campaign — very much like the response you get when you press down on the accelerator of your car. If you press the gas pedal down about halfway and hold it there, your car takes a while to get up to speed. If you then lift your foot from the gas, your car gradually slows, taking quite a while to roll to a complete stop. The speed of your car does not respond instantly to commands from the gas pedal; instead, it lags behind because of the inertia of the car.

The response to advertising and PR works the same way. Suppose you own a small grocery store and you have not been doing any advertising. Then in Week 1, you start advertising at the rate of $1,000 a week (see the upper curve in Figure 10.1 on the next page). If you were to do telephone surveys of the customers in your area, you would find that the percentage of those who recall seeing your ad gets off to a fast start (lower curve) and continues to accelerate as long as you continue to run the ads, eventually getting up to, say, 60%. (In advertising research, we often measure "percent recall" instead of trying to measure the actual sales generated by an ad campaign, because sales are affected by many other variables besides advertising. Percent recall would be measured by calling prospective customers and asking them whether they remember seeing an ad for your store in yesterday's paper, and if so, what it said. Recall may be either 'aided,' where the caller prompts the customer, or 'unaided,' which is a tougher measure because no prompting is allowed.)

In Week 5, you stop advertising, cutting the advertising spending back to zero. But the percent recall does not immediately go to zero, any more than your car stops the instant you lift your foot from the gas pedal. Instead, the percent recall drops rapidly at first, but then coasts downward for some

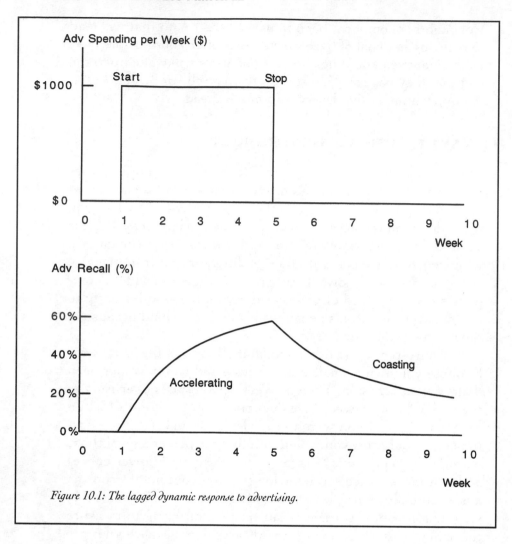

Figure 10.1: The lagged dynamic response to advertising.

period thereafter. Unlike your car, which eventually will come to a complete stop, the percent recall may level out at some value above zero and stay there for a long time, because a few of your customers may remember your ads for many months after you stop advertising. Like your car, the response to advertising and PR lags behind the stimulus.[1]

There are two important points to take away from this discussion:

1. The response to your promotional efforts, like the response to advertising spending, is not instantaneous. It builds up

over time. People take a while to learn something new, whether it is about a new car or about your newest professional achievement. And it may take even longer for people to internalize this new information, to really believe and accept what they learn from your promotional activities.

2. Similarly, people remember promotional campaigns long after the campaigns have stopped. In particular, your professional reputation will linger for years, unless something new happens to change it.

Here is another interesting effect that has been discovered by doing research on advertising. If you stretch out the learning period over a longer time, even though your weekly spending rate is lower, the percent recall decays much more slowly when the campaign is over.[2] Those things that we learn over a long period of time tend to stay with us, whereas the material we crammed at the last minute for an exam is completely forgotten a few weeks later. This means that to maximize the long-term enhancement of your reputation, build your promotional campaign slowly and steadily, rather than in a series of short bursts.

DON'T SKIMP ON YOUR PROMOTIONAL EFFORTS

There is a certain minimum 'threshold' of promotional activity that you must achieve in order for it to be effective. Research has shown that if the amount of advertising spending per week is too low, the effectiveness of the campaign never reaches the takeoff region and the ads are lost in the noise and clutter at the bottom of the curve, as shown in Figure 10.2 on the next page. As the amount of spending per week is gradually raised, the effect of the campaign (as measured by percent recall) takes off, growing rapidly with each additional increment of spending. Finally, at very high levels of spending, the curve saturates, meaning that there is very little additional value in raising the spending rate any higher.

The implication for your "company of one" is that there is a certain minimum level of on-going promotion that is necessary or the results of your efforts will be lost in the noise. You

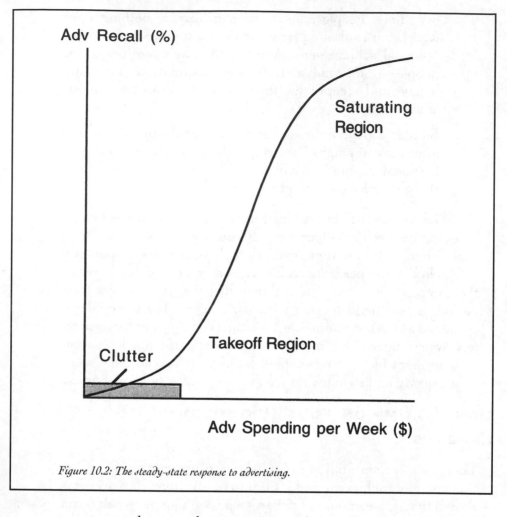

Figure 10.2: The steady-state response to advertising.

want to do enough promotion to be on the steep part of the curve, not down in the clutter.

NETWORKING AS A WAY TO MARKET YOUR "COMPANY OF ONE"

Publishing articles is one form of promotion for your "company of one"; networking is another. With the demise of the corporation's tacit commitment to offering lifetime employment, professional and managerial employees from various companies are banding together in self-help organizations that resemble the guilds of artisans and craftsmen of the Middle Ages.

Often such groups are organized by profession, such as the various professional societies of engineers and accountants. Sometimes they are formed from the alumni associations of area colleges and universities, or from the memberships of charitable or religious organizations. Occasionally they are 'alumni' of a large employer, such as the 'X-Xerox' clubs for former Xerox employees. Such self-help organizations frequently meet on a regular basis to talk about about jobs, colleagues, and changes in the local job market.

Among the benefits of such networking are:

- Gaining a sense of perspective about problems in your company.

- Learning cutting-edge practices and trends in your profession.

- Picking up industry gossip about organizations you might want to work for or avoid.

- Getting job leads.

- Raising your visibility by speaking at association conferences or writing for association publications, thus *establishing yourself as an expert in your field*.

The advantage is that you get to share ideas with a lot of smart people, and the cost is low.[3] And keep in mind that most successful professional job changes are the result of personal contacts and networking, not as the result of going through professional headhunters.

IMPLEMENTING YOUR PERSONAL MARKETING PLAN

'Brian,' 46, graduated in 1979 with a bachelor's degree in Liberal Arts and accepted a job with a small industrial supplies firm. Over the next several years he held a number of jobs with the company, eventually working his way up to Purchasing Agent at an annual salary of $15,000. He also began taking courses toward a part-time MBA degree in Marketing and Information Systems. After graduating with his MBA in 1983, he made a lateral transfer within the industrial supplies company, becoming Manager of Information Systems at $17,000.

Although he enjoyed his new responsibilities, Brian realized that his future in this small company was very limited. Rather than just moving to another company, he invested in building his reputation outside of the company. He attended professional conferences of data processing managers and served on a subcommittee that held workshops for small business owners who were struggling with the problems of bringing computers into their businesses. Before long, Brian began to receive offers to consult at night and on weekends for some of these companies, and he summarized his advice to small business owners in a printed handout sponsored by his professional association.

In time, one of his handouts was seen by a partner at a major information systems consulting company, who made Brian an offer to join the firm as an Associate specializing in computer applications for small businesses. Today, he is a Senior Consultant with the firm, with an annual salary in excess of $80,000. His advice to others is to promote yourself and develop a career strategy: "Join professional organizations and be active in these groups. Plan your career—have set goals and work toward them."

THE BOTTOM LINE

Matthew, the banker who we met at the beginning of this chapter, as well as Jean and Brian, have learned how to market themselves. They have invested in their *product* by learning new Strategic Skills, they have used the techniques of *promotion* to make others inside and outside of their companies aware of their new skills, and in the cases of Matthew and Brian, they are being paid salaries that reflect the premium *prices* the market is willing to pay for these skills.

By adding Personal Marketing Skills to the organization chart of their "company of one" (Figure 10.3), these young professionals have taken the right steps to ensure that present and prospective employers will be fully aware of what they can offer.

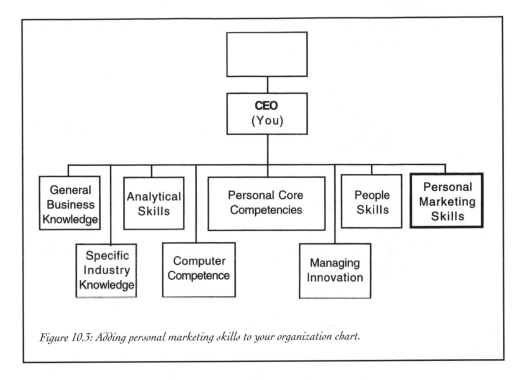

Figure 10.3: Adding personal marketing skills to your organization chart.

THOUGHT QUESTIONS FOR YOUR PERSONAL MARKETING CAMPAIGN

1. What is the objective of your promotional campaign? (Recall how Jean's objective was to reposition herself, from 'just another secretary,' to a talented professional in the book publishing industry with unique computer skills and management potential.) How do you want to position yourself in the professional and managerial job market—as an engineering genius, a super salesperson, a financial whiz?

2. Who is the target audience for your promotional campaign? What media will you use to reach this target audience?

3. What supporting evidence can you offer to support your positioning strategy? What have you accomplished that is interesting and persuasive, that will add credibility to your "company of one"?

4. What is your timetable for this effort?

5. How will you use networking to support your marketing campaign?

....

1   Figure 10.1 is a graphical representation of the Vidale-Wolfe advertising response model.

2   Zielske, H.A., "The Remembering and Forgetting of Advertising," *Journal of Marketing*, January 1959, pp. 239 - 243.

3   Lancaster, H., "Managing Your Career," *The Wall Street Journal*, January 16, 1996, p. B1.

SELECTING AND CULTIVATING MENTORS

In our research study, respondents reported that the help and advice from senior managers who served as mentors was as valuable to their professional success as the content of the MBA courses they took. In the organization of your "company of one," mentors serve as a board of directors, sharing their experience and wisdom, and using their professional relationships to open doors.

'Peter,' who has an undergraduate degree in Political Science and a master's degree in Economics, was in his mid-20s when he lost his job as a financial analyst as the result of a corporate reorganization that closed his division. Through a referral from a mutual acquaintance, he was hired as an administrative assistant to the CEO of a $500 million company, a position he soon leveraged into Director of Acquisitions and Planning, still reporting to the same CEO. Through hard work, creativity, and dedication, he was promoted again while still in his early 30s, this time to Vice President of Finance and Administration—again, still reporting to the same CEO. It was clear throughout the organization that the CEO was not only his boss, but also his mentor. Both Peter and his mentor benefited from the relationship.

Successful mentoring relationships like this don't just happen—they have to be developed and managed. Sometimes an exchange is implied: the mentor offers advice and counsel; the younger manager offers loyalty, long hours of hard work, and occasionally technical skills such as computerized spreadsheet analysis.

THE NEW MENTORING

The old model of mentoring is changing. Peter was fortunate to latch on to a single powerful mentor who guided him over the years as he worked his way up to a top management post. But in today's complex organizations, you should aim to have a *group* of mentors with differing skills and positions both inside and outside the company to provide the function of a board of directors for your "company of one," for several reasons:[1]

- A single mentor is unlikely to have a wide enough scope of expertise, experience, and contacts to help you maximize your progress and professional growth. Just as a corporation appoints a number of experienced advisors to its board of directors, so you need a number of advisors on your board of mentors. You will require a portfolio of skills and expertise on your board, which you can only get from a diversified group of mentors.

- In today's turbulent workplace, senior executives—like everyone else—are concerned about holding on to their own jobs, and many do not have the time or the patience for extensive mentoring of younger colleagues. You can't count on receiving hours of coaching from just one individual. Some potential mentors may even feel threatened that they might lose their jobs to the eager, young, lower-paid persons they are counseling if they were to share everything they know.

- By having more than one mentor, you are building a constituency of potential supporters who will advance your cause when it comes time for them to offer recommendations for filling that big opening.

- You are also spreading your risk by not being too closely identified with just one mentor who might be bounced out of the company tomorrow.

- You need the advice and support of mentors who are outside of your company, as well as a few selected insiders, to provide you with a broader view of your industry and how well your company is perceived to be doing within the industry. But be careful about getting too close to key people who work for direct competitors—if you are seen having lunch with the sales manager of your number one competitor, people will assume you are planning to leave.

- Generally, you will be better off not involving your inside mentors in extended discussions of your personal strengths and weaknesses. "What you don't want," warns Harvard Business School professor Rosabeth Moss Kanter, "is a lot of inside coaching on your weaknesses. You don't want them to become a topic of conversation within the company. Let your outside mentors help you work on them."[2]

SELECTING YOUR BOARD OF MENTORS

Who should be invited to join your board of mentors? The basic selection rule is that you want people who will have your interest at heart, who have relevant knowledge, wisdom, expertise, and contacts, and who will level with you when you ask for advice and counsel. In selecting your board, consider the following candidates:

- *Your boss* (ex officio). Like it or not, your boss is a member of your board of mentors by virtue of his power over your future. You don't have to always take your boss's advice, but you should listen. In most companies, a manager's success is measured in part by how well he develops subordinates, and often a manager is not considered for promotion until he has trained his replacement. So your boss does have an interest in your success.

- *Another senior manager* (but not your boss's boss or one of your boss's enemies). This mentor can give you a wider picture of what is happening within the company, and she may be able to tip you off about choice jobs that are opening up elsewhere in the firm. But avoid your boss's boss

(this will make your boss nervous) or his political enemies (this will be viewed by your boss as being disloyal).

- *A peer* from another functional area of your company. In
  organizations, knowledge is power, and the more you
  know about what is going on in other areas of the company, the more effective you will be. Sharing information is
  a necessary strategic skill in today's flat organizations. In
  the process, you will absorb some useful cross-training
  about key issues in other functional areas of the company,
  such as what it takes to build a good dealer organization.

- *A subordinate* who will level with you. From time to time,
  you need to know how you are regarded by the troops. If
  your people are restless or unhappy, they can find a hundred ways to make you look bad—and you'll never know.

- *A computer guru.* Information technology is changing so
  rapidly that you need to have informal access to an expert
  you can trust to steer you to new software and hardware
  that will make you more effective in your job, while
  warning you away from new information technology that
  has proven to be troublesome.

- *An industry expert.* In Chapter 4, we underscored the
  importance of knowing what is going on in your industry,
  and how well your company is doing relative to its competition. Staying in touch with one or two industry leaders at trade shows and by telephone keeps you well
  informed about trends and opportunities in the industry,
  as well as the latest gossip. But use good judgment about
  how much you tell. Don't share confidential information
  with competitors, and avoid situations that might give
  even the appearance to someone in your company that
  you are sharing sensitive information or looking around
  for a job. You want to know what is going on, but you
  don't want to be branded as disloyal.

- *A former classmate.* College and business school alumni
  often form close friendships that continue long after graduation. A special bond exists between alumni that can
  open doors at critical times in your career, such as when
  you are attempting to line up capital for a new venture.

Staying in touch with one or two classmates lets you keep track of who is working where, and provides a convenient way to benchmark your career progress against your peers.

RECRUITING YOUR MENTORS

Unlike a company board of directors, which periodically meets as a group, you will meet with your mentors separately. After you choose a list of likely candidates, invite your would-be mentor for coffee or lunch, and see if you share a commonality of interests. If one of your candidates is someone you haven't met, have a mutual friend or colleague set up a lunch for the three of you. Recognize that a successful mentoring relationship has many of the characteristics of a personal strategic alliance, so it will be worthwhile to re-read the section on "Strategic Alliances and Networking" in Chapter 8. Bear in mind that your mentoring relationship is professional, and that you are selecting people for their expertise and objectivity. Don't limit your search to personal friends who will tell you only what you want to hear.

Some companies have established formal mentoring programs that pair younger managers (known as protégés) with more seasoned mentors who offer different sets of talents and experiences. Created initially to provide a helping hand to women and minority managers, such formal mentoring programs typically are now open to all young managers. Leading firms such as Avon, Xerox, and General Electric are finding that formal mentoring is a low-cost way to develop young managers they want to keep.[3]

RENT-A-MENTOR

Another change: Not all mentors are volunteers anymore. Now there are also paid outside mentors, such as 'Doug,' a former IBM executive who specializes in coaching professional women.

'Anne,' a computer analyst who has been coached by Doug for about a year, says that he helped her identify obstacles in her career path. For example, he helped her realize that she was not being recognized for her accomplishments. "I'd give credit to everyone, diminishing my accomplishments," she said. Doug also helped her eliminate the technical jargon from the accomplishments she listed in her latest performance review, taught her to pick her fights more carefully, and, perhaps best of all, educated her on how to "read" her bosses.

Working with 'Kathy,' a planning executive for a computer company, Doug taught her to cut her losses when a project went sour, and also when to keep her mouth shut ("I'm very blunt," says Kathy). He also pushed her to take on more challenging projects.

ADVICE FOR WOMEN

As an outside executive coach, Doug offers this advice for women who seek to break the glass ceiling: Look for some common ground, something you can talk about with your bosses as an icebreaker to make them feel more comfortable. Brush up on your presentation skills; you should not come across as weak or uncomfortable in front of groups. Don't try to do it all; pick the things that will have the most impact on your career and farm out the rest. Push for assignments where you'll get noticed. And finally, try to find an inside mentor. Outside executive coaches can't provide the same degree of sponsorship and protection as a senior executive who takes an interest in your career.[4]

THE BOTTOM LINE

Selecting and cultivating a board of mentors (see Figure 11.1) requires judgment and sensitivity. Mentors can be as valuable to your career as the course content of an MBA program, and coaching by mentors is an essential part of the leadership development process. In the end, successful mentoring relationships come down to personal chemistry and mutual trust.

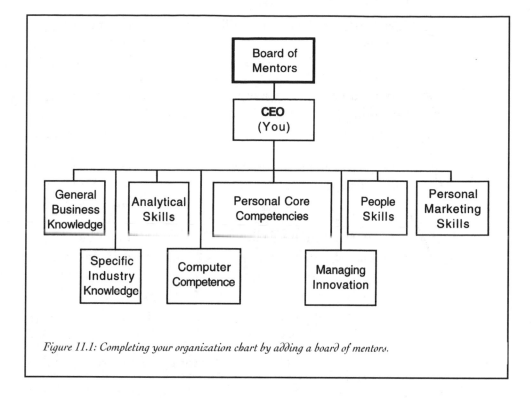

Figure 11.1: Completing your organization chart by adding a board of mentors.

A BALLOT FOR NOMINATING MEMBERS FOR YOUR BOARD OF MENTORS

Remember, you are selecting these mentors on their potential to provide you with clear, objective, well-thought-out advice.

☐ A senior manager (but not your boss):   1st choice _____

2nd choice _____

3rd choice _____

☐ A peer from another part of your firm: 1st choice _____

2nd choice _____

3rd choice _____

☑ A subordinate (one who will level with you):

1st choice ____
2nd choice ____
3rd choice ____

☑ A computer guru (to keep you up-to-date)

1st choice ____
2nd choice ____
3rd choice ____

☑ An industry expert (for the latest gossip)

1st choice ____
2nd choice ____
3rd choice ____

☑ A former classmate (who's working where):

1st choice ____
2nd choice ____
3rd choice ____

....

[1]   See Loeb, M., "The New Mentoring," *Fortune*, November 27, 1995, p. 213.

[2]   Ibid.

[3]   Ibid.

[4]   Lancaster, H., "Managing Your Career," *The Wall Street Journal*, November 14, 1995, p. B1.

SHOULD YOU INVEST IN AN MBA DEGREE?

'Edward,' who is 41, is a portfolio manager for a medium-sized investment firm located in New York's financial district. He earns $935,000, an increase of 25% over the previous year.

Edward was awarded his bachelor's degree in Economics in 1976 and immediately entered a full-time MBA program, graduating in 1978 with an MBA in Finance. Following graduation, he began his career with a bank as a management trainee at $24,000 a year.

He puts in a very reasonable 40 hours a week at the office, averages two hours a week at business-related social functions, brings work home infrequently, and enjoys spending ten hours a week on golf and tennis.

The most important skills he acquired from his MBA program were "quantitative cost/benefit analysis and capital market pricing theory." He credits the MBA with giving him the confidence to pursue his career plan, and given the choice to do it over again, he would definitely pursue an MBA degree at the same business school. He rates his job satisfaction on a 1-to-5 scale as a "5."

Edward does not advocate moving from firm to firm, nor does he endorse the current tendency to seek cross-functional training in different areas. His advice to current MBA students is, "Start with a prestigious large company and learn as much as you can."

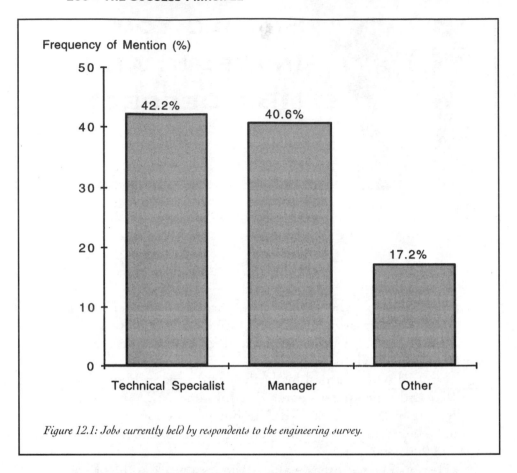

Figure 12.1: Jobs currently held by respondents to the engineering survey.

A DIFFERENT GOAL—THE FREEDOM TO LEAVE AND RE-ENTER THE WORKFORCE

Edward has leveraged his investment in an MBA degree to achieve great success in earnings and professional accomplishment. Some who pursue the MBA degree have other goals, however. Consider the case of 'Donna,' age 43, who earned a bachelor's degree in Mathematics in 1974 and continued on for her MBA, graduating in 1976.

Her first job after graduation was as a staff accountant at a national public accounting firm. After a few years, she moved on to another large organization where she had the opportunity to travel widely, which she enjoyed.

When her children were born, Donna dropped out of the workplace for a number of years to care for them. Now that her

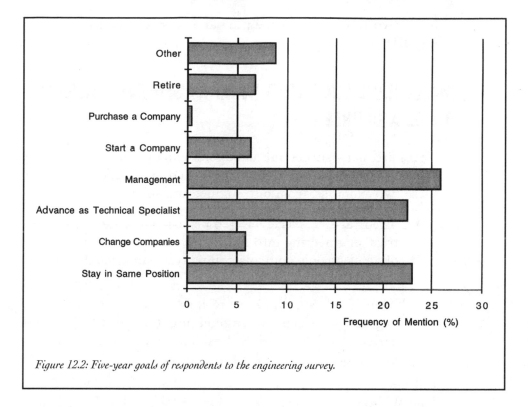

Figure 12.2: Five-year goals of respondents to the engineering survey.

children are older, she has returned to her profession as an accountant, but for her local church rather than for a "Big Six" public accounting firm. Her annual salary, $25,000, is very modest by MBA standards, but she loves her work and gives credit to her MBA degree for providing the skills and credentials to return to the workplace in a job of her choice after raising her family.

NOT EVERYONE SHOULD PURSUE AN MBA DEGREE

The MBA is a management degree, and not everyone is interested in becoming a manager. For example, analysis of the data from the *engineering* survey showed that the respondents were split almost equally between management and non-management jobs (see Figure 12.1).[1]

Furthermore, the number of engineering respondents who plan to advance professionally as technical specialists is nearly equal to those who intend to move into management (Figure 12.2). Unless management is clearly your career choice, it may not be worth it to invest the time and energy necessary to earn an MBA.

MANY HAVE SUCCEEDED IN MANAGEMENT WITHOUT AN MBA DEGREE

There are many successful managers who do not hold an MBA degree, particularly in technology-based companies. Consider these two examples from our engineering survey:

- 'Fred,' age 47, has leveraged his bachelor's degree in electrical engineering into the top job as President and CEO of an electronic controls company, at an annual salary of $150,000.

- 'Dan,' 57, has a Ph.D., as well as bachelor's and master's degrees, in electrical engineering (but no MBA) and earns $200,000 as Vice President of the Semiconductor Group of a large chip manufacturer.

Bill Gates, Apple Computer founder Steve Jobs, Wal-Mart's Sam Walton, GE's Jack Welch, David Packard—all are giants of American industry who have done extremely well without the benefit of an MBA degree.

The best MBA students (in terms of grades) are not necessarily the most successful. More than 25 years ago, J. Sterling Livingston reported that an individual's long-term success on the job cannot be predicted by grades in school or even by the number of degrees a person holds.[2] Along the same line, research by one of my graduate students shows no significant correlation between an individual student's GMAT score and his or her post-MBA starting salary.[3]

Livingston found that the "need for power"—the desire for prestige and high income, the love of competing, and the satisfaction gained from the power to control others—is what drives a few men and women to become top managers. The skills learned in MBA programs may be helpful to such individuals but these skills are not indispensable, and in some cases, not even necessary for their success. People such as Bill Gates and Jack Welch will be successful, with or without an MBA.

OVERWHELMING CUSTOMER SATISFACTION AMONG THOSE WHO HAVE EARNED AN MBA

For most aspiring managers, however, there *are* a number of reasons for pursuing an MBA degree. Financial gain is only one. Others include the enhancement of your knowledge for its own sake, the opportunity to learn how to structure and critically analyze complex problems, the security of adding an MBA to your professional credentials, and the fun of meeting and working with outstanding young professionals.

The most powerful endorsement for investing in an MBA degree comes from those who already have made this investment, and have seen it pay off. Respondents to the MBA survey were almost universal in reaffirming their choice to pursue an MBA degree. When asked, "If you had it to do over again, would you still go for an MBA degree?," 91.5% of the MBA survey respondents answered "yes," only 2.9% said "no," and the remaining 5.6% were not sure (see Figure 12.3)—an overwhelming level of customer satisfaction.

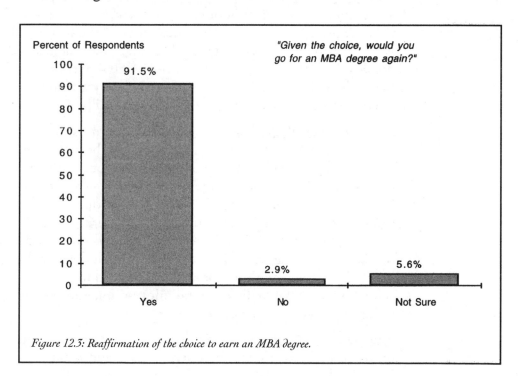

Figure 12.3: Reaffirmation of the choice to earn an MBA degree.

Changes in the new economy will affect you whether or not you have an MBA. The relevant question is whether you will be better equipped to deal with these changes *with* an MBA or without one.

MBA PROGRAMS AND THE 10 STRATEGIC SKILLS FOR PERSONAL SUCCESS

In the preceding chapters, we learned the importance of developing competence in the 10 Strategic Skills for Personal Success. For some of these 10 Strategic Skills—but not all—an MBA program at a quality business school is a proven, disciplined way to become proficient in these areas:

1. Taking charge of your career as CEO of your "company of one." In today's workplace, you are on your own. The first Strategic Skill is learning to *manage* yourself as a "company of one," and the MBA is a *management* degree.

2. Obtaining general business knowledge. To be effective as a member of a multifunctional team, you must have a basic knowledge of how the various parts of the business work, beyond your own functional area. Accounting, Economics, Finance, and Marketing are essential parts of the core curriculum of all MBA programs, and pursuing an MBA is an excellent way to acquire these skills.

3. Acquiring specific industry knowledge. You must understand your own industry in great depth—who your key competitors are, how the companies in your industry compete, and how your company has positioned itself to satisfy its customers. The MBA degree provides the tools for analysis (such as Porter's model of competitive industries, as discussed in Chapter 4). But beyond giving you the tools, pursuing an MBA won't be of much direct help here. Using the techniques of analysis learned in business school, you'll have to dig out vital information about your industry on your own.

4. Sharpening your analytical abilities. Depending solely on intuition and experience for business decision-making is

no longer sufficient in today's fast-paced world. Developing analytical skills is where MBA programs really shine. More than any other, this is the Strategic Skill that a good MBA program will develop and hone to a fine edge.

5. <u>Building computer competence.</u> Having grown up with computers, young managers have a huge natural advantage to be at the leading edge in their companies in the application of computers to business opportunities. An MBA program will get you started, but computer technology is moving so rapidly that you will have to work constantly at keeping up. Remember, it is the obsolete managers who get the pink slips first.

6. <u>Learning to manage innovation.</u> Innovating with new products and services is the way companies make most of their profits in today's technology-driven economy. But many business schools have been slow to teach the management of the innovation process—perhaps, because like many companies, they too have trouble understanding how it works. This is an area where outside reading of business periodicals can be of great help.

7. <u>Developing skills for working with people.</u> Although management is the art and science of accomplishing things through other people, developing people skills such as leadership, teamwork, and written and oral communications cannot be accomplished entirely within the framework of an MBA program. Much skill development in this area comes with coaching and practice. Business schools can help you determine what to do, but the skills for working with others are refined by years of practice.

8. <u>Polishing your personal core competencies.</u> This is what you do for your company that clearly sets you apart from others. It is a strategy of specialization. By picking and choosing from the specialized elective courses in an MBA program, you may be introduced to an area where you want to build your core competencies. But to become truly outstanding in your field, you will have to continue to learn about your chosen field on your own. Your business education will be of help, because in a good MBA

program you will learn the process of how to learn on your own.

9. <u>Learning to market your Strategic Skills.</u> To get the most value from your investment in your personal core competencies, people have to be made aware of them. A business degree program can contribute in two ways here: 1) By helping you build a network of faculty experts and professional colleagues that you can call on for the rest of your career, and 2) By publicly announcing that you have achieved a recognized level of proficiency in the field of management and have been awarded a graduate professional degree that certifies this high level of competence.

10. <u>Selecting and cultivating mentors.</u> Survey respondents reported that advice from senior managers who served as mentors was as valuable as the content of all of the MBA courses they took. Business school faculty have often served as mentors for young managers, but today's management professional needs a *board* of mentors, and faculty members can fill only a limited role in mentoring.

To summarize, pursuing an MBA degree can accelerate the process by which you become proficient in most of the 10 Strategic Skills for Personal Success. But you must also recognize that the MBA degree by itself is not a substitute for the hard work, enthusiasm, commitment, and imagination needed to succeed in today's turbulent economy.

THE FINANCIAL REWARDS OF HAVING AN MBA

Although financial gain is not the only reason for pursuing an MBA, it is an important one. As we learned in Chapter 5, the total investment, including foregone salary, to earn an MBA in a two-year full-time program can easily exceed $100,000. As we also learned in Chapter 5, the investment in an MBA from a top business school easily pays for itself in a few years. But does it pay to earn an MBA from a school that is not in the Top 10?

According to a recent study carried out at Harvard and MIT, the median pay in 1993 for men 30 years old with only a

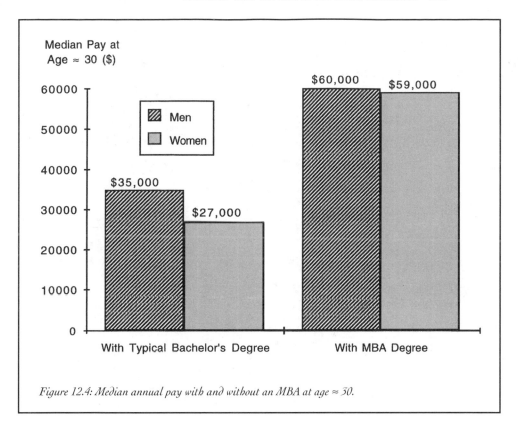

Figure 12.4: Median annual pay with and without an MBA at age ≈ 30.

bachelor's degree was $35,000, and for women age 30 with only a bachelor's degree was $27,000.[4]

From our MBA survey of graduates of the Simon School (an excellent business school, but not in the Top 10), men between the ages of 28 and 32 earned median pay of $60,000 in 1994 (71.4% more than with just a typical bachelor's degree) and women in the same age bracket earned $59,000 (118.5% more). Compared to pay levels with just a typical bachelor's degree, the investment in an MBA begins paying off early in one's career (see Figure 12.4).

Unlike holders of the typical bachelor's degree, electrical engineers—even those with only bachelor's degrees—are highly paid early in their careers. Respondents to the engineering survey between ages 28 and 32 reported making almost as much as the MBA respondents in the same age bracket (Figure 12.5 on the following page). (There were too few women electrical engineers in the sample between the ages of 28 and 32 to make

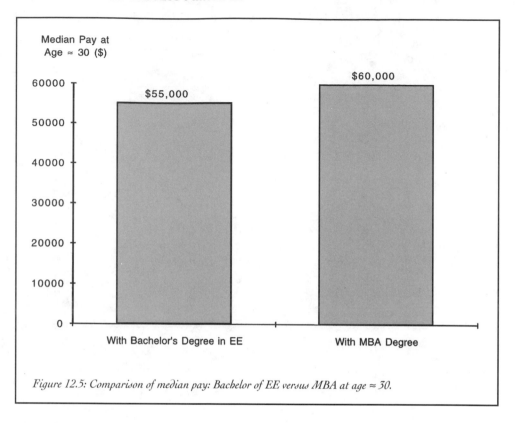

Figure 12.5: Comparison of median pay: Bachelor of EE versus MBA at age ≈ 30.

it meaningful to break out the median pay of men and women separately.)

However, above age 30, the gap in pay between the MBA respondents and the engineering respondents widens. Compare Figures 12.6 and 12.7.

In Figures 12.8 and 12.9, outliers above $300,000 per year in the MBA data have been removed and the vertical scale expanded to show more detail.

RISING STARS

These graphs show that the pay patterns of the MBA respondents differ from those of the engineering respondents in two important aspects:

- The slope of the regression line of pay versus age in Figure 12.8 is 32% steeper for the MBAs than for the engineers. At age 45, the MBAs are averaging $99,000 a year, whereas the engineers average about $79,000.[5]

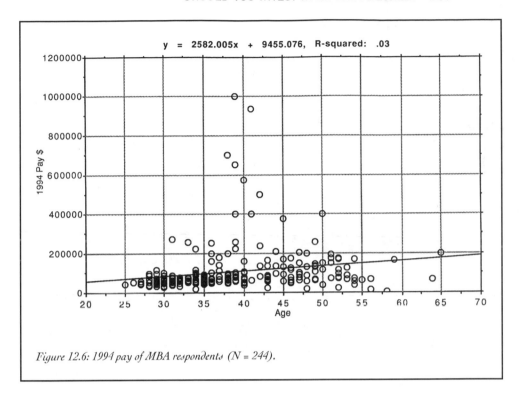

Figure 12.6: 1994 pay of MBA respondents (N = 244).

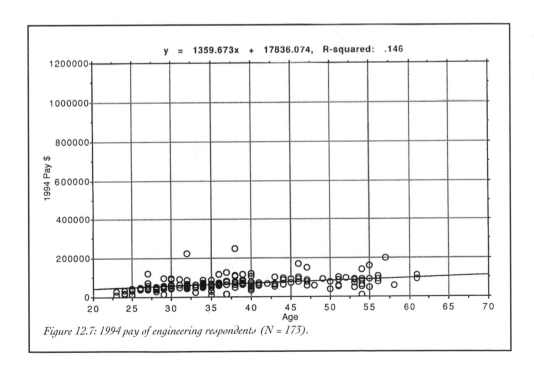

Figure 12.7: 1994 pay of engineering respondents (N = 173).

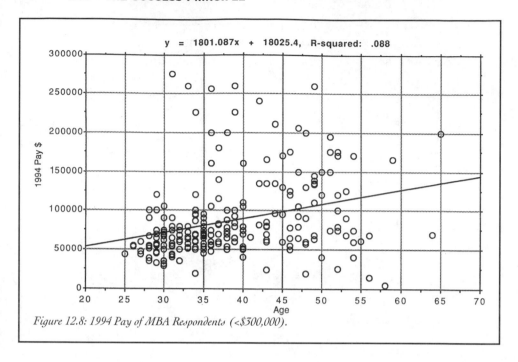

Figure 12.8: 1994 Pay of MBA Respondents (<$300,000).

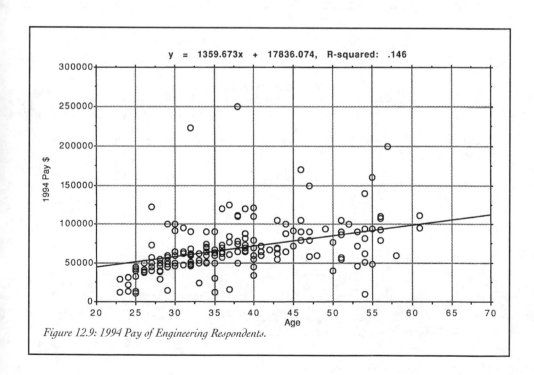

Figure 12.9: 1994 Pay of Engineering Respondents.

- There is a marked qualitative difference in the patterns. While both groups show an effervescence of 'stars' rising above the rest of the sample, this phenomenon is much more apparent with the MBA respondents. Not only are there more MBA stars (Figure 12.8 versus 12.9) but they tend to rise higher (Figure 12.6 versus 12.7).[6]

Note also another interesting phenomenon with both the MBA and the engineering respondents that shows up clearly in Figures 12.8 and 12.9. Beginning at about age 40, the tightly packed clusters of points seen at lower ages seem to explode. (Although it may not be obvious, about half the data points in each graph lie to the right of age 37, since the median age of the MBA respondents is 38 and of the engineering respondents is 36).

The reason for this "exploding" phenomenon is not clear — perhaps it has something to do with a mid-career crisis where many people feel the urge to break out of the straight-and-narrow corporate jobs and do something more adventuresome and risky in the second half of their careers. As students of the stock market know, with increased risk comes increased volatility of financial returns.

Even in the relatively high-paying profession of electrical engineering, adding the MBA degree offers higher financial returns. To demonstrate this, the pay of electrical engineering respondents with MBA degrees was compared to those of EEs with just the bachelor's degree, using multiple regression. EEs with MBAs averaged $16,741 more per year, a result that is highly significant. For those with bachelor's degrees in fields that pay less than electrical engineering, the financial advantage from the MBA degree is even greater.

Does more money imply greater job satisfaction? In general, the answer appears to be "yes." Greater job satisfaction and higher pay are positively correlated. There was a highly significant positive statistical association between the responses to the five-point job satisfaction question in the MBA questionnaire and reported levels of 1994 pay.[7] Moreover, 11 of the 12 highest paid stars from the MBA survey—all earning more than $300,000 in 1994—rated their job satisfaction as a "5."

HOW MUCH MORE WILL YOU MAKE?

How much more will you make if you earn an MBA degree? There are two effects that will tend to increase your earnings:

- At the time of graduation from business school, your pay typically will 'step up' about 50% to 70% above the level of your pre-MBA pay.

- During the first five years on the job, your pay is likely to grow considerably faster than the 5% raises that are the norm in today's economy.

THE SALARY "STEP UP RATIO"

The size of the "step up ratio" depends on a number of factors. Your choice of business school can be a major factor (typically, Top 20 schools offer post-MBA salary "step up ratios" of 50% or more over pre-MBA pay).[8] Other factors are your area of concentration and the kind of post-MBA job you choose. (Consulting pays the highest starting salaries.)[9]

A comparison of the pre-MBA pay (in constant 1994 dollars) and post-MBA starting pay (in constant 1994 dollars) of respondents to the MBA survey from the full-time program at the Simon School shows a mean salary "step up ratio"—averaged over the past 30 years—of +51.4%. (This compares closely with a value of 55.1% in *current* dollars calculated for the Simon School from MBA salary information collected by *Business Week* for the Class of '92.[10])

To illustrate the application of the "step up ratio," suppose you are earning $36,000 in the year before you enroll in the MBA program at the Simon School. How much could you expect to earn when you graduate? The answer is 51.4% more than $36,000.

Pre-MBA pay = $36,000

Step up ratio = +51.4% for the Simon School (*long-term historical value*)

Therefore, expected post-MBA starting pay = $36,000 × 1.514 = $54,500

But this calculation may understate your expected post-MBA pay, for two reasons:

- First of all, the calculation was done in constant dollars. If inflation is assumed to be 2.5% per year during the two years you are in business school, then your starting pay in *current* dollars will be $54,500 × 1.025 × 1.025 = $57,260.

- Secondly, the survey data showed that the step up ratio has been rising over the years for the Simon School. (This may be happening for other quality MBA programs, as well.) Based on this rising long-term trend, the calculated value of the step up ratio for the year 1994 for the Simon School full-time MBA program (in constant dollars) is +60.6%. Again, if we assume 2.5% inflation per year during the two years in business school, the rising long-term trend value of the step up ratio in *current* dollars becomes +68.7%. (Using an entirely different database and method of calculation, *Business Week* reported a step up ratio for the Simon School for 1994 in current dollars of +69.9%, very close to our value of +68.7%.[11]

Repeating the calculation with the rising trend value of the step up ratio gives:

Pre-MBA pay = $36,000

Step up ratio = +68.7% for the Simon School (*rising trend* value in current dollars)

Therefore, expected post-MBA starting pay = $36,000 * × 1.687 = $60,700

So how much more would you make? If you are a full-time student and your pre-MBA pay is about the same as that of other incoming students (in the range of $35,000 to $40,000), you could expect an increase of 50% to 70% over your pre-MBA pay.

POST-MBA SALARY GROWTH

The second factor that affects the economic value of an MBA degree is the high rate of salary growth during the first few years following graduation.

Analysis of the survey data showed that the MBA respondents from the full-time Simon School program experienced post-MBA pay growth at an average compounded rate of 14.4% per year (in constant 1994 dollars) during the first five years following graduation. This was based on calculations using their reported 1994 pay, their reported post-MBA start-ing pay (in constant 1994 dollars), and the number of years since they graduated.

At the current inflation rate of about 2.5%, the 14.4% real growth works out to calculated *current dollar* average annual pay raises of 17.3% during the first five years on the job. (This is in the middle of the range of current dollar post-MBA pay growth rates of graduates from the top business schools for the first five years after graduation, as calculated using *Business Week* data.[12])

When asked in a separate question at the end of the survey about the size of their pay raise for the year 1994, the mean value *reported* by those respondents who graduated from the full-time program within the past five years was 17.5% (almost identical to the *calculated* current dollar rate of 17.3%), and the reported median value was 12%.

As with starting pay, post-MBA salary growth rates can be affected by many factors, not the least of which are the energy and competence the new graduate brings to the job. As a con-servative estimate, figure on 10% to 15% annual raises during the first five years after graduation.

PRE-MBA WORK EXPERIENCE—IS IT ESSENTIAL?

Should you wait to get work experience before applying to business school? Almost all of the top business schools strong-ly prefer that incoming students have three or four years of work experience—a preference that shows up in higher starting pay. A separate study of 169 Simon School students graduating in 1993 showed that each year of work experience added an average of $1,400 to post-MBA starting pay.[13]

Analysis of the MBA survey data shows a similar premium for full-time graduates between 1985 and 1994 with work expe-rience: a statistically significant $1,201 (in constant 1994 dol-lars) for each year of pre-MBA work experience.[14] (This value is lower because it is the average of data collected for those who graduated over the past ten years. The premium for work expe-rience has risen in recent years because the preference of cor-porations for MBA graduates with work experience has increased.)

Over the long term, however, the picture is very different. There was no statistically significant relationship whatsoever between *long-term* pay levels (as represented by 1994 pay) and pre-MBA work experience for full-time students who graduated within the past ten years.[15] In other words, pre-MBA work experience has a significant positive effect on starting pay, but it appears to have no measurable effect on *long-term* pay.

You will probably command a higher starting salary if you wait to gain work experience and you will find it easier to land a job, but if you are in a hurry and can get accepted by a good school, it could be to your benefit to get started on your MBA as soon as possible. The earlier you begin compounding that higher post-MBA pay, the better, and starting early won't do any harm to your long-term pay levels.

PART-TIME MBA PROGRAMS—ARE THEY WORTH IT?

A part-time MBA program makes financial sense if you currently have a good job you want to keep—i.e., you have a high opportunity cost—or if your family responsibilities make it impractical for you to drop out of the job market for two years. In 1994, there were over 118,000 students—about 64% of all those seeking MBAs—studying in part-time MBA programs.[16]

There are five major advantages of a part-time MBA program:[17]

- Because most people who take part-time programs do so at a local business school, there's no need to move. You avoid the cost and disruption of having to live somewhere else for two years to get an MBA.

- You continue to make a salary while you are in school. The biggest cost of a full-time MBA is not the tuition—it's the salary you give up for the two years you are in school. This is a major cost of getting an MBA that you can avoid. There's no need to take out loans to go to business school.

- There is little risk of being unemployed after you graduate. The new MBA grad from a *full-time* program is thrown on the market and has to scramble for a job. And if you *do* plan to change employers after getting a part-time MBA, the job change can take place at *your* convenience.

- You can start your part-time MBA right after you finish your undergraduate degree, and you'll have your MBA by age 26 or 27—about the age most full-timers are just beginning their programs (because most full-time programs now require 3-4 years of prior work experience). This means that you can start compounding the advantages of having the MBA degree 3-4 years earlier.

- For most part-time MBA students, the employer will pick up part or all of the tuition cost. But even if the company doesn't, it's still less costly than a full-time program, because you continue to earn a salary.

As a result, there's no "breakeven" point in a part-time program because there is no investment to recover. Furthermore, you can immediately start applying what you are learning in class to your job. You're ahead from day one.

The most serious problem that part-timers face is getting their employer to recognize their new capabilities. Your boss may expect you to continue in your old job with little or no change in pay or responsibilities, and you may find that you have to leave the company to capture the benefits of your new MBA degree. But even if it is necessary to leave, you can take the time to carefully plan your move, and you can do it on your own terms and timetable. Evidence from the survey shows that the typical part-time graduate does realize a substantial increase in pay following graduation.

PART-TIME VERSUS FULL-TIME: A LOOK AT THE NUMBERS

Of the respondents to the MBA survey, 28% were part-timers. As with the full-timers, the part-time students reported a "step up ratio" in post-MBA pay relative to their pre-MBA pay level. In constant dollars, the average "step up ratio" over the past 30 years for part-time students has been +27.2%—a value that has been slowly growing. Using the long-term upward trend, the 1994 calculated "step up ratio" (in constant dollars) for part-timers in 1994 was +37.5%.

In the case of part-time students, however, part of this step up would be the result of normal pay increases during the three to four years it takes to complete the program—at 5% per year, a total of some 15% to 20% over the period. Therefore, perhaps only half the observed step up is the direct result of earning an MBA degree.

POST-MBA PAY GROWTH FOR PART-TIMERS

Post-MBA pay growth for part-timers in the first five years following graduation was calculated to average 10.3% per year in constant dollars (or about 12.8% in current dollars)—about 4 percentage points less than post-MBA pay growth of full-timers.

When asked in a separate question about the size of their 1994 pay raise, respondents who had graduated from the part-time program within the past five years reported a mean raise of 13.0%, with a median value of 10%—again, about 3 percentage

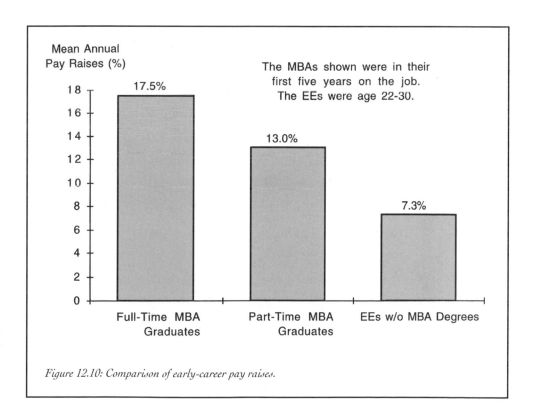

Figure 12.10: Comparison of early-career pay raises.

points less than for full-timers. By comparison, however, electrical engineering respondents from the *engineering* survey *without* MBA degrees and between the ages of 22 and 30 reported a mean raise in 1994 of only 7.3%, with a median value of 5% (see Figure 12.10).

Based on the numbers, part-time students appear to realize a substantial economic gain from their MBA degree—not as much as their colleagues in the full-time program, perhaps, but certainly more than their peers without an MBA. And when the convenience, reduced risk, and lack of financial investment for part-time programs are all factored in, a part-time MBA degree from a quality business school is well worth the time and effort.

CREDENTIALS AND CONFIDENCE FOR A COMPETITIVE JOB MARKET

In addition to the financial rewards for investing in an MBA degree, many respondents noted the importance of the MBA as a credential, a certification of competence in the field of management. 'Edward,' the portfolio manager introduced at the beginning of this chapter, credited the MBA with giving him "the confidence to pursue his career plan."

Women in particular reported valuing the MBA as certification of their competence as managers:

- 'Jill,' age 40, earns $50,000 per year as an industrial engineer for a large automotive manufacturer. Although she finds the auto industry to be male-dominated, she wrote on her questionnaire that the MBA "has given me the confidence and the ability to stand up and compete with my male co-workers."

- Another woman who responded to the survey, 'Mary,' 31, is paid $65,000 as an Assistant Vice President at a hospital. She wrote that her MBA has provided her with "credentials and confidence." She continued that the MBA "has given me the confidence to seek out other opportunities and allowed me to do so at a much higher level than before."

- 'Patricia,' age 35, earns $65,000 as a Financial Director for a large photographic company. She stated that the MBA was "[the] ticket to apply for bigger and better jobs, a major plus in stiff competition."

- Finally, 'Joanne,' 39, a Senior Product Manager earning $85,000 a year for a large healthcare company, wrote that "[I] have more credibility with key managers. The President of the Division believes my recommendations now."

These women, as well as many of the men who responded to the survey, have come to appreciate the value of their MBA as a widely-accepted certification of their skills. In the knowledge-based industries of the new economy, credentials count.

CAREER CHANGING

Many respondents noted that the MBA opened up new career choices for them. 'Harold,' for example, was a math teacher in a local high school earning $14,000 a year when he began working on his MBA part-time. After graduation in 1982, he took a job as a training instructor with a small industrial automation manufacturer. A few years later, he made another career change, to the field of financial services.

Today, at age 45, Harold earns $130,000 as an Assistant Vice President of a large financial services firm, a job he rates as a "5" in satisfaction. On his questionnaire, he wrote, "The MBA gave me the opportunity to move from the public sector (non-profit) into the private sector with some credibility and competitive advantage over other job candidates."

Here is a another example of using the MBA to change careers. 'Ted,' 28, earned his undergraduate degree in computer engineering in 1987 and worked for a year as a software engineer at a high technology company, for an annual salary of $30,000. He returned to business school as a full-time MBA student, graduating in 1990 with concentrations in Accounting and Finance. Currently, he works in sales and trading for a major investment bank, where he earns $100,000. Regarding his career change from engineering to finance, he wrote, "[The MBA] allowed me to change career paths. It has enabled me to earn more money than my previous career and has provided more opportunities for going forward."

INNOVATION IN MANAGEMENT EDUCATION—THE MBA OF THE FUTURE

Business schools sometimes are slow to practice what they preach. In spite of efforts to modernize their curricula with new course offerings on Business Process Reengineering and Total Quality Management, traditional MBA programs have not kept up with changing customer requirements. Ten years ago, MBA students were mostly young men in their early 20s with little or no work experience, mainly from the U.S., who were seeking entry level jobs at major American corporations. Today, most MBA students are in their late 20s and have significant work experience. A third are women, 25% are foreign students, and a fair number hope to land jobs with small businesses and entrepreneurial startups rather than giant corporations. Enrollment in entrepreneurship courses is soaring.[18]

Although the leading business schools have changed the content of many of their courses, most have been slow to abandon the same one-size-fits-all, two-year MBA programs they have offered for years. While business school professors expound on the benefits of accelerated product development methods for bringing new cars and computers to the market in half the time, it still takes two years to produce an MBA graduate in their full-time programs—just as it did 30 years ago.

But today, major opportunities abound for accelerating the MBA process. For students with extensive prior work experience, the second year of the MBA program can be like a country club. A *Wall Street Journal* article noted that in the second year, "Students now can spend up to 20 hours a week searching for the sweetest job offer at an endless round of corporate presentations, wine-bar receptions, and fly-in/fly-out interviews . . . . Many students spend much of their final year crisscrossing the country for interviews. 'It was nonstop flying,' [said one second-year student at a Top 20 school]."[19]

While this partying may be fun, it can be very costly to students. Students with substantial work experience—or those

iness school on leaves of absence from their fami-
r corporate employer—may not want or need to
is time during their second year pursuing a job.
graduating sooner, these students can get an early
iing big money in their new, higher-paying jobs—
ra to pay off those student loans in many cases.

SEIZING THE OPPORTUNITY TO INNOVATE

A few leading business schools have seized the opportunity to differentiate their programs to provide increased value to their more experienced students, mainly by reengineering wasted time out of their schedules. For example, the University of Rochester's Simon School has pioneered a thriving optional January admission program that allows students to complete their MBA in 18 months, or even as little as 15 months if they squeeze in a full course load during the summer. Harvard has introduced a 16-month MBA option that starts in January.[20] In mid-1995, when Cornell's Johnson Graduate School of Management introduced a unique one-year MBA program for scientists and engineers who already hold at least one other graduate degree, there were five times as many applications as there were seats.[21] In the summer of 1996, the Crummer Graduate School of Business at Rollins College in Winter Park, Florida, rolled out an entirely new, highly-selective one-year MBA program especially designed for exceptional students who have at least three years of relevant work experience, or who are on a one-year professional leave of absence from their employer.

Questions arise, however, about the quality of such accelerated programs. According to *The Wall Street Journal*, "Many [schools] now offer compressed 18-month schedules, and a few have one-year MBA programs—which some observers disparage."[22]

THE QUESTION OF QUALITY

How good is the quality of one-year programs? For those experienced students who qualify, there is no fundamental reason why a well-designed one-year program cannot provide an education that is the equal of today's less efficient two-year

MBA programs. Most top business schools have for many years offered a high-quality two-year executive MBA program that delivers a first-rate education to experienced students who continue to work four days a week in their regular jobs, so it is reasonable to assume that they could also develop an efficient one-year program for experienced MBA students who are not working and are on campus full time. But just as U.S. automakers had to learn from the Japanese how to design efficient, high-quality cars, so U.S. business schools may have to learn from the best European schools.

INSEAD, for example, which is located just outside of Paris, has a 10½ month MBA program that some consider comparable to Harvard's two-year program. In 1994, average starting salaries at INSEAD were the equivalent of $90,000, which would rank it among the top five business schools in the U.S. Average starting pay at another one-year European MBA program, IMD in Lausanne, Switzerland, was the equivalent of $107,000, higher than any U.S. business school. Both schools are highly selective and require entering students to have extensive work experience.[23]

The bottom line is that for qualified students with appropriate work experience, the European business schools have shown that a one-year MBA program can provide a high-quality educational experience.

DESIGNING A NEW ONE-YEAR MBA PROGRAM FROM SCRATCH: A CASE HISTORY

Designing a first-rate one-year MBA program involves more than just compressing a conventional two-year schedule into 12 months. Rollins College's Crummer School began by doing extensive marketing research, first by studying the strengths and weaknesses of other accelerated programs, and then by carrying out focus group interviews of current MBA students and mail surveys of prospective students who met the high admissions standards of the proposed new program. (Crummer has also continued its two-year MBA for students with less work experience.)

The Advantages: Out a Year Earlier, and Ahead by More Than $90,000

From their research, Crummer learned that prospective students correctly perceive that the major cost of a two-year MBA degree is not the tuition but the extra year of foregone salary. Using spreadsheet simulations, the researchers found that with a typical post-MBA starting salary of $60,000, a student graduating from a one-year program will be—within a few years—*more than $90,000 ahead of a graduate from a conventional two-year program* ($60,000 of the $90,000 is from the extra year of salary, and the rest is the result of beginning the compounding of post-MBA salary growth a year earlier).

The research also showed that prospective students valued the saving of a year's time even more than the extra money.

TIME FOR INTERNSHIPS AND JOB SEARCHES

One of the biggest challenges for the program designers at Crummer was to reserve time for internships and job searches. In conventional two-year MBA programs, summer internships can be very valuable experiences for MBA students because they give students the chance to try out what they have learned in the first year of the program with actual companies. For those who are planning a major career change, such as from Engineering to Finance for example, a summer internship in their new field can be an important stepping stone to building a relationship with a new employer.

But not all summer internships are successful. Sometimes career changers find that when they get into their summer internship, their chosen new field really is not to their liking. Because students have only one summer internship opportunity in a conventional two-year program, if they choose the wrong field they do not get a second chance.

Students also lose out when the companies they intern with are unable to come up with truly challenging and meaningful projects and they end up doing mundane tasks—such as entering mountains of data into a computer—that do not draw on their newly-acquired MBA skills. More than one student has returned to school in the fall muttering that their summer internship turned out to be a complete waste of time.

Internships with Faculty Supervision: the Medical School Model

The program designers at Crummer recognized that internships with companies would be more efficient and more valuable to students if they also were supervised by faculty, just as internships in medical schools are closely supervised by medical school faculty. Consequently, many of the elective courses in the new program were designed with two components: a six-week theory component followed by an optional six-week internship component, during which the students apply these theories to carry out actual projects with cooperating companies under faculty supervision, for which they earn academic credit.

For example, in the first part of the new Security Analysis elective course, students learn the theory of building financial portfolios. In the optional second part, they develop proposals for managing actual portfolios with investment officers from local financial institutions, under the watchful eye of their finance professor. Similarly, in the first six weeks of the Marketing Research elective, teams of students develop research strategies and survey questionnaires for marketing research studies that are actually carried out with cooperating companies in the second part of the course, again under faculty supervision.

Because these mini-internships occur as part of *advanced* courses such as Security Analysis and Marketing Research, they provide a richer learning experience than the usual summer internship that is taken in traditional two-year MBA programs after the students have completed only the basic core courses.

Multiple Internships in a Variety of Fields

Instead of spending their entire summer working with only one company on a single internship project that might or might not provide a true learning opportunity, students in the new one-year program have the opportunity to work with three or four companies on a variety of internship projects, with the assurance that the supervising faculty member will make each project a valuable learning experience. This flexibility also allows students who choose to concentrate in two areas, such as Finance and Marketing, to carry out supervised internships in both areas—a feat that is impossible with a conventional summer internship.

Students who plan to change careers but are unsure about which areas they want to pursue can try internships in several areas before making a final commitment. And as they go forth to their job interviews, armed with bound copies of their internship final reports, students are able to impress prospective employers with documented evidence of their ability to apply what they have learned in these advanced courses to real business problems.[24]

BREAK PERIODS FOR RECRUITING TRIPS

To provide time for students to visit these prospective employers, break periods are scheduled after each six-week term—two one-week breaks in the fall and a three-week break between mid-February and early March, during the peak of the recruiting season. Between interviewing trips, students may elect to use these break periods to carry out international internship projects with companies, again under faculty supervision.

ONE-YEAR MBA PROGRAMS: A CASE OF SUCCESSFUL REENGINEERING

One-year MBA programs are new, and they are not for everyone. Students without significant work experience will be better off spreading the MBA educational process over the traditional two years. Moreover, it may take a few years for U.S. employers to recognize what their European counterparts already have discovered—that the quality of the incoming students is more important than the length of the MBA program.[25]

If these innovative new one-year programs deliver as promised—a high-quality educational experience while gaining a year's time and $90,000 or more in additional earnings—the competitive market in MBA education will cause them to attract the best and the brightest incoming students. Those students who *are* able to meet the high standards for admission to these new one-year programs can look forward to receiving a quality graduate business education while realizing immense savings in time and money.

THE BOTTOM LINE

The responses to the survey showed that an MBA degree is a very profitable investment for most people. If you decide to enroll in a full-time MBA program at a quality business school, you should expect:

- A 50% to 70% increase in pay when you graduate, compared to your pre-MBA salary.

- Annual pay raises in the 12% to 20% range during your first five years after graduation.

If you choose a quality part-time program, you should expect:

- A 15% to 20% pay raise when you graduate, assuming you are successful in convincing your employer to recognize your new competence and credentials, and to pay the market rate for MBA graduates with your years of experience.

- Annual pay raises in the 10% to 15% range during the first five years following graduation.

SHOULD YOU INVEST IN AN MBA DEGREE?

In this book, we have examined 10 Strategic Skills for Personal Success. These are skills that the more than 450 successful men and women who responded to our survey are using to thrive in today's turbulent workplace. Many of these skills can be mastered without the benefit of an MBA degree. But it is my observation that earning an MBA makes it easier.

Let me close by summarizing my belief about the overall value of the MBA degree for one's career:

I believe that for men and women pursuing a career in management, the MBA degree from a good school is a superb investment in one's professional capital. Jobs and promotions may come and go, but the knowledge and the credentials from a graduate degree in business are permanent assets.

Business has become too complex and too competitive to wing it. If one is truly serious about a career in management, the education and the credentials of the MBA are indispensable.

The world of business is changing. It's fashionable these days to talk about "the learning organization." But organizations don't learn; people do. And lifelong learning will be greatly enhanced by a thorough grounding in the fundamentals, which is best acquired through the formal process of education. To paraphrase Louis Pasteur:

"Change favors the prepared mind."

---

1   Throughout this chapter we make comparisons between electrical engineering graduates and MBA graduates, both alumni groups of the University of Rochester. Electrical engineers make an interesting reference group because like MBAs they are professionally trained and they tend to be bright and career-oriented.

2   Livingston, J., "Myth of the Well-Educated Manager," *Harvard Business Review*, January-February 1971.

3   Daum, M., "Predictors of MBA Starting Salaries," MBA summer research project, William E. Simon

Graduate School of Business Administration, August, 1993, showed no significant correlation between the starting salaries of *individual* graduates and their GMAT scores. However, when GMAT scores of the graduating classes for the top business schools are *pooled*, the average GMAT for each school does correlate with the economic success of that school's graduates, as measured by the average NPV of that school's MBA degree (see Chapter 5).

4   Koretz, G., "Is a Sheepskin Worth It All?," *Business Week*, September 4, 1995, p. 28.

5   If the regression line in Figure 12.6 is used instead, the slope for MBAs is 90% steeper, and MBAs average $126,000 per year at age 45. However, Figure 12.8, which has the outliers above $300,000 removed, provides a more conservative estimate of the value of the MBA degree.

6   For the job descriptions of some of these stars, see Appendix A.

7   The coefficient of the regression equation was positive and highly significant ($t = 4.072$, $p = 0.0001$).

8   For a listing of the historical salary step up ratios of the top business schools, see Yeaple, R., *The MBA Advantage*, Bob Adams Inc., 1994, p. 37.

9   Ibid. pp. 284 - 285.

10   Ibid. p. 37.

11   Byrne, J., *Business Week Guide to the Best Business Schools*, 4th Edition, 1995, McGraw-Hill, Inc., p. 57.

12   Yeaple, p. 38.

13   Daum, M., "Predictors of MBA Starting Salaries," MBA summer research project, William E. Simon Graduate School of Business Administration, University of Rochester, August, 1993.

14 The slope of the regression equation was positive and highly significant (t = 2.843, p = 0.0057).

15 The slope of the regression equation was negative and not significantly different from zero (t = 0.19, p = 0.8496).

16 Levenson, E., "Part-time B-School is a Full-time Grind," *Business Week*, August 21, 1995, p. 82.

17 Adapted from Yeaple, 1994, p. 175.

18 Almost half of the graduating class of the Stanford Graduate School of Business finds employment with companies having fewer than 1000 employees, and 17% choose firms with fewer than 50 employees. See Yeaple, 1994, p. 57. See also Mehta, S., "More Students Start Businesses While in School," *The Wall Street Journal*, May 6, 1996, p. B1.

19 Markels, A., "Marketing 101," *The Wall Street Journal*, December 15, 1995, p. A1.

20 Byrne, J., "Harvard B-School's Professor Fixit," *Business Week*, May 20, 1996, p. 93.

21 "Trading Microscopes for Microeconomics," *Fortune*, April 17, 1995.

22 Markels, p. A8.

23 *Business Week Guide to the Best Business Schools*, 4th ed., McGraw-Hill, 1995, pp. 55, 309, 313.

24 "Ability to apply MBA education in a practical work setting" is the most important attribute corporate recruiters use in selecting the business schools at which they recruit. See *The MBA Advantage*, p. 220.

25 As we learned in Chapter 5, the most important factor in explaining the relative success of the various leading business schools is the quality of their incoming students, as measured either by pre-MBA pay or by GMAT scores (see Figures 5.4 and 5.5).

APPENDIX A

ANSWERS TO THE MOST FREQUENTLY-ASKED QUESTIONS ABOUT CAREER STRATEGY

Over the years, I have been asked many questions by students and young professionals about career strategy. The next several pages contain a number of the most frequently-asked questions with answers based on evidence from the research study.

1. **Q:** *I was brought up to believe that if you do outstanding work, your career will take care of itself. But I have been working for the same company in the same area for eight years and my career doesn't seem to be going anywhere; furthermore my company doesn't seem to care. What should I do?*

   A: Our MBA survey respondents agreed that in today's economy, you cannot rely on your company to promote you, even if you do excellent work (see Figure A.1 on the following page).

   The answer is to stop depending on your employer, and to take charge of your own career. Think of yourself as the CEO of your "company of one." Develop a set of core competencies that will give you a real edge in the job market in the event you have to change companies (see Chapter 9). This is not being disloyal to your present employer. These core competencies will make you a more valuable employee if you stay, and a more marketable person if you have to leave.

2. **Q:** *I have been told that I should find a mentor in my company to provide advice and to open doors for my career. How does one go about finding a mentor?*

   A: This is good advice. Our survey respondents reported that counsel and support from mentors was as valuable to their success as the content of all their MBA courses. But in today's turbulent job market, you need more than one

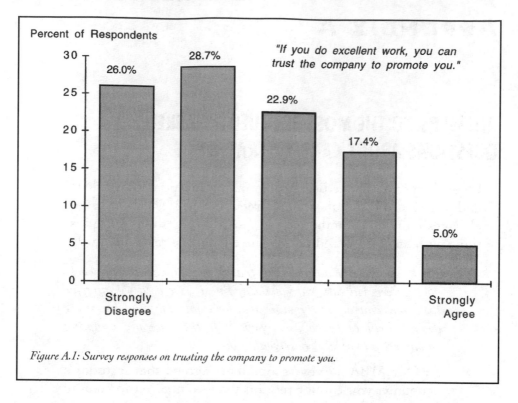

Percent of Respondents

"If you do excellent work, you can trust the company to promote you."

26.0%
28.7%
22.9%
17.4%
5.0%

Strongly Disagree

Strongly Agree

Figure A.1: Survey responses on trusting the company to promote you.

mentor. You should think about developing a *board* of mentors for your "company of one," much like the board of directors for a corporation. The checklist at the end of Chapter 11 describes the kind of people you should look for as mentors.

3. **Q:** *Is it better to work for a variety of companies, or to stay with one firm?*

A: Our survey respondents were almost equally divided on this one, with 32% in favor of working for a variety of firms, and 38% in disagreement (the rest were not sure). The answer is that it depends on two factors: 1) How well are you progressing in your present job—in particular, are you still learning useful skills?, and 2) Are you on a path that leads to your long-term career goals? If you have not decided on your career goals, read Chapter 2, particularly the section on "Objectives and Mission Statements."

If you are in the very early part of your career, you are better off starting with a prestigious large company in your field and staying to learn as much as you can, a strategy strongly recommended by our survey respondents.

4. **Q:** *I have a degree in engineering, but after working for five years as a design engineer, I think I would like to go into management. Will I need a graduate degree? If so, which would be a better investment, an MS degree in engineering or an MBA?*

A: You don't absolutely need a graduate degree to advance as a manager, particularly if your company is high-tech, but it will improve your chances. An MS is a good investment if you intend to advance as a technical specialist, which is the career goal of about half of our engineering respondents. Analysis of the survey data shows that acquiring an MS degree will not significantly improve your pay, however. But an MBA added to your undergraduate degree in engineering will increase your earnings about $17,000 a year, and much more if it causes your career as a manager to really take off.

If you are sure about management as a career goal, go for the MBA. If you are not sure, take a couple of graduate management courses in the evening at your local college and see if management is really a field you are interested in before you make the commitment to pursue an MBA.

5. **Q:** *My company has offered me the chance to make a lateral move from marketing to manufacturing, as part of a new cross-functional training program. Should I take it?*

A. Our survey respondents were strongly in favor of cross-functional training (see Figure A.2 on the next page).

There are two reasons why cross-functional experience is so valuable. In the short run, it will make you a more effective member of the cross-functional teams that are becoming so important in companies today, because you will have an appreciation of the capabilities and limitations of the other functions represented on the teams.

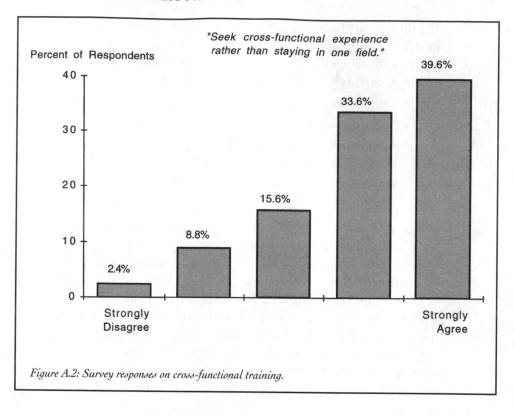

Figure A.2: Survey responses on cross-functional training.

And cross-functional experience is excellent preparation for general management.

Unless your career strategy involves intensive concentration in a very narrow functional specialty, take the offer. You'll learn a lot, and you will increase your market value both inside the company and on the outside.

6. **Q:** *I have been thinking about starting a part-time MBA program at a local school, but it looks like it will be a lot of work. Is it worth it? Or would I be better off to quit my job and go full time?*

A: As noted in Chapter 12, a part-time MBA program makes sense if you currently have a good job you want to keep, or if your family responsibilities make it impractical for you to drop out of the job market for two years. About 64% of those pursuing MBA degrees are doing so in part-time programs.

The survey data showed that the financial payoff for part-timers is good. Part-timers reported raises averaged 13%

a year during the first five years following graduation. Although this is not quite as high as for the full-timers at 17% per year, it is much better than the 7% per year for engineers in the same age bracket with only bachelor's degrees (see Figure 12.10 in Chapter 12).

7. **Q:** *Over the past five years I have developed outstanding expertise in an area of software development that is very important to my company, but I am worried that the technology of the industry is changing and my expertise will not be as valuable in the future. I might even lose my job. What should I do?*

A: Obsolescence is the major reason that professional people are let go in today's competitive workplace. The bad news is that your expertise in a specialized area of software development—your core competency—is at risk of dropping in value because of technological obsolescence, not only within your own company, but throughout the industry. The good news is that you have recognized it early. Now you have to be willing to act on this information. As an expert in your field, you will be able to track this decline closely and you should be able to predict when this technology will no longer be able to support you professionally.

In the meantime, assume that you *will* have to upgrade your technical skills, and make the necessary investment in courses and self-study to stay out in front of the changes. Most transitions in technology occur over a period of years, and the reason people get left behind is more likely to be one of denial than lack of information.

8. **Q:** *I will graduate from business school in three months and I am trying to choose between going to work for a prestigious large company or an entrepreneurial startup. Both are in the telecommunications industry, which is my field of interest. I also have an offer from an internationally-known consulting firm. Which would be the best choice?*

A: It sounds as if you have three exciting career opportunities, and you should begin by realizing that you probably wouldn't go far wrong with any of them. Without knowing more about the individual companies and how

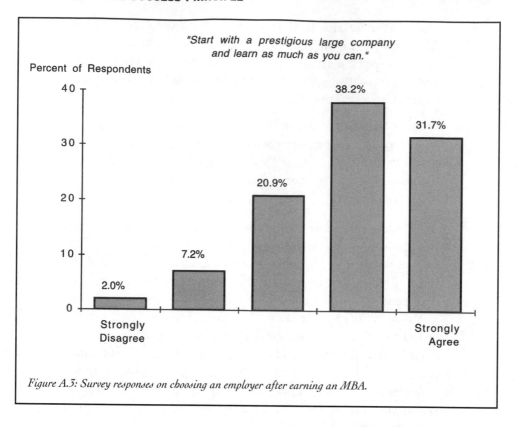

Figure A.3: Survey responses on choosing an employer after earning an MBA.

they relate to your long-term career goals, it is difficult to generalize on an answer to this question. Our MBA survey respondents were generally in favor of starting out with the best large company in the industry and learning as much as you can (see Figure A.3).

Many graduating MBAs are taking their first jobs in Consulting because of the high salaries, but our survey respondents were not as strongly in favor of this option. (I am assuming that you would be able to pursue your interest in telecommunications if you accepted the consulting job.)

The entrepreneurial startup offers high risk and high reward (see Figure 7.3 in Chapter 7). Most successful entrepreneurs learn the business first with someone else's money—by starting out with other successful companies in the industry. Three-quarters of the concepts for successful new ventures are based on ideas encountered in previous jobs. The key questions here are whether you have enough expertise this early in your career to make a real contribution to a startup company, and whether you can afford to accept the risk that goes along with working for a startup.

To make the final choice, ask lots of questions, evaluate the pros and cons of each job, and then trust your intuition. Even if you make a choice that doesn't fulfill its promise, you will learn a great deal from the experience, and you will not find it difficult to change jobs.

9. **Q:** *Which is better preparation for business school: a liberal arts degree or an engineering degree?*

A: The MBA survey data was analyzed using multiple regression to see if there was any statistical association between pay (both starting salaries right out of business school and long-term salaries) and four categories of undergraduate degrees: technical (which included engineering, math and science, and comprised 44% of the MBA graduates), business administration (20%), economics (22%), and liberal arts (14%).

There was no significant association whatsoever. Managerial success (as measured by salary levels) was found to be independent of undergraduate degree. A further look at the undergraduate degrees of the *highest paid* respondents to the MBA survey, all earning more than $300,000, showed that their undergraduate degrees were about equally divided among technical, economics, and liberal arts. Typically, however, the placement reports of most business schools show that *starting* salaries for MBAs with technical undergraduate degrees are a few thousand dollars higher.

10. **Q:** *Which areas of concentration in business school pay the highest?*

A: Based on multiple regressions of starting pay and long-term pay versus areas of concentration in business school, it appears that Accounting majors and Information Systems majors are paid significantly less at the time of graduation. However, over the long run, these differences wash out, and there are no significant correlations between long-term pay and the various areas of business school concentration.

11. **Q:** *I have heard that on average, jobs in Finance pay the most over the long run. Is this true?*

A: Not according to our survey data. Entrepreneurs are paid the most, followed by general managers, marketing managers, consultants, and then finance. But the differences in median pay across these areas of employment are relatively small, in the order of $5,000 to $10,000, and it would be a mistake to choose a professional field based solely on these numbers.

It is worth noting, however, that of the 11 highest paid MBA respondents (all making over $300,000), 7 majored in Finance while in business school and 6 currently are working either in financial institutions or as chief financial officer of their companies.

12. **Q:** *How valid are the business school rankings published by magazines such as* Business Week *and* U.S. News & World Report?

A: These two publications have contributed greatly by focusing the attention of business schools on the importance of satisfying their two sets of customers, the students and the companies that hire them. The published information on average starting salaries and GMAT scores by school is particularly useful to prospective students. The qualitative information on what it is like to be a student at the various schools, as published in the softcover book, *Business Week Guide to the Best Business Schools* (McGraw-Hill) is very helpful.

The rankings themselves, however, should not be taken at face value. For example, the student satisfaction component of the *Business Week* ranking varies randomly from survey to survey, and the corporate component is more a reflection of the size and location of the various schools than of the value added by the academic programs. Not surprisingly, corporate recruiters give higher rankings to large schools located in cities that are convenient to reach by air. (To see how these top schools compare in terms of "value added," see Table 5.6 in Chapter 5.)

Similarly, the *U.S. News* ranking is based on a complex formula that has not been validated against any measures of value added by the school.

Neither the *Business Week* nor the *U.S. News* ranking is a measure of the long-term success of the graduates, which is what really counts when comparing business schools.[1] (The most important factor in explaining the value of MBA degrees from the various top business schools is the quality of the incoming students, as measured either by pre-MBA pay or by GMAT scores, as shown in Figures 5.4 and 5.5 in Chapter 5.)

The bottom line is that all of these top schools are excellent. Don't worry too much about the rankings. The important thing is to find a school that is strong in programs that match your interests.

13. **Q:** *I received my undergraduate degree a year ago, and I have been advised to work for two or three more years before applying to business school. Do you agree with this advice?*

A: It will be difficult to get into one of the top schools without at least two or three years of pre-MBA work experience. However, it would be worthwhile to apply to a couple of your top choices, because most schools do take a few students without work experience who are exceptional in other ways, such as having high GMAT scores.

You should be aware that if you enter business school with only one year of work experience, it may be more difficult to find just the right job when you graduate, and your starting salary may be lower than that of your more experienced classmates by $3,000 to $4,000. If you are comfortable with this, by all means go ahead and apply now. Over the long run, the survey results show that you will do as well as your classmates who have more work experience.

14. Q: *I have heard that what is taught in business school is mostly useless theory, and that very little of a practical nature is learned. Would you care to comment?*

A: Sure. First of all, there is nothing more practical for a manager than a well-tested theory that relates cause-and-effect. If you are about to spend money on advertising, for example, wouldn't you like to have some way to estimate how much sales will go up as a function of the dollars you put into advertising? There are a number of useful theories that have been developed and tested over the years about how advertising affects sales, and you will make better decisions if you understand them.

Second, if all this theory is worthless, why do 9 out of 10 people who earned an MBA say they would do it again if they had it to do over? (See Figure 12.3 in Chapter 12.)

Finally, you should be aware that while a considerable amount of theory is taught in the first year of an MBA program, much of the second year is devoted to application of that theory to managerial problems. Furthermore, most schools offer projects and internship experiences with companies that give students the opportunity to try out these new concepts in an actual business setting. Nothing could be more practical.

15. Q: *Along the same line, some schools stress faculty research while others promote teaching. Which kind of school will provide the better educational experience?*

A: You can get a fine education at either kind of school. In general, however, the evidence tends to favor schools where the faculty is heavily involved in research. In carrying out research for an earlier book, I came across data which makes a strong case for research-oriented schools.

When I plotted the Net Present Value of the "value-added" for the students by their MBA degrees (from Table 5.6) versus faculty research activity (as measured by the median number of times each faculty member's research has been cited by his or her colleagues), I obtained the curve shown in Figure A.4. In general, the

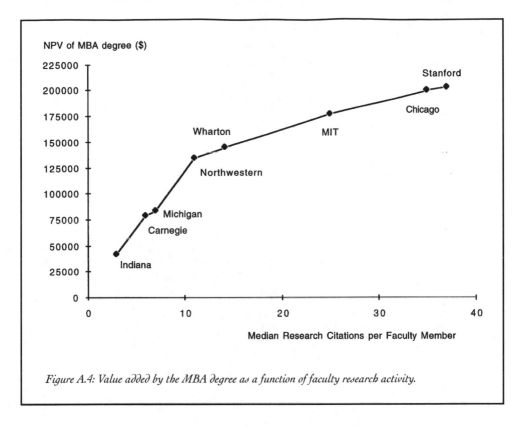

Figure A.4: Value added by the MBA degree as a function of faculty research activity.

more research activity by the faculty, the higher the value added by that school's MBA degree.[2]

----

1   For more on the limitations of magazine rankings of business schools, see Yeaple, R., *The MBA Advantage: Why It Pays to Get an MBA*, Bob Adams Inc., 1994, particularly Appendix A and Appendix B.

2   Ibid. p. 238.

APPENDIX B

HOW THE RESEARCH WAS DONE

One of the distinguishing features of this book is that it is the result of a scientific survey of the careers of nearly 500 managers and professionals across a wide range of ages and educational backgrounds.

SURVEYING THE ALUMNI

As mentioned in the Introduction to this book, in the spring and summer of 1995 I conducted two comprehensive mail surveys of alumni of the Simon Graduate School of Business Administration and of the Department of Electrical Engineering, both at the University of Rochester. A total of 550 questionnaires were mailed out to a random sample of Simon School alumni, all of whom have MBA degrees, and 273 usable responses were returned, for a response rate of 50%.[1]

Similarly, from a random sample of 500 electrical engineering alumni, I received 208 usable replies, for a response rate of 42%. Of the 208 engineering graduates who responded, 101 have MS degrees in engineering as well as their bachelor's degrees in electrical engineering, 30 have MBAs, and 24 have PhDs.

All told, between the two alumni groups, there were 481 usable responses for an overall response rate of 46%, which is considered excellent for a mail survey. To ensure the privacy of the respondents and to encourage frankness and candor, all replies were anonymous and no attempt was made to identify individual respondents. Those responding were also asked not to identify their current employers, as further protection for their privacy. As a token of appreciation, a $1.00 bill was enclosed with the outgoing questionnaires, a marketing research technique that has been found to double the response rate.[2]

WHY ALUMNI OF THE UNIVERSITY OF ROCHESTER?

While many books have been written about the MBA programs and alumni of such top business schools as Harvard and Stanford, these schools are among the most elite.[3] Such books are of limited practical value to a typical young professional trying to decide whether or not it pays to invest in an advanced business or engineering degree from a high-quality regional school, either full-time or through a part-time program. The experiences of MBA and engineering alumni from the University of Rochester, a top-quality regional university, are likely to be more representative and therefore more useful for personal career planning.

LIMITATIONS OF THE SURVEYS

It is important to realize that reported averages from surveys sometimes can be misleading. Although an overall response rate of 46% is excellent for a mail survey, it is possible that I heard only from the more successful alumni. Furthermore, some of those who responded may have inflated their actual earnings and accomplishments. Moreover, a few investment bankers working eighty hours a week on commission and earning $500,000 or more can distort the averages (for this reason, median salaries as well as mean salaries are reported).

EVIDENCE OF THE ACCURACY OF THE SURVEYS

Having noted these cautions, I can report that the great majority of responses were of excellent quality. As one confirmation of the accuracy of our survey, the 1994 median income from our engineering survey ($65,000) was found to be within 3% of that reported in a completely separate comprehensive national survey conducted by the largest professional society of electrical engineers, the IEEE Salary Survey for the year 1994 ($67,000).[4]

Similarly, the value of the post-MBA salary step up of +68.7% calculated from our MBA survey data is almost identical to the value of +69.6% as reported by *Business Week* for the

Simon School using an entirely different database and method of calculation.[5]

Another test of the quality of the data: The average post-MBA salary growth rate during the first five years on the job was calculated from the survey database to be 17.3%. In a completely separate question at the end of the survey, respondents who graduated from the Simon School were asked for the size of their pay raise in 1994. For those who graduated within the last five years, the mean reported value was 17.5%, almost exactly the same as the calculated value of 17.3%.

Throughout the book, unless otherwise specified, all salary information about the MBA and engineering respondents is for the calendar year 1994. For those salaries that are identified as having been earned ten or even twenty years ago, salary growth patterns are reported both in current dollars and in constant 1994 dollars to remove the effect of inflation.

It was clear that most of the respondents took the survey seriously. Many filled the margins of the questionnaire with extra comments, and a few enclosed thoughtful letters full of advice for aspiring managers.

For all those who took the time to respond to these surveys, my heartfelt thanks.

....

[1]   A random sample means that all of the alumni of the Simon School had an equal-likely chance of being selected for the study. By drawing a large random sample, the characteristics of the sample (such as the mean and median salaries) are likely to be close to the characteristics of the whole alumni body.

[2]   See Yeaple, R., "Increasing the Response to Mail Surveys Using Financial Incentives: Two Controlled Experiments," *Simon Research Review*, Fall 1989.

[3]   Two of the most recent books are John Kotter's "The New Rules" (The Free Press, 1995), about alumni of the Harvard Business School, and Peter Robinson's "Snapshots from Hell: the Making of an MBA" (Warner Books, 1994), about the MBA program at Stanford.

4   *The Institute*, published by the Institute of Electrical and Electronics Engineers, Inc., May 1995, p. 1, and "IEEE U.S. Membership Salary & Fringe Benefit Survey 1995," The Institute of Electrical and Electronics Engineers, Inc., 1995, p. 1-2.

5   Byrne, J., *Business Week Guide to the Best Business Schools*, 4th Edition, 1995, McGraw-Hill, Inc., p. 57.

INDEX